Early Keyboard Instruments
in European Museums

EARLY KEYBOARD

INSTRUMENTS *in*

EUROPEAN

MUSEUMS

BY EDWARD L. KOTTICK
AND GEORGE LUCKTENBERG

Indiana University Press
Bloomington and Indianapolis

© 1997 by Edward L. Kottick and George Lucktenberg

The paper used in this publication meets the minimum requirements of American National Standard for Information Sciences—Permanence of Paper for Printed Library Materials, ANSI Z39.48-1984.
Manufactured in the United States of America

Library of Congress Cataloging-in-Publication Data

Kottick, Edward L.
Early keyboard instruments in European museums / by Edward L.
Kottick and George Lucktenberg.
p.   cm.
Includes index.
ISBN 0-253-33239-7 (cl : alk. paper)
I. Keyboard instruments—Catalogs and collections—Europe. I. Title.
ML461.K68 1997
786'.194'0744—dc20   96-24494

I 2 3 4 5 02 01 00 99 98 97   MN

To Charles and Dorothy Freeman

CONTENTS

XVI. UNITED KINGDOM

✦ ILLUSTRATIONS

Preface

The predecessors of the modern piano have always fascinated me, but awareness of developing trends and attitudes toward antiques, and their interrelationships with keyboard repertoire, came late. Only at midlife, and in mid-career, did I fully grasp the drastic changes in perceptions about instruments and interpretation to which I had to adapt or become professionally redundant. But, without benefit of sabbaticals, summer study, or leaves of absence, how and where to go about making such changes?

Brief trips to metropolitan centers on the East Coast of the United States were quite helpful. I was received with kind forbearance by builders and restorers such as John Challis, William Dowd, Hugh Gough, Frank Hubbard, William Hyman, John Watson, and Wolfgang Zuckermann; curators Darcy Kuronen, Richard Rephann, and Edwin Ripin; and performers Albert Fuller, Paul Jacobs, and Sylvia Marlowe, to name but a few. Also, attendance at concerts, seminars, and masterclasses by Gustav Leonhardt and Malcolm Bilson, and especially Kenneth Gilbert, as well as careful listening to their recordings, were crucial to the process.

Among others, Kenneth Gilbert, Keith Hill, Virginia Pleasants, and Howard Schott gave me invaluable advice and suggested locations and instruments to visit. It took much longer than I had expected, but after a dozen excursions and much experimentation over twenty-five years, at last the insights and revelations I sought are sufficiently clarified to make my contribution to this book possible. The more I found out about historical keyboard instruments, the more I wanted to know. A delightful discovery was the extent to which a similar passion existed in kindred spirits; a thirst for firsthand knowledge and a professorial compulsion to share it with others led to the Lucktenberg Historical Keyboard Tours of Europe.

On all but my earliest ventures I have been ably abetted and seconded by my esteemed colleague Edward Kottick, whose amiable presence and broad knowledge soon made him indispensable to the endeavor. His diligent notations and photographs, and his comprehension of methods and details of construction and decoration, have made our descriptions and considerations of individual instruments effective in ways and to an extent that I could never have achieved alone.

Had we just one principal reward for our collaborative effort, it would be this: to find that it had enabled a museum visitor to say or think: " . . . look at *that!* Now I understand what it *is,* and what it may have meant to its era and to those who first played it." We ask for no more.

January 1996   GEORGE LUCKTENBERG

Acknowledgments

We are grateful to many people for their help in bringing this book to fruition. J. Bunker Clark, Thomas Hendrickson, Robert Karpiak, and Carolyn Simons made available to us slides and photos of instruments to which we had not had access. Martha Novak Clinkscale supplied us with material from her computerized relational data base, "Early Pianos, 1720–1860." Boyd McDonald shared his piano data base with us as well. Others, including Peter Bavington, Sheridan Germann, Charles Mould, John Koster, and Kenneth Mobbs, answered our requests for specific information.

We owe a great debt to Martha Novak Clinkscale, Peter Bavington, Kenneth Gilbert, and Judith Wardman, all of whom read the manuscript in draft. Their sharp eyes and expert knowledge prevented many errors and infelicities from finding their way into print, and their thoughtful suggestions helped us improve the book. Our obligation to them is not easily discharged. The same can be said of Natalie Wrubel, our editor at Indiana University Press, to whom we are genuinely beholden. Her guidance, expert advice, and unerring sense of style were invaluable.

Each museum was sent a draft of the section on its early keyboard holdings, with an invitation to respond with corrections, criticisms, and suggestions, and we want to express our gratitude to the conservators, curators, directors, and keepers who did so. We would like to thank each by name, but a few requested anonymity, and to recognize all but those would be to identify them by omission; nonetheless, that does not lessen our indebtedness to all, especially those who sent checklists, catalogs, pictures, articles, and other useful materials. To those who also sent words of encouragement, a special thanks.

We are grateful to the following for permission to include photographs of their instruments:

Mozart's Birthplace and Museum Carolino Augusteum in Salzburg

Kunsthistorisches Museum Sammlung Alter Musikinstrumente and Technisches Museum für Industrie und Gewerbe in Vienna

Museum Vleehuis in Antwerp

Museum Gruuthuse in Bruges

Musée Instrumental, IVe Département des Musées Royaux d'Art et d'Histoire, Bruxelles

National Museum in Prague

Musikhistorisk Museum og Carl Claudius' Samling in Copenhagen

Musée de la musique/Publimages in Paris

The Neumeyer-Junghanns-Tracey Collection in Bad Krozingen

Albert Ludwigs Universität in Freiburg

Staatliches Institut für Musikforschung Preussischer Kulturbesitz, Musikinstrumenten-Museum in Berlin

Bachhaus Eisenach

Händel-Haus Halle

Museum für Kunst und Gewerbe in Hamburg

Musikinstrumenten-Museum, Universität Leipzig

Deutsches Museum and Städtische Instrumentensammlung der Stadt München in Munich

Germanisches Nationalmuseum in Nuremberg

Württembergisches Landesmuseum Stuttgart

Hungarian National Museum in Budapest

Museo degli Strumenti Musicali in Florence

Museo degli Strumenti Musicali in Milan

Museo Nazionale degli Strumenti in Rome

Gemeentemuseum in The Hague

Ringve Museum in Trondheim

Museu da Música in Lisbon

Museu de la Música in Barcelona

Stiftelsen Musikkulturens främjande and Musikmuseet in Stockholm

Sammlung alter Musikinstrumente des Historischen Museums Basel

University of Edinburgh, Russell Collection of Early Keyboard Instruments

Finchcocks Collection in Goudhurst

Trustees of the National Museums & Galleries on Merseyside (Liverpool Museum)

Fenton House: The Benton Fletcher Collection; The Royal College of Music Museum of Instruments; and Victoria and Albert Museum in London

The Bate Collection of Musical Instruments in Oxford

Biographical information on builders was taken from a variety of sources, including the books by Clinkscale, Boalch, and Good and the *New Grove* paperbacks *Early Keyboard Instruments* and *The Piano*. We also referred to museum catalogs for material on the instruments and regularly consulted the books by Good, Hubbard, O'Brien, and Russell (all these sources are fully cited in the Introduction). In dealing with Flemish instruments in general and Ruckers instruments in particular, O'Brien's book was especially valuable.

Finally, we would like to declare our indebtedness to Gloria and Jean for their love and support. This book could not have been written without them.

Introduction

The practice of collecting antique artifacts as *objets d'art* has been part of Western culture at least since the sixteenth century, but that special branch involving musical instruments is a phenomenon of the last 150 years. Fétis and Snoeck in Belgium, De Wit and Heyer in Germany, Donaldson and Engel in England, Bachke and Nydahl in Sweden, Claudius in Denmark, Gallini in Italy, Gorga in Rumania—they and others gathered in not only keyboards but also woodwinds, brass, percussion, folk, and non-Western instruments by the hundreds and even thousands. It is said that antique collecting can become addictive, but the relatively small group of individuals who assembled those hoards of harpsichords, clavichords, and early pianos must have been truly obsessed. Some amassed giant collections and sold them, only to begin new ones; others started by buying individual instruments and progressed to acquiring them by the roomful—and in some cases, by the museumful.

Most of the stringed keyboard instruments in today's museums were acquired as gifts or purchases from one or more of these notables. Fétis's holdings went to the Brussels Conservatoire, now the Musée Instrumental. Claudius's went to Copenhagen's Musikhistorisk Museum, and Gallini's went to Milan's Museo degli Strumenti Musicali. The Musikinstrumenten-Museum in Berlin was created in 1888 with a purchase of instruments from de Wit. It was later augmented by a group from Snoeck, who also expanded the Brussels assemblage and even sent some items to St. Petersburg, Russia. Nydahl created a trust for his collection, Stockholm's Stiftelsen Musikkulturens främjande.

At first these harpsichords, clavichords, and pianos were viewed as antiquarian objects, precious relics evoking romantic images of an earlier time; but after World War II, with the growing desire to hear their sounds as well, many were restored to playing condition. As interest in early music and historically informed performance became stronger, the instruments were examined more seriously—and scientifically—by a widening circle of scholars, builders, and performers. What started as a trickle of professional concern became a torrent, and the growth of interest by the concert-going public has kept pace. A harpsichord on stage is no longer considered an anomaly, although audience members still gather around the instrument at intermission, attracted by the decorative elements so conspicuously lacking in modern keyboards. These same concert-goers also purchase tapes and CDs of music recorded on antique harpsichords, clavichords, and pianos—recordings that frequently provide evocative pictures of beautiful instruments, with details of their disposition and decoration. As a result, there is now a much greater awareness of the importance of antique instruments, and with that, a desire to see them.

From 1978 to 1995 the authors of this work attempted to satisfy some of that desire. For seventeen years Lucktenberg, then Kottick, guided groups of harpsichordists, clavichordists, pianists, organists, instrument builders, scholars, teachers, listeners, owners, and owners-to-be to the major cities of Western Europe—and when it became possible to do so, a number of locales formerly behind the Iron Curtain—to see early keyboard instruments. We made a determined effort to visit every large public collection about which we could obtain information. But we also visited many of the smaller ones, such as the Haydn-Haus in Eisenstadt. Descriptions of these holdings form the core of this book.

There are some extensive collections of early keyboards in North America. Washington's Smithsonian Institution, New Haven's Yale Collection, New York's Metropolitan Museum of Art, and Boston's Museum of Fine Arts are known as the "big four" in the eastern United States. The Midwest boasts the Schubert Club collection in St. Paul, Minnesota, and the Shrine to Music Museum in Vermillion, South Dakota. Still, with its unrivaled comprehensiveness and variety, Europe remains Mecca for the early keyboard enthusiast.

Having to limit our choices may have excluded many worthy museums and private collections that are open to the public. We would have preferred a systematic survey of all European museums, but had we attempted to do so we would still be at it and this book would not have been written. We have described some collections that we did not visit by using information in checklists, catalogs, and material supplied by trusted colleagues (in these cases the text makes clear the source of our information).

A considerable amount of our information came from direct observation; nevertheless, some had to be derived from out-of-date catalogs, guides, and checklists. Further, museums constantly borrow, lend, acquire, and dispose of instruments, so our listings—and theirs!—can never be completely current. And with the slow but steady ongoing research in early keyboards, attributions and dates of instruments are anything but static. We have tried to present our material accurately, but in a book of this nature total accuracy is unachievable.

We submitted drafts to each museum herein, requesting comments and corrections. Most provided helpful information, although a few did not reply. While we do not mean to evade responsibility for errors, to some extent our accuracy depends on the quality of a museum's response. If a museum official told us a harpsichord's buff stop is not original, or that a certain piano dates from 1810 rather than 1800, we accepted that statement, even if it is contradicted by the museum's own publications or inscriptions on its placards. Accordingly, the reader should consider this book a snapshot of the holdings of institutions, rather than a scholarly catalog or comprehensive overview.

Museums change displays, and instruments seen today could be in storage tomorrow. Further, curatorial philosophies change: the current trend is to display fewer items and to insulate them from public contact by placing them on platforms or behind barriers. But even when we have fairly complete information on an institution's holdings, we rarely provide a description of every early keyboard instrument it owns; to do so would turn this guide into a vast and unwieldy catalog. On the contrary, our intent is to alert the reader to the items in each collection that could be considered interesting, unusual, or important.

These qualities cannot be measured by size, complexity, or beauty alone. For example, Oslo's Norsk Folk Museum has only a few early keyboards, and aside from a Hass clavichord and a Shudi & Broadwood harpsichord, none seems particularly interesting. Among them, however, is a small and rather nondescript clavicytherium, of uncertain age and provenance. But it has a partial soundboard, and clavicytheria with this feature are considered the prototypes for later exemplars. One of only three such early versions extant, it is an important artifact, although without some prompting it might receive less than a passing glance from the casual observer.

While almost any instrument can be interesting or important in some way, a guide such as this must be selective. For example, anonymous Italian harpsichords are fairly common; to describe each one in every museum would be redundant. Northern harpsichords, on the other hand, are more individualistic. There are fewer of them, more are signed, and as a group they show greater variety in their dispositions and decorative schemes; consequently, they are usually described in greater detail. Square pianos and seventeenth-century German clavichords, notable more for similarities than for their less obvious differences, are often simply mentioned in passing.

We have tended to focus our descriptions on easily observable characteristics such as range, disposition, number of keyboards, and unusual mechanisms, as well as elements of decoration such as lid and soundboard paintings, chinoiserie, veneers, marquetry, and stands. Decorative aspects are more easily understood and appreciated, while the comprehension of technical elements such as striking points, soundboard barring, case construction, scaling, and minutiae of piano actions usually require specialized knowledge. Furthermore, before the advent of mass-produced pianos, an instrument's decoration was sometimes considered even more important than its musical values. The distinction we make here is an important one and speaks directly to our intent to guide and inform, rather than present technical details best found in catalogs and scholarly studies.

Finally, since we limit this volume to a discussion of stringed keyboards, we have not included organs, except the occasional organ-harpsichord or organ-piano combination.

There are other books that may be useful to those contemplating a visit to European museums. Donald H. Boalch's *Makers of the Harpsichord and Clavichord, 1440–1840*, 3d ed., edited by Charles Mould (Oxford: Oxford University Press, 1995), is invaluable. Boalch lists all known signed harpsichords and clavichords under their makers' names, with locations and comments. An equally useful work, whose purpose parallels Boalch's, is Martha Novak Clinkscale's *Makers of the Piano, Vol. 1: 1700–1820* (Oxford: Oxford University Press, 1993; reprinted with corrections, 1995). Clinkscale is preparing a second volume, for pianos from 1820 to 1860.

This book is aimed at readers who are interested in the history of keyboard instruments, whether or not they are planning a European trip. Nevertheless, those contemplating a pilgrimage would profit from some preparatory reading before embarking, particularly in two important sources that update information found in *The New Grove Dictionary of Musical Instruments*, 3 vols., edited by Stanley Sadie (London: Macmillan, 1984), itself a revision of the material in *The New Grove Dictionary of Music and Musicians*, 20 vols., edited by Stanley Sadie (London: Macmillan, 1980). The first is Edwin Ripin et al., *Early Keyboard Instruments*, The New Grove Musical Instruments Series (New York: W.W. Norton and Co., 1989), which contains a concise and detailed history of the harpsichord along with biographies of such builders as Hass, Ruckers, Taskin, and Zenti. The other is Philip Belt et al., *The Piano*, The New Grove Musical Instrument Series (New York: W.W. Norton and Co., 1989). Like *Early*

Keyboard Instruments, this paperback contains the most current details outside the scholarly literature.

Another useful source is Edward Kottick's *The Harpsichord Owner's Guide* (Chapel Hill: The University of North Carolina Press, 1987). The first three chapters introduce the various regional styles of harpsichord building and give information on how the harpsichord works. Sheridan Germann's authoritative article, "Regional Schools of Harpsichord Decoration," *American Musical Instrument Society Journal* 4 (1978), pp. 54–105, is an excellent introduction to that subject. Two basic works that are somewhat out of date but should be read by anyone who wishes to gain a more detailed knowledge of the instruments are Frank Hubbard's *Three Centuries of Harpsichord Making* (Cambridge: Harvard University Press, 1967); and Raymond Russell's *The Harpsichord and Clavichord*, 2d ed. (London: Faber and Faber, 1973). A book that became a classic upon publication is Grant O'Brien's *Ruckers; A Harpsichord and Virginal Building Tradition* (Cambridge: Cambridge University Press, 1990). It has been consulted regularly in the preparation of this book and is worth careful reading. Another fine scholarly effort is Stuart Pollens's *The Early Pianoforte* (Cambridge: Cambridge University Press, 1995).

Dominic Gill's *The Book of the Piano* (Ithaca: Cornell University Press, 1981), a splendid coffee-table book, has a strong historical bias. A more technical work, but also highly recommended, is Edwin M. Good's *Giraffes, Black Dragons, and Other Pianos* (Stanford, CA: Stanford University Press, 1982).

When the books by Boalch, Clinkscale, Hubbard, O'Brien, and Russell are mentioned in the text, they are cited only by the name of the author. Noted in the same manner are two monographs in volume 3 of *The Historical Harpsichord*, edited by Howard Schott (Stuyvesant, NY: Pendragon Press, 1992): Hubert Henkel's "Bartolomeo Cristofori as Harpsichord Maker" (pp. 1–58); and Denzil Wraight's "The Identification and Authentication of Italian String Keyboard Instruments" (pp. 59–161). Other sources referred to in the text are provided with full citations.

During most of the period covered in this book, spelling—even of proper names—was not standardized; witness Cristofori, Cristofai, Cristofani, Christofani, and Cristofali. A hundred years later the piano builder Caspar Katholnik, who also spelled his first name Casper, signed various of his instruments with Katholnick, Katholnig, Katolnig, and Katholning. Also, builders often Latinized one or more of their names when putting them on an instrument; thus we find Antonius Patavinus appearing on a virginal as Antoni Patavini, and John Player invariably signing his first name as Johannes. To avoid confusion and to provide a modicum of standardization, we have taken Boalch and Clinkscale as our authorities in the spelling of builders' names.

Octave designations are referred to by the system commonly used by organologists, which runs from C through B, with middle C as c^1. An octave below that is c, the next is C, then CC. Accordingly, if the lowest note of a harpsichord is FF, the octave above is F, the next is f, then f^1, f^2, and so on.

CHAPTER I

*A*USTRIA

EISENSTADT

🏛 Burgenländische Landesmuseen

Encompasses three museums: Burgenländische Landesmuseum. Address: Museumgasse 1-5, A-7000 Eisenstadt; hours: 9 A.M.–Noon, 1 P.M.–5 P.M. Tuesday to Sunday; telephone: 2682 62652; fax: 2682 62715 30.

Joseph Haydn Museum. Address: Haydngasse 21, Eisenstadt; hours: 9 A.M.–Noon, 1 P.M.–5 P.M. daily, from Easter to the end of October. Closed May 1; telephone: 2682 62652 29.

Franz Liszt Museum. Address: Lisztstrasse 46, A-7321 Raiding (near Eisenstadt); hours: 9 A.M.–Noon, 1 P.M.–5 P.M. daily, from Easter to the end of October. Closed May 1; telephone: 2619 7220.

The Burgenländische Landesmuseen, situated in the main building of the Burgenländisches Landesmuseum, has two branches: the Joseph Haydn Museum, also in Eisenstadt; and the Franz Liszt Museum, in nearby Raiding. Among these three locations there are four keyboard instruments, all pianos.

Eisenstadt is now the capital of the Austrian province of Burgenland, but in the eighteenth century it was a royal free city of Hungary and a two-day carriage ride from Vienna. From 1761 to 1766, the young Joseph Haydn worked at its Esterházy court as Vice-Kapellmeister (in 1766 he became Kapellmeister and the court was moved to Süttör)—reason enough for the city to have a Joseph Haydn Museum. The only piano here is a 1780 Anton Walter, similar to the one owned by Mozart.

A Paris Érard of 1850–51 came from Liège, Belgium, where it is claimed Franz Liszt played it in 1886, the year he died of pneumonia. Logically, this piano is located in the Franz Liszt Museum. Liszt was born in Raiding, which was then part of Hungary.

The remaining two instruments, by Viennese builders, are in the main museum: a Ludwig Bösendorfer, ca. 1880, and a Michael Rosenberger, ca. 1820, the latter said to have been played by Liszt during a visit to Eisenstadt in the 1840s.

Correspondence regarding any of these instruments should be directed to the Museumgasse 1–5 address.

SALZBURG

Mozart's Birthplace

*Address: Getreidegasse 9, A-5020 Salzburg; hours: 9 A.M.–6 P.M. daily;
telephone: 84 4313; fax: 84 0693.*

It is almost impossible to visit the city in which Mozart was born without paying him homage. His birthplace is primarily a tourist attraction, but it exhibits a keyboard instrument of great significance, an early 1780s Anton Walter fortepiano with hand-operated moderator and two knee levers for split dampers. It was owned by Mozart, who performed with it after he moved to Vienna in 1781. One feels a sense of awe in the presence of the instrument upon which the master daily laid his fingers. It has been restored and used in recordings, and has served as a model for many modern copies.

Museum Carolino Augusteum

*Address: Museumplatz 6, A-5020 Salzburg; hours: 9 A.M.–5 P.M. daily;
telephone: 0622 891 139 or 0622 893 195; fax: 0622 841 134 10.*

Founded in 1834, the Museum Carolino Augusteum is one of the oldest institutions of its type in Europe. Although still occupying its original site, it is no musty mausoleum and is appropriately lit and airy. Its modest number of early keyboard instruments is displayed in spacious surroundings. Six plucked keyboards, five clavichords, and twenty-four pianos are listed in its literature, with important instruments in the first and last classifications.

Seventeenth-century South German harpsichords are rare, but the Carolino Augusteum has two. The earlier, built in Stuttgart by Johann

Ca. 1780 piano by Anton Walter

Mayer in 1619, is a handsome exemplar of its type. About six and a half feet long, with a deeply curved bentside, it has a short brass scale, an elaborate, gilded geometric rose, a sparse soundboard painting, and a flamboyantly ornate keywell. The thin walnut case has applied moldings overhanging both sides, and molded sections are also used on the exteriors. The interior case walls are paneled with contrasting woods.

The jackrail and the keywell are similarly paneled, and are inlaid with mother-of-pearl. The jackrail's most obvious feature, however, is its expanding wedge shape. Disposed 2×8′, the instrument has three rows of jacks. The front and middle rows can both pluck the same 8′ choir, al-

1619 harpsichord by Johann Mayer

though not at the same time, and the back row plucks the other 8′ choir. The three registers, which fan out from one another, are close at the treble and separated in the bass. At the spine the front row has angled forward, closely paralleling the nut, while the rear row has moved away from the relatively straight middle row. The point of all this is to produce three distinct tonal qualities: the middle row makes a "normal" harpsichord sound; the front is a *nasal*, or lute stop; and the back has a more rounded sound, with a strong fundamental and few upper partials. Over these rows of jacks, the "expanding jackrail" goes from a width of about three inches in the treble to twice that in the bass. The registers pass through the cheek and terminate in nicely turned brass knobs.

The other seventeenth-century South German instrument is a claviorganum made in 1639 by the Linz builder Valentin Zeiss. An imposing box, nearly square, with the pipes inside the Prussian blue case, it sits on a low walnut platform. A ten-note pedal board projects from the player's end. The harpsichord soundboard also serves as the top of the organ case. A lid covers the case, with a classically inspired column standing guard at each corner. Although the decoration is richest on the exterior of the box—it is more organ than harpsichord—the harpsichord part has much the same visual and design characteristics as the Mayer instrument. It is without an expanding jackrail, however: disposed 2x8', the two rows of jacks are close and parallel.

Another of the Carolino Augusteum's holdings is an anonymous early seventeenth-century thin-walled polygonal virginal, possibly German, with inset keyboard and a scale of intermediate length. Only three similar virginals are known to be extant, all sixteenth-century Flemish: the 1548 and 1550 instruments by Ioes Karest in the Musée Instrumental in Brussels and the Museo Nazionale in Rome and the 1591 Hans Ruckers in the Gruuthuse Museum in Bruges. A number of paintings showing such virginals also survive. These instruments represent a significant link between a thin-case International style and the newer heavy-case style developed by the Flemish.

Another anonymous early seventeenth-century instrument, a false inner-outer triangular octave spinet with a painting of "Orpheus charming the beasts" on the lid is also probably German. It is unusual for several reasons. For one, a curved left side gives the instrument the appearance of a half-triangular, half-bentside spinet; more startling, though, is the bass end of the keyboard. Although it appears to be a typical broken short octave, with split-sharp C/E bass, there is an additional key below the C/E key, which is covered in ebony with a tripartite decorative pattern inlaid in ivory. In fact, it is a triply divided key, sounding GG, AA, and BB-flat from front to back. Further, the C/E key is also split, playing BB-natural in front and C in back. The split sharps sound D–F-sharp and E–G-sharp, as expected. Interestingly, the rest of the bass end of the case is filled with a wide endblock, so it would have been perfectly possible for the builder to have assigned those last three notes to separate, full key heads. This strange key pattern is seen on some other instruments: a ca. 1800 South German grand piano in Halle's *Händel-Haus*, a 1747 harpsichord by Johann Christoph Pantzner in Vienna's *Kunsthistorisch Museum*, a 1755 harpsichord by the Viennese Johann Leydecker in the *Schloss Eggenberg* in Graz, a harpsichord-piano conversion in Nuremberg's *Germanisches Nationalmuseum*, and an anonymous harpsichord in Prague's *National Museum*.

A 2×8' inner-outer (no outer) harpsichord is signed "D. Francisci Nerii Ariminensis MDCVC," but it may have been an enharmonic instrument built as much as one hundred years earlier and rebuilt by Neri. Its slab-cut cypress soundboard contains an elegant upside-down wedding-cake rose. The case interior and nameboard are beautifully inlaid with leaf patterns, and the cheeks are carved with acanthus leaves.

The Carolino Augusteum has an anonymous bentside spinet with a six-octave range dated 1843, well past that moment early in the nineteenth century when, according to conventional wisdom, harpsichord building came to an end. There was a resurgence—or perhaps a continuance—of virginal building in Italy in the 1830s, but this instrument bears no similarity to the instruments of that school. It is probably German, and looks rather crude. In the absence of further evidence, it should probably be considered an anomaly.

The museum has three small, fretted, short-octave, four-octave anonymous German clavichords, with meager soundboard areas, from the seventeenth and early eighteenth centuries. A 1794 Christoph Friedrich Schmahl clavichord is also fretted, but it is much larger because of its five-octave compass and more generous soundboard. Schmahl, from Regensburg (whose cousin Johann Matthäus Schmahl of Ulm also made clavichords), was better known for his "lying harp" square pianos with a "bentside" at the wrestplank. As befits a Central German instrument, the clavichord is unadorned and finished in natural wood.

A late eighteenth-century anonymous five-octave clavichord in natural wood, with a floating-panel lid, also looks Central German. Because it is unfretted, and therefore has a more extensive string band, it is five inches wider than the Schmahl. It belonged to Joseph von Berchthold zu Sonnenburg, who married Mozart's sister in 1784.

The museum's collection of pianos is important for the work of the eighteenth-century Salzburger Johann Evangelist Schmid, who was also court organ builder. Leopold Mozart evidently thought highly of Schmid, since he recommended him for the court position and even purchased one of his pianos as a wedding present for his daughter, Nannerl. Of the four instruments in the museum that are signed by Johann Schmid, three (ca. 1790, 1794 and 1803) are fortepianos. There are also two instruments by his son Joseph, one of which (ca. 1815) is a fortepiano. Although they appear to be similar to the pianos of Johann Andreas Stein—hardly surprising, since the elder Schmid worked for Stein at Augsburg—they include some of Walter's ideas as well. Both father and son utilized floating-panel lids, but Johann's cases have rounded tails and vertical-grain veneer, while Joseph's has a mitered tail and horizontal grain. Both seemed to use the same pattern for their turned legs.

The ca. 1790 piano has a separate soundboard, strings, and action on the instrument's bottom, and an attached eighteen-note pedalboard. The piano's compass is the standard five-octave FF–f^3, but the pedalboard has a C/E short octave, indicating that even at the end of the eighteenth century that stratagem was still known and employed when appropriate. Schmid built at least three pedal instruments (the others are in New York, at the Metropolitan Museum and in Nuremberg at the Germanisches Nationalmuseum). Mozart wrote for such an instrument; his Walter was

Ca. 1790 pedal piano by Johann Schmid

originally supposed to have had a pedal division. This Schmid is said to have been owned by the daughter of Franz Xaver Gruber, the composer of "Silent Night."

Of the three other Schmids, the 1803 fortepiano was owned by Joseph Haydn's younger brother Michael, a respected church musician who played an important role in Salzburg's musical life. An 1800 pyramid is noteworthy for the unusual horizontal louvers on the door covering the soundboard and the front of the case. A square, dated ca. 1815, looks quite substantial but was evidently designed as a traveling instrument or for tight quarters, since the keyboard disappears into the case when not in use.

The only other Salzburg pianos are an 1845 grand by Ludwig Mooser and a mid-1800s square by Johann Dumel; but the museum holds four more grands, two uprights, and a square by Viennese builders. Two early nineteenth-century grands, by Joseph Böhm (also known as the inventor of a pedal-operated page-turning device) and Ferdinand Comeretto, are both multi-pedaled (seven for the first, six for the second) with Janissary stops; but the similarities stop there. The Comeretto is relatively plain and work-a-day in appearance (as is the ca. 1835 Comeretto square also in this collection); but the Böhm is encased in carefully chosen vertical-grain book-matched veneers, with a lighter, contrasting wood on the interior. A scene of young women in a wooded glen is lacquered on its gracefully back-curved nameboard, and other figures appear on the raised plaques on either side of the keywell. Ebony and gold caryatids sit on tapered square legs, and the unusual lyre, supported by a bow attached at either end to the front legs, shows a fanciful ebony and gold seascape. All in all, the Böhm is typical of the most refined, elegant, and tasteful piano building of the early 1800s.

The 1824 six-octave giraffe by the Viennese builder Heinrich Janszen is a particularly graceful instrument, with uncluttered lines and a restrained use of contrasting veneers. A well-executed statue of Orpheus stands on a little platform on the right, in the crook of the bentside. With crossed legs, draped in a gold cloth and holding a golden lyre, Orpheus lazily leans his elbow against the bentside. The statue's languid pose both parallels the piano's graceful shape and contrasts with its restrained decoration. Five pedals control a bassoon stop, moderator, dampers, a second moderator and the *una corda*.

An 1838 cabinet piano by the Viennese builder Johann Pottje is an early example of an upright form in which the case descends to the floor, thus shortening the overall height. The cabinet doors open to reveal not only the soundboard, bridge, and strings, but also shelves connecting bentside and case wall. Like most upright pianos in which the keyboard bisects the case, some of the strings are tuned from below the keyboard, some from above. Other Viennese pianos include an 1841 Johann Baptist Streicher and an 1870 Streicher & Son. A 1797 square by Nicholaus Rumel and an early nineteenth-century grand by Johann Frenzel are from nearby Linz. The museum has one early twentieth-century piano, a 1910–18 grand by Julius Blüthner of Leipzig.

A 1787 organized square piano by Michael Bogner of Freiburg has pipes in a shallow chest, forming an apron upon which the piano sits. Other squares include a mid-nineteenth-century Kaim & Günther of Stuttgart and a 1775 Christian Baumann of Zweibrücken. The last, said to be the first known piano in Salzburg, was owned by Hieronymus Colloredo, the

1824 giraffe piano by Heinrich Janszen

1838 cabinet piano by Johann Pottje

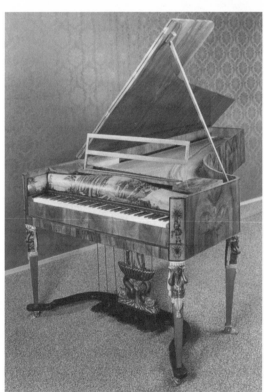

Early 19th-century piano by Joseph Böhm

Archbishop of Salzburg and the employer of Mozart and his father, Leopold. (In 1781, unhappy with what he considered were working conditions of near-servitude, Mozart requested release from his position of cathedral organist. At first Colloredo refused, but when Wolfgang persisted, he literally had him kicked out.) An octave square and an octave grand, both anonymous early nineteenth-century, may have been children's instruments.

The museum's yearbook for 1988 is dedicated to the keyboard instruments: Kurt Birsak, *Salzburger Museum Carolino Augusteum, Jahresschrift*, Band 34/1988 (Salzburg: Salzburger Museum Carolino Augusteum, 1990). A mine of information, it contains detailed descriptions of scales, plucking points, and dimensions. It has many color and black-and-white photos, instructive articles, restoration reports, and historical information of all sorts.

VIENNA

🎔 Kunsthistorisches Museum

Address: Neue Burg, Heldenplatz, A-1010 Vienna; hours: 10 A.M.–6 P.M. Wednesday to Monday; telephone: 1 521 77 471; fax: 1 533 55 13.

Vienna's Art History Museum is housed in several imposing multi-storied buildings with enormous entryways and spacious courtyards. In addition to its outstanding collections of Western, Egyptian, and Oriental art, it possesses an impressive corpus of early keyboards—seven harpsichords, a dozen clavichords, and almost sixty pianos. These, along with many non-keyboard instruments, are displayed in high-ceilinged marbled galleries. One could easily spend several days exploring the treasures of this renowned institution.

The clavichords, all German or Austrian and almost all fretted, date from the end of the seventeenth century through the eighteenth. An unsigned instrument of 1783 had been attributed to the great South German builder Christian Gottlob Hubert, but it is no longer considered to be his work. An anonymous late eighteenth-century clavichord is thought to be by Johann Heinrich Silbermann of Strassburg, nephew of Gottfried Silbermann. The museum has a rare octave clavichord, sounding at 4′ pitch. Closed, it resembles a book, thus joining the ranks of other instruments similarly disguised, such as "bible-regals" and "bible-spinets."

A 1587 combined spinet-regal, the first at 2′ pitch, the second at 4′, by the Augsburg builder Anton Meidting, is another "bible" instrument. The top of each half doubles as a game board, and the entire construction folds

1587 combined octave spinet and regal by Anton Meidting

Clavicytherium by Martin Kaiser, second half of the 17th century

up into a "book." The keys on this complex and expensive little curio are quite small, suggesting that it was built for a child or as a precious object intended primarily for display.

There can be no question that the early seventeenth-century 4' spinet built by a later Augsburger, Samuel Biderman, was intended as a precious object. Veneered with parquetry, it fits into an ornately carved seven-foot high ebony chest richly decorated with tortoise shell, marble, gold and semi-precious stones. This spinet, like others of Biderman and his two sons, has a wind-up clock-work mechanical action that plays six tunes.

A pyramid clavicytherium by Martin Kaiser of Düsseldorf (formerly dated ca. 1675, but now simply attributed to the second half of the seventeenth century) is another elaborately decorated instrument. Standing almost seven feet high, its expanse of tortoise shell, ivory and mother-of-pearl inlays, and ornate bronze mounts is dazzling. This harpsichord has two bentsides and two bridges arranged symmetrically on the soundboard, with the two longest strings placed in the middle. The strings then alternate, until the two shortest are found at the extreme left and right. An organlike roller-board system allows the jacks to pluck the appropriate strings. We know of only one other instrument with two bridges and a roller board, an anonymous Italian pyramid clavicytherium in Rome's Museo Nazionale di Strumenti Musicali.

The Kunsthistorisches Museum has two Italian harpsichords. One was built in 1559 by Joseph Salodiensis of Venice; the other, an anonymous instrument, also Venetian, is from the seventeenth century. Although the latter is now disposed 2×8', it was originally built 1×8', 1×4'. The line of the 4' bridge, which was probably removed in the seventeenth century, can still be seen faintly but clearly on the soundboard.

The mid-eighteenth-century Flemish builder Johann Daniel Dulcken did not leave a large body of work. In his late twenties he moved his shop from Antwerp to Brussels, and he died at the age of thirty-three. Still, he must be considered among the important late Flemish builders. His two-manual harpsichord with five-octave range, disposed 2×8', 1×4' plus lute, is typical of his work. Dulcken favored draw knobs under the wrestplank for register changers, rather than the more usual fulcrum-action levers on top of the wrestplank. His instruments also have a unique interior bentside framework that may have been intended to take some stress off the soundboard.

One of the stranger harpsichords in the Kunsthistorisches Museum is a 1747 single by the otherwise-unknown Viennese builder Johann Christoph Pantzner. The case is made of natural wood, with a deeply curved bentside, a mitered tail, and slanted cheeks; its stand, like that of

1745 harpsichord by Johann Daniel Dulcken

1765 octave clavichord by Johann Moyse

the anonymous harpsichord in Prague's National Museum, is a harpsichord-shaped set of drawers. Also like that instrument, its keyboard appears to descend to C, without C-sharp, and with split keys for F-sharp and G-sharp. However, the apparent C sounds FF; the apparent D is divided into three keys and sounds (from front to back) GG, AA, and BB-flat; the apparent E is twice divided, sounding C and BB-natural. The F-sharp and G-sharp keys follow the normal broken short-octave scheme, with the front portions sounding D and E, and the backs the apparent notes. Other instruments known to have this split bass-octave scheme are cited in connection with the anonymous seventeenth-century triangular octave spinet in Salzburg's Museum Carolino Augusteum.

Another important harpsichord is a 1775 Shudi & Broadwood, one of the largest and most impressive instruments to come from the English tradition. Its five-and-a-half-octave range descends to CC, and it has a Venetian swell, a machine stop, and pedals to operate each mechanism. It is beautifully decorated in English style, with contrasting veneers. Shudi and his partner sent their instruments all over the world; they were owned by Handel, Frederick the Great (who had three), Empress Maria Theresa, Thomas Gainsborough, and other notables.

Most of the pianos in the collection are of local origin. Viennese fortepianos from 1790 to 1820 are well represented, with thirteen by Brodmann, Graf, Hoffman, Jakesch, Kober, Könnicke, Rosenberger, Schantz, Schweighofer, Matthäus Andreas Stein, and Walter—an impressive array. From the same period are a 1791 Johann Andreas Stein (Augsburg), an 1803 Érard (Paris), and an 1807 Broadwood (London). Later pianos include instruments by Blüthner, Bösendorfer, Brodmann, Érard, Ehrbar, Graf, Schweighofer, Steinway, Stodart, and Streicher.

The ca. 1815 instrument by Joseph Brodmann is another example of the rare pedal piano. In this instance the pedal division is in a separate, slant-sided case that sits on the floor and is straddled by the piano itself. Since normal piano pedals would get in the way, the instrument is equipped with knee levers, which were otherwise out of fashion on grands by this date. It is nicely decorated, with Egyptian-inspired legs, and in the keywell, a bronze frieze of a mythological scene features Apollo with his lyre.

An 1839 Conrad Graf, with wood framing, straight stringing, and leather-covered hammers, was not a particularly advanced piano for its time, nor is it especially beautiful; but it is of considerable historical significance. It is the instrument Graf presented to Clara Wieck, one of the first great women virtuosi, on the occasion of her marriage in 1840 to Robert Schumann. After his death Clara gave the instrument to their close friend Johannes Brahms. In 1873 Brahms, who had a keenly

Ca. 1800 piano by Johann Schantz

1840 down-striking piano by Johann Baptist Streicher

1867 piano by Bösendorfer

developed sense of history, donated it to the Vienna Gesellschaft der Musikfreunde, whose collection of early keyboards came to the Kunsthistorisches Museum on loan in the 1930s. Most of the instruments were returned after World War II, but some, like the Graf and the earlier-mentioned Shudi & Broadwood, have remained here.

There are five Bösendorfer pianos: the first, built in 1867 and made for Kaiser Franz Joseph I, is decorated almost to a fault, with elaborate marquetry, ivory bas reliefs, and bronze mounts. It is probably the most ornate piano known. Another (owned by the Gesellschaft der Musikfreunde), dated 1875–76, has an octave coupler. Pianos with such devices, and even with two keyboards that could be coupled, were occasionally produced late in the nineteenth century but were never popular. Although they made the playing of thunderous Lisztian octaves too easy, they made the action unacceptably stiff. A third Bösendorfer, dating from 1909, has a thoroughly "modern" look with its Art Nouveau legs and lack of ornamentation.

The museum owns two rather nice giraffe pianos, one by Franz Martin Seuffert, the other by Kulmbach, both built around 1819, and an equally pleasing ca. 1820 pyramid by the Bohemian Johann Friedrich Reitz. Two upright consoles, by Filippi and Lorenz, are from the latter part of the nineteenth century. Hugo Wolf is said to have owned the Lorenz and composed many of his songs on it.

Surviving square pianos are fairly numerous; the Kunsthistorisches Museum has nineteen. As with the grands, most of the builders represented were Viennese: Bösendorfer, Graf, Heubeck, Katholnik, Kober, Ledezki, Schantz, Stein, and Walter, plus a few anonymous examples. Other builders represented are J. S. Heubeck (Nürnberg, probably related to the Heubeck noted above), Warth (Stuttgart), and more anonyme. There are two from England, one anonymous from 1778, the other an Adam Beyer dated 1790. Most of these instruments are small—true *Tafelklaviere.*

The 1816 instrument by Johann Heinrich Stein—son of Johann Andreas and brother of Nannette—is actually shaped like a table, with drawers under the keyboard for stationery. Schubert is assumed to have played on the 1820–25 Walter, since he appears to be doing so in a painting by Wilhem Rieder. Several of the anonymous instruments are little nighttable pianos, providing a minimum keyboard for the boudoir. The 1885 J. S. Heubeck is a large square grand.

Finally, the museum has two organized pianos: one is by Longman & Broderip (London, late eighteenth century), the other by Franz Xaver Christoph (Vienna, ca. 1785). Organized pianos were intended for home use, and they all look like large cubes with keyboards.

An aging but still useful catalog of the keyboard holdings, *Katalog der Sammlung Alter Musikinstrumente, I. Teil: Saitenklaviere* (Vienna, 1966), lists all the instruments with information on builders, former owners, size, range, registers, action, decoration, and additional literature. It also has thirty-two black and white photos of some of the outstanding specimens.

Technisches Museum für Industrie und Gewerbe

Address: Mariahilferstrasse 212, A-1140 Vienna; hours: 9 A.M.–4 P.M.
Tuesday to Friday, 9 A.M.–1 P.M. Saturday and Sunday;
telephone: 833 618.

Vienna's Technisches Museum is much like the Smithsonian Institution's National Museum of American History: an enormous edifice with all sorts of large, impressive technological and scientific displays, including sailing ships, flying machines, railroad engines, automobiles, generators, and dynamos. A suite of rooms on the second floor contains an intriguing collection of pianos. That the piano should occupy space in such a museum is not surprising—it was one of the most technologically oriented artifacts of the nineteenth century.

One instrument in this assemblage is not a piano at all, but a *Streich-klavier*, a pianolike instrument whose strings are stroked by some sort of bowing mechanism—in this case, rosined leather belts. It was made early in the twentieth century by the Viennese firm of Hofmann & Czerny. There are other extant Streichklaviers, but to our knowledge only one, a Baudet *piano-quatuor* in the Stuttgart Württembergisches Landesmuseum, has been restored to playing condition.

Two pianos have jarring visual features. One is an anonymous Viennese fortepiano from ca. 1800 that looks and sounds normal in all respects, except that its bentside is on the left, rather than the right! It is difficult to avoid the suspicion that such an instrument cannot really exist. The same sense of wrongness is felt with the other piano, a Bösendorfer from ca. 1840, which looks perfectly ordinary until the lid is lifted. Then the eye is greeted by the case framing normally found underneath the soundboard, and the soundboard is in the position usually occupied by the framing. Another unusual piano is an upright console fitted with a Janko keyboard.

The Technisches Museum owns two pianos with down-striking actions by Nannette Streicher and her son, Johann Baptist, that are undated but are probably from the 1840s. Judging from the number of down-strikers still extant, they must have enjoyed at least a brief popularity. Other pianos include a Nannette Streicher of 1819, with four pedals (*una corda*, bassoon, moderator, and damper, which were fairly standard for that time), and two from 1820—a Brodmann *Tafelklavier* and a Clementi grand. Four instruments are from 1840: a small square by Leopold Herr with a compartmented jewel-box lid, a grand by Graf, a combined piano-harmonium, and a Bösendorfer grand. Late nineteenth-century grands include an 1870 Rosenberger, an 1870–95 Hoffman, and an 1890 Bösendorfer. Even the twentieth century is represented, with a ca. 1920 New York Welte Mignon player piano.

$\mathcal{B}$ELGIUM

ANTWERP

🎕 Vleeshuis Museum

Address: Vleeshouwersstraat 38, 2000 Antwerp 1;
hours: 10 A.M.–4:45 P.M. Tuesday to Sunday except for holidays;
telephone: 03 233 6404; fax: 03 231 4705.

The Vleeshuis is not as large as some museums, but its solid brick and stone structure is imposing. Originally a sixteenth-century butchers' guild hall, the museum is now a repository of all manner of Flemish artifacts. The large main floor is impressive, with a colorful array of banners, armor, statuary, paintings, furniture, weapons, costumes, bells, and instruments. The collection of early keyboards, most of which are on the upper floors, is not large: eleven plucked instruments and nineteen pianos; but the harpsichords and muselars form an important assemblage, since all but one were built in Antwerp, with six by members of the Ruckers-Couchet family.

The Ruckers dynasty—Hans Ruckers (ca. 1550–ca. 1598), his sons Ioannes (1578–1643) and Andreas (1579–ca. 1645), Andreas's son Andreas II (1607–ca. 1668) and Andreas II's cousin Ioannes Couchet (ca. 1611–1655)—dominated Antwerp harpsichord building in the late sixteenth and early seventeenth centuries. By 1700 their instruments had achieved legendary status throughout western Europe, heavily influencing eighteenth-century French, English, and North German makers. In view of the illustrious role played by Antwerp craftsmen, the Vleeshuis, with its important collection of Antwerp instruments, has rightly deemed itself the repository of the Ruckers-Couchet legacy, and for many years it has sponsored research into the history of Flemish harpsichord building.

The two muselars in the Vleehuis represent early and late examples of

1650 muselar virginal by Ioannes Couchet

the genre. The first, from 1611, by Ioannes Ruckers, is the earliest known full-size stand-alone muselar from the Ruckers family (two earlier instruments, the 1581 in New York's Metropolitan Museum and the 1591 in New Haven's Yale Collection are mother-and-child muselars, and the 1604 in Brussel's Musée Instrumental is about a foot shorter in length and pitched a tone higher). The second, a 1650 muselar by Ioannes Couchet, is the last-known virginal to come from this workshop. Despite the forty-year gap between them, the instruments, with four-octave, short-octave compasses, are remarkably similar in their musical resources. They are now partially redecorated, but they would have been similar in appearance as well: both sheathed in Flemish papers, with soundboard paintings and the exteriors imitating green porphyry marble. On the 1650 muselar, the location of a portion of the blue scalloped border painted on the sound-board, near the right bridge, reveals that the instrument originally had an arpichordium stop. This beautiful-sounding as well as striking-looking muselar has been recorded many times. Its fine lid painting shows a view of seventeenth-century Antwerp.

The four Ruckers harpsichords also span the years during which the family was most active. Andreas I is represented by a single from ca. 1605 (his first-known instrument), a 1615 double, and a 1644 single (his last-known). The fourth harpsichord is a 1646 single by Andreas II. Both the 1615 and the 1646 still have their painted reddish marbled exteriors. While all Ruckers harpsichords originally had either the marbled finish or, less often, iron strapwork painted on a red ground, few escaped repainting in later *ravalements* (although frequently the case and lid papers and sound-board painting were retained, perhaps to validate the claim that they were indeed by members of the Ruckers family). Otherwise, like the muselars described above, differences between these instruments are slight. Harp-sichord building at any time was conservative, and the Ruckerses were bound by guild regulations that discouraged experimentation and change. Nevertheless, their instruments were prized throughout Europe (and even known abroad: the 1581 mother-and-child muselar in New York's Metro-politan Museum was originally owned by a Peruvian nobleman—a gift, it is thought, from Philip II of Spain).

The Vleeshuis also has a "1629" single with a Ioannes Ruckers rose, but it is from a later date and is not a Ruckers. Many harpsichords, but particularly those of Ruckers and Couchet, were rebuilt, enlarged, and redecorated during the seventeenth and eighteenth centuries, often more than once. The reputation of Flemish instruments was so potent that an enlarged Ruckers could command a price twice or three times that of a new one. Consequently, although many Ruckerses and Couchets have sur-vived, practically none are in original form. When genuine instruments became scarce many builders—even those with reputations, like Blanchet and Taskin—placed real or counterfeit Ruckers roses into old Flemish (but non-Ruckers) harpsichords and even into new ones, and passed them off as authentic. The story of the Ruckers dynasty and the rebuilding and counterfeiting of their instruments is told in detail in O'Brien.

The heyday of harpsichord building in Antwerp ended about the mid-dle of the seventeenth century; still, harpsichords continued to be built there. The Vleeshuis Museum has three important ones dating from a century later: a 1747 single by Johann Daniel Dulcken, a 1763 double by Jacob van den Elsche, and a 1779 single by Joannes Peter Bull. Dulcken,

1646 harpsichord by Andreas Ruckers

1763 harpsichord by Jacob van den Elsche

of German origin but born in the Dutch town of Maastricht, moved to Antwerp before building this harpsichord. Bull, also German, came to Antwerp in 1745 and apprenticed with Dulcken. The 1763 double is the only surviving instrument by van den Elsche (another, in Berlin's Staatliches Institut, was destroyed during World War II). These three large, powerful harpsichords have five-octave ranges and 2×8′, 1×4′ dispositions. The Bull and the van den Elsche both have lute stops and two knee levers (on the Bull they control the buff stop and the dogleg 8′; on the van den Elsche the lute stop and the dogleg 8′) as well as hand stops. The Dulcken has an interior framework paralleling the bentside. This interior bentside, perhaps designed to take some of the tension of the soundboard, is common to all his instruments. The registers are changed by draw knobs working under the wrestplank. While removed from the more rigid 1×8′, 1×4′ Ruckers sound-world, the eighteenth-century tradition from which these harpsichords derive nevertheless owes much to those earlier examples.

The last of the plucked instruments, a pretty little anonymous seventeenth-century inner-outer octave spinet, is probably of North German, or possibly Italian, origin.

The collection of pianos (eleven squares, three grands, five uprights) contains some interesting examples, including two from Antwerp: a graceful 1840 square by Mannekens and a larger, late nineteenth-century square by G. Van Deurme. Two other squares, one anonymous and the other by Karel Kadel, both dated ca. 1840, are from nearby Brussels. In addition, two of the uprights, an anonymous 1850 and a 1917 by P. Hans, are Belgian. The earliest piano in the collection, an anonymous 1760 *Tafelklavier*, has been given a new stand with cabriole legs.

A square with the spine sloping toward the left side and with a bentside at the right was the trademark of Johann Matthäus Schmahl of Ulm. As can be seen from the museums's ca. 1790 example, the bentside is mainly a decorative affectation, since it is the wrestplank, rather than any soundboard area, that is contoured. The shape, known as the "lying harp," was popularized by Schmahl and a few others. Most of them had hand stops for various effects; this one has five. Other squares are by Sébastien Érard (Paris, 1802), John Broadwood (London, ca. 1806), Endrès (Paris, 1826), Jean-Henri Pape (London, 1834), and Simrock (Cologne, no date). The Pape, with its unusual swirling-grain veneer, is particularly attractive.

The grands include one by Graf (Vienna, 1823); two by Pleyel, Wolff & Cie, 1884 and 1899; and a rare *tête-à-tête* piano—a huge, unlikely looking oblong structure with a keyboard at each end.

The museum has published an attractive, illustrated descriptive catalog:

Catalogus Muziekinstrumenten (Antwerp: Museum Vleeshuis, 1981). It also publishes the proceedings of symposia it sponsors from time to time.

🏵 Plantin-Moretus Museum

Address: Vrijdagmarkt 22, B 2000 Antwerp; hours: 10 A.M.–5 P.M.
Tuesday to Sunday except for holidays;
telephone: 03 233 02 94, and 03 232 24 55; fax: 031 226 25 16.

The Plantin-Moretus Museum was a famous print shop in Antwerp when the Ruckerses were building their equally famed harpsichords. Although now a printing museum, it displays one instrument: a unique double-manual harpsichord with a quint virginal built into the bentside, made in 1734 or 1735 by Johannes Josephus Coenen, an organist and amateur harpsichord builder from Roermond. As far as we know, Hans and Ioannes Ruckers were the only other builders to make such an instrument: Hans made one in 1594 (in Berlin's Schloss Köpernick) and Ioannes made two, one undated (in Berlin's Staatlisches Institut) and the other in 1619 (in Brussels, at the Musée Instrumental). Since the 1619 is the only one of the three to have two manuals and a quint (the others are singles with octave virginals), it may well be that Coenen's harpsichord is the first known example of what we would today call a historical copy. The imposing combination, with its lid painting of St. Cecilia at the organ (a copy after Rubens by C. and F. Bender), is supposed to have been housed in the museum building since it was made.

BRUGES

🏵 Gruuthuse Museum

Address: Dyver 17, 8000 Bruges; hours: 9:30 A.M.–Noon, 2–5 P.M. daily in
summer; 10 A.M.–Noon, 2–5 P.M. Wednesday to Monday in winter;
telephone: 050 44 87 11; fax: 050 44 87 78.

The city of Bruges is something of a museum in itself. In the fourteenth century it was one of the busiest and most prosperous ports in Europe, but in the next hundred years its waterways silted up and most of the trade had moved to Antwerp. Bruges never recovered its former glory; but with its Gothic architecture and a system of canals and bridges, the city has retained some of its Renaissance flavor.

1591 polygonal virginal by Hans Ruckers

Containing treasures of Belgium, the Gruuthuse's holdings include paintings, sculpture, furniture, *objets d'art*, some magnificent tapestries, a huge, ominous-looking guillotine, and a few musical instruments. It has two Ruckers, a 1591 virginal by Hans and a 1624 harpsichord by Andreas. The latter was originally a two-manual harpsichord with unaligned keyboards, but it was later rebuilt into a single. This is precisely the opposite of what usually took place when such instruments underwent *ravalement*: many single-manual harpsichords and almost all unaligned doubles were later turned into aligned doubles. Presently, this one has no keyboards at all.

The 1591 is a rare and much-discussed example of a Flemish spinet virginal in polygonal form. Only two other Flemish polygonals exist, both by Ioes Karest, an Antwerp predecessor of Hans Ruckers, dating from 1548 (in Brussels at the Musée Instrumental) and 1550 (in Rome's Museo Nazionale). Similar virginals can be seen in both Flemish and German paintings; perhaps the best-known example is van Falckenburg's *Musical Society at Nuremberg* in Nuremberg's Germanisches Nationalmuseum. Both the virginals in the paintings and the Karest examples are thin-case instruments; in fact, like thin-walled Italian harpsichords and virginals, both Karests have outer cases. The Ruckers, on the other hand, is a thick-walled instrument and differs from the Karest virginals in other ways as well. Aside from the fact that its two rear corners have been "eliminated," in size, string scale, and decoration it is very much like the oblong virginals normally built by the Ruckerses. The outside of the case still shows the painted green porphyry marble that constituted the usual Ruckers finish for members of the virginal family. The interesting relationship between all these instruments is explored in detail in O'Brien.

The Gruuthuse also has an anonymous Italian harpsichord more in pieces than together, and square pianos by Christian Fuhrmann of Ghent (1777), Guillaume Le Blond of London and Dunkirk (1792), and Jean-Joseph & Eugène Ermel of Bergen (1798).

The museum has published a catalog: *Catalogus van de Muziekinstrumenten* (Brugge, 1985).

BRUSSELS

🎵 Musée Instrumental de Bruxelles

Address: 17 Petit-Sablon, Brussels B 1000; hours: 2:30 P.M.–4:30 P.M. Tuesdays, Thursdays, and Saturdays; 10:30 A.M.–12:30 P.M. Sundays; telephone: 02 511 35 95; fax: 02 512 85 75.

François-Joseph Fétis died in 1871, and the next year his heirs sold his collection of more than 7,000 books to Belgium's Royal Library. The purchase included his large assemblage of musical instruments, which the government stored in the attics of the Brussels Conservatoire, where they became the basis for the Conservatory collection, established in 1877. (Fétis was a larger-than-life composer, conductor, theorist, musicologist, and bibliographer. For almost forty years, he was director of the Conservatory. His crowning achievement was a highly original treatise on music theory, *Traité complet de la théorie et de la pratique de l'harmonie*, published in 1844.) Three other substantial collections were added to Fétis's: part of the holdings of Abel Régibo, a lawyer from Renaix; most of the instruments of the Venetian Giovanni Correr; and a large and important group from the Belgian collector César Snoeck, who also sold instruments to Berlin and St. Petersburg. The collection had always been part of the Conservatory, but in 1992 it was separated and became a department of the Royal Museum of Art and History. Faced with more than seventy plucked instruments, well over 150 pianos, a dozen clavichords, and a *Geigenwerk*, we cannot discuss the entire collection; but we will describe the more important of these treasures, most of which have been on display in the past.

With its proximity to Flanders it is not surprising that the Musée Instrumental has seventeen Flemish virginals, eleven of which are by members of the Ruckers clan. Many of the various sizes and types of virginals the family produced are represented here, including muselars at normal pitch (Andreas, 1620 and 1633; Ioannes, 1614 and 1638), a step higher (Ioannes and Andreas, 1604), quart- (Ioannes, 1629) and quint- (Andreas, 1613, 1613, and 1632) spinett-virginals, and mother-and-child muselars (Ioannes, 1610 and 1628, the last converted to a normal muselar). The earliest instrument, the 1604 muselar a step above normal pitch, has been repainted but otherwise little altered. It has a Hans Ruckers rose, but the names of his sons Ioannes and Andreas are prominently displayed on the jackrail. Although the inscription is not original, the instrument was indeed built by the brothers (Hans was dead by that time). The rose is made of *papier mâché*, but gilded like the normal Ruckers lead roses. The 1610 mother-and child muselar and the 1614 muselar, both by Ioannes, present interesting contrasts in the way they were later redecorated. The 1610 was painted an unattractive brown; but the 1614, while also repainted, was decorated by Aespin van de Passe with figures derived from a 1599 woodcut of animals and people playing instruments and dancing.

Of the museum's three non-Ruckers virginals the most important is a 1548 polygonal instrument by Ioes Karest, the earliest surviving Flemish harpsichord of any kind. Looking little like later virginals and muselars, it more resembles the 1591 Hans Ruckers polygonal virginal in the Gruuthuse Museum. Its thin-case inner-outer construction bears a superficial likeness to the unpainted Italian instruments of the time. (It has been fairly well established that the earliest Flemish harpsichords were derived from early German and International prototypes, which admittedly had much in common with Italian models.) This instrument, with its polygonal form, thin sides, inset keyboard, and separate outer case, shows much of that influence. Another virginal by Karest, dated 1550, is in Rome's Museo Nazionale. It has painted decoration on natural wood, with motifs similar to those on the papers later used during the time of the Ruckerses, but the exterior of the Brussels virginal is decorated with a Latin motto painted on the natural wood. The soundboards of the Karest virginals were also decorated, although only traces of that painting still exist. Karest, who was born in Cologne but moved to Antwerp in his teens, was an important figure. He headed the list of harpsichord makers who requested, and gained, admission to the St. Luke's guild in 1557. Interestingly, the guild was concerned with the decorative arts.

1548 polygonal virginal by Ioes Karest

Another significant non-Ruckers virginal is a ca. 1580 instrument by Johannes Grouwels, one of the two existing Flemish virginals with its keyboard placed in the middle. The Ruckerses put them on the right or, less often, on the left; but there are no extant Ruckerses with the keyboard in the middle. A builder named Joris Britsen is represented by two virginals, a 1676 muselar and a 1686 octave instrument. (The Britsens were a family of Antwerp builders, three of whom were named Joris. They left few examples of their work, and none can be ascribed with certainty to a specific Joris.)

Of some twenty surviving English virginals, the Musée Instrumental owns the earliest, built in 1641 by Gabriel Townsend. It is an excellent example of a genre which, like the Flemish virginal, was largely derived from Germanic and International models. Like the Flemish instruments it so much resembles, this virginal has papers on the exterior and interior of the case and a decorated soundboard; but it also has molded frames on the exterior of the case and a coffered lid. The oak case is left natural on the exterior. A naive painting of Orpheus charming the beasts graces

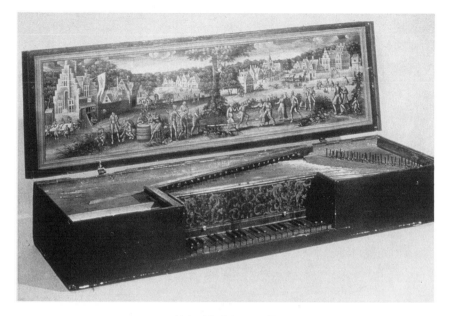

1580 virginal by Johannes Grouwels

Ca. 1631 bentside spinet by Girolamo Zenti

the interior of the lid. The English placed the keyboard at the left of the case, as did the Flemish in their spinett-virginals.

Other virginals, spinets, and octave instruments include two by Albert Delin, sixteen from Italy, and three anonymes from France and one from Germany.

Girolamo Zenti, one of the most peripatetic of harpsichord builders, was born near Rome. He worked in that city on at least one occasion, but he also built instruments in Stockholm, London, and Paris, where he died in 1668. He is credited with inventing the bentside spinet, and the Musée Instrumental owns what may indeed be the first example of that type, dated 1631. Another bentside spinet is an unusual eighteenth-century anonymous French instrument at 4′ pitch.

The museum owns one of the three extant harpsichord-virginal combinations mentioned in connection with the "copy" in the Plantin-Moretus Museum: the imposing 1619 Ioannes Ruckers two-manual harpsichord with a quint virginal built into the bentside. It has been so over-restored that very little is original—not the striking Flemish papers or the lid painting. Nevertheless, it is something to see, and it makes one wonder what the builders had in mind with such a combination.

Five more harpsichords (1612, 1637, 1639, and two undated) are attributed to the Ruckers family (the 1639 to Andreas, the others to Hans), but they are either genuine Flemish, non-Ruckers instruments into which counterfeit Ruckers roses have been placed (one of the undated, the 1637, and the 1639), have no rose at all (the other undated), or are perhaps entirely counterfeited (the 1612). One of the undated instruments is intriguing because it has a set of 16′ strings; it is little more than a conglomeration of parts of other instruments and never really had an original state. An inscription on the 1612 says it was rebuilt and enlarged by Taskin in 1774, but O'Brien (p. 278) believes that Taskin may have built the whole thing. It is worth noting that these "fakes" are not bad or worthless instruments simply because they were passed off as Ruckerses; some of them are quite fine. A seventeenth-century non-Ruckers Flemish harpsichord is by Simon Hagaerts.

A 1646 Couchet double, repainted a nondescript off-white, is one of the finest-sounding antique harpsichords we have heard. Evidence of its *ravalement*, where extra wood was placed onto the bentside and nameboard to expand the treble register, can easily be seen.

The museum has seven Italian harpsichords: by Dominicus Pisaurensis (sixteenth century), Alessandro Trasuntino (1538), Giovanni Boni (1619), Girolamo Zenti (ca. 1656), Nicolaus de Quoco (1694), and two seventeenth-century anonymes. The 1619 Boni, a single-strung inner-outer, has a broken C/E short octave and split keys on all its E-flats and G-sharps; the purpose was to allow the player access to D-sharps and A-flats as well, since accidentals are not enharmonic in mean-tone tuning.

A 1679 Vincent Tibaut, one of the few extant seventeenth-century French harpsichords, shows a strong influence of the International School. Its bentside is deeper and the case walls thinner than found on Flemish models. Like most northern harpsichords, it has a painted soundboard. This beautiful two-manual instrument is completely covered with mar-

1734 harpsichord by Hieronymus Hass

quetry, inside and out. Its solid ivory sharps are typical of French harpsichords of the time.

The two other French harpsichords in the collection are a 1709 Marius *clavecin brisé* and a Pleyel, Wolff from the 1880s—one of the earliest instruments of the harpsichord revival.

Probably the most physically imposing instrument in the Musée Instrumental is the 1734 two-manual harpsichord by Hieronymus Hass. He and his son Johann Adolph were organ, clavichord, and harpsichord builders in Hamburg. They made some complex harpsichords with 16′ stops. This instrument is disposed 1×16′, 2×8′, 1×4′ plus lute, and with everything going its sound is organlike and majestic. The tortoise shell, ivory, and ebony contrasts in the keywell are typical of the care the Hasses took with the visual element of their instruments; and the ebony and ivory chevrons on the sharps are particularly striking. Despite its colorful interior and classically inspired lid painting, the exterior is painted a dull grey, although this may not be the original finish. It is a massive instrument, with a thicket of bridges and hitchpin rails blanketing its painted soundboard. Like all such Hasses, the 16′ strings have their own bridge on a separate section of soundboard.

A 1773 Shudi & Broadwood represents the complete late English harpsichord, with machine stop and Venetian swell, although its exterior is not as elegant as some other English instruments of this vintage. A 1751 single by the Tournai builder Albert Delin is a clavicytherium, taking no more floor space than a virginal. With the soundboard only inches away from the performer's head, these instruments resonate about the ears in an exhilarating fashion. The other two extant Delin clavicytheria are in Berlin's Staatliches Institut and The Hague's Gemeentemuseum.

The museum owns three harpsichords by Johann Daniel Dulcken, a 1755, a 1769, and an undated one from ca. 1750. The last has lost its exterior paint, providing an opportunity to study the case joinery. The through-mortises of the wrestplank, for example, are easily visible. The instrument still has its lid painting, signed by the artist Bigée. Other late Antwerp harpsichords include 1776 and 1789 instruments by Dulcken's student Johann Peter Bull.

Three interesting clavichords are housed in Brussels. The first is an anonymous sixteenth-century thin-walled instrument designed to go into an outer case. Polygonal in shape, with a sloping soundboard and three bridges, it is characteristic of sixteenth-century Italian clavichords. The range is short-octave C/E–f^3, the same four and a half octaves found on Italian harpsichords and virginals of that time; in the next century that range was reduced to short-octave C/E–c^3 on both plucked instruments and clavichords. The second clavichord looks like a rather normal, if nondescript, seventeenth-century German fretted instrument, but it betrays its Flemish origins in two ways: Flemish papers decorate the case lid, toolbox lid, and cheeks; and each boxwood-covered natural has two sets of double-scored lines, with a dimple between the two sets on each side of the key, a decorative gesture characteristic of Flemish keyboards. An additional feature of this clavichord, to our knowledge not found on any other instrument, is the imaginative knuckle-like carving on the key levers.

The third clavichord is by Hieronymus Hass, the same Hass who built the museum's large 1734 harpsichord. This 1744 instrument is also large, with an expansive soundboard area and a five-octave range. The bottom octave and a half has a third set of strings, at 4′ pitch, to brighten the sound of the deepest bass strings. Its lid decoration appears to be something we might identify today as calendar art—scenes printed on paper and glued onto the lid.

With roughly twenty-five grands, seventy squares, fifty upright consoles, some assorted cabinets, and a pyramid, Brussels has one of the world's largest collection of pianos. Most of them are in storage, so we must of necessity confine our descriptions to a few specific instruments. Only one grand, an 1835 by T. J. Dumoulin of Liège, is from Belgium. Most of the others are from France, and of these, the majority are by Érard and Pleyel, and the many partners they took on from time to time. The rest are from Germany (with a 1786 Stein), Austria, and England. In fact, most of the grands produced in the nineteenth century came from France, Germany, Austria, and England, while local manufacture tended to concentrate more on squares and, later, upright consoles. Accordingly, twenty-five of the squares are Belgian, with over half from Brussels. The upright consoles are in about the same proportion.

Covered with beautiful marquetry, a tall, slender 1745 pyramid piano by Christian Ernst Friederici is an impressive piece of furniture, the first of his three surviving pyramids. Although he is said to have invented the genre, Friederici was not the first to build a piano in upright form; that honor probably goes to Domenico del Mela, a Sicilian builder whose sinuous 1739 upright piano is in Florence's Museo degli Strumenti Musicali.

A 1783 square by Johann Gottlob Wagner of Dresden has a cover over the soundboard, which is hinged at the back and operated by a knee lever. When the lever is pressed the lid rises, after the fashion of a nags-head swell, assisting the effort toward *crescendo*. Swells like this were not uncommon on small squares. The museum also has a ca. 1785 "lying harp" *Tafelklavier* by Johann Matthäus Schmahl of Ulm.

Finally, among that richness of early keyboards is the only extant *Geigenwerk*, a type of "bowed" stringed keyboard instrument invented by the Nuremberg builder Hans Heiden. Attempts to build a keyboard instrument in which sounds could be sustained as on bowed strings go back as far as Leonardo da Vinci, but Heiden was the first to have developed a successful model. Instead of jacks, hammers, or some other plucking or beating mechanism, it had rosined wheels that protruded through the gap. Pressing a key pulled the string down to the wheel, and, in the manner of a hurdy-gurdy, the rotating wheel set the string into vibration. The string would continue to sound as long as the turning wheel was in contact. The museum's instrument is a rather crude version of Heiden's design, with a slantside rather than a bentside. It was built in 1625, by a Spaniard named Raymundo Truchado. Other than the mechanism itself, with its four protruding wheels, and the hand crank protruding from the tail, its most fascinating feature is its stubby legs.

Instruments in the Musée Instrumental have been the subject of several exhibition catalogs, all of which describe and picture some of the keyboards. One, in French, describes an exhibition held in the Hôtel de Sully: *Instruments de musique des XVIe et XVII siècles* (Paris, 1969). Another, for

1745 pyramid piano by Christian Friederici. IRPA-KIK-Brussels.

1625 Geigenwerk by Raymundo Truchado. IRPA-KIK-Brussels.

a 1972 exhibition, was published in Dutch and French. The Dutch title is *Catalogus van de Tentoonstelling Gewijd aan Musiekinstrumenten uit de XVIe en XVIIe Eeuw Behorend tot het Instrumentenmuseum van Brussel.*

The last, for an exhibit in Brussels, December 1985–January 1986, is *Instruments de musique anciens à Bruxelles et en Wallonie—17e–20e siècles*. This catalog may still be found in bookstores, but the others are out of print. Also out of print for many years, and quite dated, is Victor Mahillon's *Catalogue descriptif et analytique du Musée instrumental du Conservatoire de musique de Bruxelles*, 5 vols., 1880–1922. Mahillon was a Victorian-era curator of the museum, and his work is one of the earliest comprehensive museum catalogs. It was reprinted in 1978.

CHAPTER III

CZECH REPUBLIC

PRAGUE

National Museum, Music Instrument Museum

*Closed to the public. For information write to
Department of Musical Instruments, Lázeňská 2, 118 01 Prague 1;
telephone: 245 101 14; fax: 242 264 88.*

Bohemia, as this fertile area in Central Europe is called, was long part of the Austro-Hungarian Empire. After World War I it became part of Czechoslovakia, the union of Czechs and Slovaks; but the independent Czech Republic was created in 1993, after the breakup of Czechoslovakia.

Because of lack of support—a situation not uncommon in many former Eastern-bloc countries—the contents of Prague's Music Instrument Museum are now in storage. This is especially unfortunate because, although it has some plucked instruments and clavichords, its holdings in nineteenth-century pianos by Bohemian and Viennese builders are significant. The instruments still exist, however, and by writing ahead, those with bona fide credentials may still be able to see some things of specific interest. And perhaps, with better times to come, the collection may be reopened one day. We were not able to view this museum before it closed; our information comes from the checklists described at the end of this section and from photographs and descriptions supplied by colleagues.

The museum has six harpsichords, a virginal, and two bentside spinets, although only three of the harpsichords, the virginal, and one of the spinets are what we would normally consider antiques. The one signed harpsichord is a 1722 double by Johann Heinrich Gräbner the elder of Dresden, the patriarch of a family of organists and instrument builders, most of whom engaged in both activities. It now has a five-octave range of EE–e³, but the orginal compass was a more normal FF–d³. The ornate carved stand is not original. This instrument is said to have been played in a private palace by Mozart in 1787, presumably when he was in Prague to mount *Don Giovanni*.

The two anonymous antique harpsichords are interesting. The earlier one, dating from ca. 1700, has many characteristics of the seventeenth-century International School and could be of Viennese or possibly Bohemian origin. A small 2×8′ single, finished in attractive wood veneers, it has a deeply curved, thin-walled bentside and a rounded tail, but neither a rose nor a soundboard painting. Like the 1747 Johann Christoph Pantzner harpsichord in Vienna's Kunsthistorisches Museum, it has slanted cheeks and sits on a harpsichord-shaped cabinet decorated with the same veneers and in the same style as the instrument it supports. It also has the same short octave as the Pantzner: FF/C; G, AA, BB-flat/D; C, B/E; etc., although this keyboard has mother-of-pearl naturals and tortoise shell sharps.

The second anonymous harpsichord is a 2×8′ FF–f³ single from the late eighteenth century, possibly by the inventive Florentine Vincenzio Sodi. In 1792 Sodi had the distinction of producing the last surviving Italian harpsichord—at least, as far as we know. The extant Sodi instruments resemble one other, and this harpsichord is no exception. They all have elegant long cases, deeply curved bentsides, slanted cheeks, rounded

Late 18th-century harpsichord attributed to Vincenzo Sodi

tails (Sodi is the only Italian maker who appears to have done this), and plain but prominent bottom moldings. This instrument is strikingly finished in gold and black chinoiserie on a red ground.

Chronologically, Prague's next harpsichord, by Ignatz Lutz of Vienna, is dated from the last third of the nineteenth century. If so, it is one of the very few instruments built at that time, when the revival of the harpsichord was barely in its infancy.

For many years now, harpsichords from the early twentieth century have been finding their way into museums. A different breed from the antiques, they draw strongly on piano technology, with an emphasis on a wide tonal palette and the use of pedals to shift quickly from one tone color to another. They were heavily built and braced like pianos, without bottoms and often with metal frames. Such instruments went out of style in the 1960s, and today few people are familiar with them. Prague's two remaining harpsichords, doubles by Gaveau (Paris, 1923) and Neupert (Bamberg-Nuremberg, 1935), are examples of this genre. One of the bentside spinets, by E. Klingler, Vienna, 1799, is an antique; the other, by Hanns Neupert, is a twentieth-century version.

The museum has thirteen clavichords, all but two fretted. There are seven anonymous instruments, late eighteenth- or early nineteenth-century, including a small, portable clavichord, a 1683 Johann Baumgartner (Bolzano), and an unfretted ca. 1800 clavichord by Klingler. Four examples are of Bohemian origin: two early nineteenth-century instruments by T. Wokurka & A. Kunz, an 1821 (the second unfretted) by Ignaz Kunz, and an 1839 by K. Kunz.

The real strength of Prague's Music Instrument Museum lies in its collection of more than one hundred pianos, consisting of grands, squares, pyramids, giraffes, upright consoles (including a quarter-tone version), and desk pianos. We have observed that antique instruments tend to be found near the locales of their origins. Accordingly, many Bohemian pianos are located in Prague; but there are also instruments here from Vienna, not only because of its geographical proximity to Bohemia, but also as a result of Austrian hegemony in that area in the eighteenth and nineteenth centuries. Of the collection's seventy-five grands, about a third are from Prague and only a few less have Viennese origins, with the remainder either from Germany or other towns in Bohemia. Most are nineteenth century, with several late eighteenth and a handful of early twentieth, including a pair of New York Steinways from 1926 and 1927.

Some of these pianos were either owned by or otherwise associated with famous composers and performers. Mozart is supposed to have used a 1787 Viennese fortepiano by Ignatz Kober, probably in 1787, the same year he played the Gräbner harpsichord. A Viennese Bösendorfer of 1862 is said to have belonged to Antonín Dvořák, and a ca. 1901 grand by the same firm is connected with the Bohemian violinist and composer Joseph Suk, who was a student of Dvořák and his son-in-law. A ca. 1840 J. B. Streicher with down-striking action was played by Franz Liszt in an 1846 recital, and two 1870 pianos by the Prague builder A. Ullrich were used by Bedřich Smetana.

Upright pianos in the museum include two anonymous pyramids and one Bohemian pyramid by A. Hief, all early nineteenth century; and two anonymous, one Bohemian (J. F. Reyez), and two Viennese giraffes (Franz Martin Seuffert, and Seuffert & Seidler), all from the early 1800s. One of the anonymous giraffes, a small instrument, is a curious combination of stark, squared, unmolded woodwork with a facing of gold and white grillework-like motifs (perhaps Bohemian in origin) on a blue background.

Of the seventeen squares, six are anonymous early nineteenth-century instruments, five are from various places in Germany (including one, by Meyer of ca. 1800, from as far north as Hamburg), two are Viennese, and the rest are Bohemian, with only one from Prague. Almost all are early nineteenth century. Except for one by Gräbner, all nine pianos are Bohemian. Three more pianos are classified by the 1992 checklist as "upright pianos with case," which we are calling "desk pianos," that is, upright consoles on which sit desklike cabinets. One of these, by the Viennese builder Michael Rosenberger, has a superstructure consisting of little drawers perched on top of the instrument's case. A Prague example from the same era, by Leopold Sauer, is surmounted by a tall case with doors.

Some of the pianos are eye-catching. A Viennese Walter & Sohn from ca. 1820–30 has graceful proportions and a case and lid covered with beautiful burl veneer. Its hexagonal legs are enlivened by blue paint and gold leaf. A blue-and-gold lyre supports six pedals, and an ivory leaf motif repeats itself around the lower case molding. A monochromatic outdoor scene is painted on the back-curved nameboard. Visually, the instrument is an elegant and harmonious example of the finest piano making of the time. An 1819 grand by Jacob Weimes of Prague, although also impressive and of high quality, is less graceful than the Walter. The mahogany case with its plain veneer appears deeper in relation to the length, its massive legs are tapered squares, and a contrasting but unrefined pattern of objects resembling *fleurs-de-lis* runs around the perimeter of the bottom part of the case. Its back-curved nameboard also has a painting, but it is more exuberant than the one found on the Walter. Less care, planning, and expense seem to have gone into the Weimes, but it was probably not as expensive a piano. Of its musical qualities, of course, we know nothing.

There are two checklists for this collection. The latest, in Czech, with a few words translated into English, is entitled *Soupis hudebních nástroju v Muzeu české hudby/KLÁVESOVÉ CHORDOFONY I./ Strunné klávesové nástroje* [*The inventory of musical instruments collection at the Museum of Czech Music/ CHORDOPHONES I/ Hammered and plucked keyboard instruments*], compiled by Bohuslav Čižek (Prague, 1992). The earlier list is a forty-eight-page booklet printed in German for an exposition of Prague's museums in 1970 and 1974. There seem to be three separate titles: the most official-looking and certainly most descriptive is *Katalog der Dauerausstellung der Musikinstrumente der Musikabteilung des Nationalmuseums Praha*. The one on the cover and the first page reads, *Musik Instrumenten Museum, Nationalmuseum, Praha*; and the title on the back of the booklet is *Katologe der Expositionen des Nationalmuseums, Praha*, 1974. The catalog specifies the contents of each room in the museum: fourteen of the early keyboard holdings, the only ones displayed, are listed in Room One, where they remained until the recent closing of the collection.

CHAPTER IV

$\mathcal{D}$ENMARK

COPENHAGEN

Musikhistorisk Museum og Carl Claudius' Samling

Address: Åbenra 30, DK-1124, Copenhagen; hours: 10 A.M.–3 P.M. Monday to Friday; telephone: 33 11 27 26; fax: 33 11 60 44.

Founded in 1897, the Musikhistorisk Museum owes many of its keyboard holdings to the activity of a single collector, Carl Claudius; indeed, those original items are still referred to as the Claudius Collection. Although the museum has some interesting harpsichords and pianos, its choice assemblage is of clavichords, particularly those of the Hass family. A caveat is in order: our checklists are incomplete, so this account may be less than accurate. Nevertheless, a visit to this museum will reward the early keyboard lover with many engaging sights.

Five of Copenhagen's clavichords bear the Hass name—a significant percentage of the approximately twenty-five extant signed by that family. The 1743, with a lovely "Apollo and the Muses" lid painting, is by Hieronymus Hass. The others are by his son Johann Adolph: one from 1755 and three from 1761. The 1743 and the 1755 are unfretted, but the three later ones are all at least partially fretted. It is easy to assume that unfretted clavichords, in which every course of strings has its own tangent, are superior to fretted ones; and we might think it strange that having built examples of the former, Hass should continue to make the latter. But performers might not have been so eager to give up fretted clavichords. Since their cases did not have to carry the tension of a full set of strings, they were lighter and more stable. And since they were not as wide, their key levers could be shorter, providing a more responsive touch. Moreover, with fewer strings, tuning was easier; and with less tension on the soundboard, fretted clavichords tended to be somewhat louder. Their inability

1743 unfretted clavichord by Hieronymus Hass

to play some adjacent notes simultaneously was more likely regarded as a mild annoyance than as a serious flaw.

The 1755 Hass has an unusual lid painting: a striking black, red, and white chinoiserie on a yellow ground. Neither the red finish on its case exterior nor its stand, with the exaggerated cabriole legs favored by the North Germans, are original. The same is true of the 1743 instrument: neither its pale yellow exterior nor its stand are original. The stands on both these clavichords are practically identical, and may have been made at the same time, perhaps as copies of some original stand. Interestingly, the lid decoration on one of the 1761 instruments consists of two tiers of papers, the upper containing eight portraits of famous historical personages, the lower, five hunting scenes. Its stand, with turned legs and bottom stretchers, is much more sedate. All the Hass clavichords in this collection have an octave-and-a-half or more of 4' strings in the bass, to brighten the sound of the bass strings.

Although the decorative elements were not as flamboyant, Scandinavian clavichord building closely followed the North German school, and, in fact, continued well after the time they were no longer being built in

Hamburg. The case decoration and lid painting of the 1769 clavichord by Hartwich Müller of Copenhagen, though typical in this sense, are not original. The decor of the light-colored case could be described as "French provincial," and the lid painting depicting country pleasures, done in 1918 by H. Larsen, is handsomely executed in a style derivative of Watteau and his French contemporaries. Like most North German and Scandinavian builders, Moritz Georg Moshack made organs as well as harpsichords and clavichords. His 1770 instrument has the same 4' bass strings found in Hass clavichords. A 1777 clavichord is by Johan Jesper Jørgensen of Odense, Denmark.

Otto Joachim Tiefenbrunn was born in Germany but migrated to other lands to ply his craft. He settled in Copenhagen, and his 1793 clavichord remained in the family of the original owner until 1963, when it was sold to the Musikhistorisk Museum. This instrument sits on a stand showing strong English influences in its Chippendale-style legs and fretwork corner brackets; one should be suspicious of clavichord stands, however, since many of them are replacements built in the late nineteenth and early twentieth centuries.

Marcus Gabriel Sondermann, represented by a 1796 clavichord, built instruments in Rendsburg, Germany, near the Danish border. The youngest clavichord in the Copenhagen collection is a five-and-a-half-octave 1798 instrument by the Stockholm builder Pehr Lindholm. Its severe decor shows that by the end of the century the restrained ideas of German classicism had reached Scandinavia. Finally, there are two anonymous seventeenth-century four-octave short-octave fretted clavichords (one is "signed" on the lid with the initials JBH), probably from Germany.

Copenhagen has a nice collection of Italian plucked instruments, many of them undated and unsigned. Among them are two inner Italian polygonal virginals with C/E–f^3 range, indicating that they probably were made in the sixteenth century. (This four-and-a-half octave compass was then common in Italy, even though virtually no music was written there requiring the highest notes. The range was later reduced to the four-octave C/E–c^3, for reasons probably having to do with stringing materials, pitch levels, and transpositions.) One of these, from Venice, has a traditional fully projecting keyboard, but the other, half-projecting, possibly came from Milan, where that sort of keyboard placement was common. There are two other anonymous and undated polygonal virginals, one with the shorter C/E–c^3 compass and one at 4' pitch.

An early nineteenth-century instrument, finished in gold, with cabriole legs, looks like an anachronistic French square piano, but it is indeed a virginal. There was a minor late-Italian resurgence of virginal building,

Anonymous 18th-century harpsichord

long after plucked keyboards had given way to pianos. Others of this type include a ca. 1820 virginal in a private collection in Italy and two virginals by Alessandro Riva: an 1836 in Milan's Museo degli Strumenti Musicali and an 1839 in Leipzig's Musikinstrumenten-Museum.

One of the harpsichords is also anonymous, and the plainness of its decor suggests that it dates from the eighteenth century. Another is signed Dominicus Pisaurensis, but that attribution is considered false. A clavicytherium from the late seventeenth century is the last of the anonymous Italians.

Dated and signed instruments include a 1592 Donatus and two harpsichords by Nicolaus de Quoco of Florence, dated 1612 and 1615. Both de Quocos are inner-outers, but only the 1615 has an outer case. The 1612 has a curious device called a *Cornettzug* (cornet stop, most likely referring to its octave quality), which looks somewhat like a misshapen 4' bridge and may have been added after the instrument had been built. Little upright points of hard felt, when moved by means of a stop knob at the front of the case, contact the strings of one of the 8' courses exactly in the middle of their sounding lengths. Like a guitarist producing harmonics by pressing lightly on a string's nodal point, the pressure of the leather points cause the touched strings to sound an octave higher when plucked. Thus, when the device is activated, the instrument sounds 1×4' or 1×8', 1×4'; otherwise it plays 1×8' or 2×8'. The *Cornettzug* is mentioned briefly in an obscure 1773 treatise by Peter Sprengel, *Handwerk und Künste in Tabelen*, and is cited by Hubbard, p. 270.

Octave harpsichords in grand form are rather rare, perhaps because their bentsides—really just the upper half of a normal full-size harpsichord—look so extreme. Copenhagen's 2×4' example is no exception in this regard; yet someone went to considerable effort to create a congenial match of case and stand. The case is nicely painted and decorated, although perhaps not by the builder; but the stand dominates the ensemble. It is a complex structure with two bronzed *putti* supporting the front of the instrument on their heads; their faces are wreathed in frowns, and their bodies are contorted by their burden.

The Musikhistorisk Museum owns a 1×8', 1×4' one-manual Andreas II Ruckers harpsichord, which it acquired from the Dutch harpsichordist Gustav Leonhardt. Although the instrument has been considerably altered, its papers and soundboard painting are still in fair condition. It is a "strapwork" Ruckers, one of the few whose original case painting consisted of a red ground criss-crossed with imitation-iron grey-black straps, with large gemstones at their intersections.

The collection's most distinctive harpsichord is a large, two-manual Hieronymus Hass instrument of 1723. The exterior of the case is decorated in a bronze and polychrome chinoiserie bordered with green *faux* tortoise shell; the interior of the lid has a wide gold-on-red border, and the colorful painting depicts an outdoor concert alongside a formal garden. The keywell is embellished with more polychrome chinoiserie on an ivory ground. The sharps are bone or ivory over a light wood, and the naturals are covered with tortoise shell, with arcades of thin ivory traceries over red paint. The visual effect of such a profusion of color and design is riveting.

This Hass has a rarely found 3×8', 1×4' disposition. Usually, 3×8' instruments use two nuts at different levels: a higher one for the normal two

1723 harpsichord by Hieronymus Hass

8′ strings and a lower one for the third. A 4′ choir, if there is one, would have a lower nut at yet a third level. That is essentially the case here, except that the two 8′ nuts are combined into one nut with two levels, with a 4′ nut at the third level. The 4′ jacks are doglegged and available from either manual. Thus, one could choose either 1×8′ or 1×8′, 1×4′ on the upper manual, while the disposition of the lower manual could vary from a single 8′ to all four registers. Hubbard (p. 332) mistakenly claims that the coupler has off, on, and intermediate positions.

A 1786 Gottlieb Rosenau of Stockholm convincingly demonstrates the extent to which Scandinavian builders were influenced by the Hamburg school. It has the typical thin-walled North German double bentside (although the tails of the Scandinavian instruments tended to be slimmer, as is this one's), the natural wood case interior contrasts with the painted exterior, and the keywell is enhanced with natural wood veneers in herringbone and burls. The lid is decorated in gold chinoiserie on a blue ground, and the case exterior is a plain red. Musically, the instrument is disposed 2×8′, 1×4′ with coupler, the resources of most North German harpsichords. It originally had a lute stop, which was also common in Hamburg instruments, but that register has been removed and its gap has been closed.

Three other plucked keyboards are owned by the museum: an ordinary bentside spinet of ca. 1710; a counterfeit square octave spinet by Franciolini, and an octave clavicytherium, spuriously signed "Angiolus Migliai, Florence, 1590."

As might be expected, the Musikhistorisk Museum has many Danish pianos. Two giraffes and a grand by Peter Christian Uldahl, all from around 1810–20, are the only known extant pianos by that maker. One of the giraffes looks rather strange: it is short in height, with simple lines and no trace of the typical giraffe's "head." Further, the long side of the case is on the right rather than the left, giving the uneasy impression that the bass strings are shorter than the treble's. But in short-case pianos of this type the strings generally canted from lower left to upper right; thus, the bass strings are even longer than they would be if they were parallel to the long side of the case.

A ca. 1818 grand and a ca. 1820 giraffe by the builders Richter & Bechmann are also products of Copenhagen. The grand, which has a Janissary stop, was played by Carl Maria von Weber in Copenhagen's royal theater in October 1820, and one can imagine how he delighted the audience with its drum, cymbals, and bells. Other Danish pianos include a square from the first half of the nineteenth century, by the Copenhagen builder Andreas Marschall, that belonged to Danish composer J. P. E. Hartmann and was kept in his summer home as a practice piano.

Two other Hamburg instruments in Copenhagen are a delicate-looking square by Meincke & Pieter Meyer from the turn of the nineteenth century, and a 1798 *Tangentenflügel* by Johann Wilhelm Berner. The latter is one of the few tangent-action pianos not made by Späth & Schmahl, but Berner is reported to have studied with Schmahl. Other than its action, the instrument, with floating-panel lid, is indistinguishable from end-of-the-century Viennese fortepianos. It belonged to the Danish king Christian VII, whose stormy reign was exacerbated by mental illness.

Another Germanic instrument is a ca. 1820s Conrad Graf whose soundboard was labeled by the maker "Opus 1245." This could represent a true chronological serial number, since Graf built about 3,000 pianos during his productive lifetime. He was one of the first piano makers to employ the techniques of mass production, having purchased a dance hall and converted it into a factory in 1826.

The two English pianos in Copenhagen, by Broderip & Wilkinson (the successor to the firm of Longman & Broderip) and Van Olst, are both ca. 1800 squares. A more unusual instrument, with ornate keyboard supports, nameboard, and gallery on the lid, is a "console" piano by Jean-Henri Pape. Born in Hanover as Johann Heinrich, he emigrated to Paris, where he gained a reputation as an innovative builder. Among his inventions was this instrument, a precursor to today's upright console.

Among the other pianos in Copenhagen, anonymous and of unknown provenance, are a late 1800s upright instrument looking like a clavicytherium, with a simplified hammer action and no dampers; a ca. 1820 desk piano with shelves and drawers; a small sewing-box piano with mirror and compartments for sewing items; and an early nineteenth-century upright grand with shelves on the right.

The catalog for the Musikhistorisk Museum og Carl Claudius' Samling is Angul Hammerich, *Das Musikhistorische Museum zu Kopenhagen*, German translation by Erna Bobé (Copenhagen, 1911). A supplement by Mogens Andersen, *Supplement zum Katalog von Angul Hammerich* (deutsche Fassung 1911) was published in 1960. There is a catalog for the Claudius collection alone: Carl Claudius, *Carl Claudius' Samling af gamle Musikinstrumenter* (Copenhagen, 1931).

CHAPTER V

*F*RANCE

PARIS

 Musée de la Musique

Address: 221 avenue Jean-Jaurès, 75019, Paris; hours: Tuesday, Wednesday, Friday, and Saturday, Noon–6 P.M.; Thursday, Noon–9:30 P.M.; Sunday 10 A.M.–6 P.M.; telephone: 44 84 46 00; fax: 44 84 46 01.

With the triumph of the *bourgeoisie* in the French Revolution, harpsichords, with their fancy gilt stands and elaborately painted surfaces, were considered undesirable reminders of the *ancien régime*'s wealth and power. It has been reported that many of these instruments were confiscated from the nobility and stored in the attic of the Paris Conservatoire; that during the cold winters of the early 1800s these magnificent instruments were broken up for firewood and burned; and that about one hundred harpsichords were disposed of in this way in the winter of 1816. However, the Musée tells us that in 1796, three hundred of the confiscated instruments were sent to the Conservatoire de musique, where a portion were sold or destroyed, with twenty burned in 1816. Whether twenty or a hundred, such vandalous acts were probably innocent: by that time the harpsichord was "obsolete," and no one could have guessed that future generations would be obsessed with the desire for relics of what was deemed an unsavory past. But whatever the motives, many French harpsichords we might otherwise have had simply disappeared.

A substantial number of those that remain are still in Paris, as part of the collection once housed in the Conservatoire National de Musique. However, a new facility, the Musée de la Musique, recently opened on the outskirts of Paris, is one of the great exhibit spaces in Europe, worthy of its distinguished collection of more than a hundred pianos and fifty plucked keyboards. At the heart of the latter group are ten French double-

1612 harpsichord by Ioannes Ruckers. Collection Musée de la musique/Cliché Publimages.

manual harpsichords, all beautiful examples of the builders' art, both visually and aurally.

Two are *ravalements* of Ruckers harpsichords, but by the time the rebuilding process was completed they had become French harpsichords in
almost every way except birth. In fact, a newly minted French harpsichord
with a five-octave range was normally described as *mis à grand ravalement*.
The first of these Ruckerses, a 1612 Ioannes, started life as a non-aligned

double with a strapwork finish. It was enlarged by adding wood to both the spine and the bentside to provide space for the increased range, now FF–f³. Additional wood was added to the soundboard, which was carefully painted in the appropriate Ruckers style. New keyboards, guides, and jacks were installed; the exterior of the case was repainted with outdoor scenes; and the instrument was supplied with an elaborate gilt stand. One would never suspect that it had been born as a much smaller Flemish harpsichord, except that the spine still retains its original strapwork decoration. It would normally stand next to a wall, so despite the careful attention given to every other aspect of the rebuilding and redecorating process, the spine was left untouched.

The second, a large 1646 Andreas Ruckers now decorated in *vernis martin*, was an instrument O'Brien calls an "extended-compass 'French' double," with unaligned keyboards of GG–c³ (the "normal" pitch) on the lower manual and F–f³ (pitch a fourth lower) on the upper (p. 269). It was first rebuilt with aligned keyboards ca. 1710. Ca. 1756 it was ravalled again, widened, and given new keyboards, perhaps by Blanchet. Finally, in 1780, Taskin extended the compass to its present five octaves and added the *peau de buffle*, the machine stop and a set of *genouillères* to control the registers.

Ruckers harpsichords were so influential in the eighteenth century that French, English, and to some extent North German harpsichord building was dominated by Flemish ideas. But in the seventeenth century, French builders—and English and German, too, for that matter—followed an International School. Their instruments tended to have deeper-curved bentsides; case walls overlapping the bottom boards; thinner bentsides, tails, and cheeks; painted soundboards; and geometric parchment roses. The double-manual Gilbert Desruisseaux, built in Lyons after 1678, is one of the most elaborate of these early French instruments. Its bucolic lid painting is extremely well done, its geometric rose is gilded, and its soundboard is decorated with the usual floral patterns. Above the soundboard, the interior walls of the case are lined with colored papers. The GG/BB–c³ keyboard, although not original, is characteristically international in style, in both range and materials—naturals of ebony and sharps of solid ivory or bone. Its unpainted twist-legged stand is also typical of the time.

Paris has a 1691 Vincent Tibaut harpsichord. Unlike the other two extant Tibauts (one from 1679, described above in the Brussels Musée Instrumental collection, and the other from 1681 in private ownership, pictured in Claude Mercier-Ythier's *Les Clavecins* [Paris: Éditions Vecteurs, 1990] p. 74), except for the nameboard its walnut case is without marquetry.

1678 harpsichord by Gilbert Desruisseaux. Collection Musée de la musique/Cliché Publimages.

A Nicolas Dumont double was built in 1697; but with its red paint, gold bands, five-octave range, *peau de buffle*, machine stop with *genouillères*, and Louis XV stand, it looks convincingly like an elaborate eighteenth-century harpsichord. It was rebuilt by Taskin in 1789, after it had been in service for almost a hundred years. Although parsimony was undoubtedly part of the reason—there is ample evidence that harpsichord builders reused every piece of wood that came into their shops—more likely it reflects the philosophy that a fine old instrument was an inestimable commodity, and rather than discard it when its range, sound, or decoration became outdated, it should be rebuilt and "modernized." This process of *ravalement* was most often carried out on Flemish instruments—particularly those of the Ruckerses and Couchets—but it was by no means limited to them.

Since a rebuilt and updated Ruckers harpsichord could command four times and more the price of a new instrument, it was inevitable that builders would make new instruments look as though they had gone through *ravalement*, fit them with a real or counterfeit Ruckers or Couchet rose, and sell them for considerably more than they would otherwise have brought. The Musée owns a beautiful double, finished in black lacquer and gold chinoiserie, on an elaborate gilded stand, with *peau de buffle*, machine stop, and *genouillères*. It bears the inscription "Hans Ruckers me fecit Antverpiae" on the nameboard, an HR (Hans Ruckers) rose, and the date 1590 on the soundboard. Moreover, marks are discernable in the construction, ostensibly where new wood had been added in carrying out the *ravalement*. But when the instrument was opened for repairs in the twentieth century, the signature of the respected Parisian builder Jean-Claude Goujon was found on the reverse side of the soundboard, and the date of 1749 on some of the jacks. It was then discovered that what appeared to be joints between new wood and old were no more than artfully placed score marks. It is a fine instrument, but such was the power of the Ruckers name that Goujon undoubtedly received far more for it than if had he identified it as his own (although it has been suggested that rather than attempting to deceive, Goujon was merely paying tribute to an illustrious predecessor). Goujon's "Ruckers" underwent some *ravalement* of its own; O'Brien (p. 278) indicates that its original range of GG–d³ was subsequently enlarged to FF–e³. In 1784 the top f³ and the *genouillères* were added by another builder, Jacques Joachim Swanen.

Henri Hemsch, the better known of two brothers, was born near Cologne and worked in Paris. The Musée's 1761 double is a fine example not only of his work but of Parisian harpsichord building in the middle of the eighteenth century. The decorative scheme is typical, with a black exterior,

1749 harpsichord by Jean Claude Goujon. Collection Musée de la musique/Cliché Publimages.

wide gold bands, gilded moldings, and a red interior. It sits on a graceful black and gold Louis XV stand. Curiously, the inside of the lid is unfinished, perhaps in anticipation of a painting that never materialized. It is a much-copied instrument.

Joseph Collesse (whose brother was also a builder) was an organ and harpsichord maker in Lyons until his death in 1776. The Musée's harpsichord, started in 1775, was finished in 1777 by a Jean Franky. Paris was the hub of French harpsichord building in the eighteenth century, but Lyons was probably the most important of its few provincial spokes; consequently, any instrument built in that area is important to our overall understanding of French building practices. Like the 1761 Hemsch, Collesse's harpsichord is decorated in black with gold bands; but the interior of its lid is finished, in pale green and gold bands. The inside case walls are more ornate than Hemsch's: garlands and swags on the sides over the soundboard and in the keywell, and a *faux marbre* jackrail. Its Louis XV stand is embellished with raised and gilded floral designs. The soundboard painting is particularly beautiful. Instead of a rose, there is a painting of a bouquet of roses in a vase on a marble block—a witty visual pun. The soundboard also lacks the traditional bird scene; a boating vignette takes its place.

Sébastien Érard was born in Strasbourg, but he came to Paris while still in his teens and apprenticed himself to a harpsichord builder. Best known for the piano-building firm he founded, Érard also built some harpsichords, including the 1779 double owned by the Musée de la Musique. It is a fully equipped late Parisian model, with a *peau de buffle*, machine stop, and pedals.

An anonymous instrument from the seventeenth century completes the Musée's impressive collection of double-manual French harpsichords; but there are other French instruments as well. Jean Marius, the Parisian who claimed to have invented the folding harpsichord, is represented by two of his early eighteenth-century *clavecins brisés*. Hinged in three sections, they fold up into suitcase-sized packages. Their utility no doubt balanced their somewhat dubious musical worth. Frederick the Great is said to have taken one with him on his military campaigns.

Finally, there are two polygonal spinets. A Michel Richard is dated 1623, but that may be too early, since that builder's other extant instruments date from much later in the century. The other is a 1672 octave instrument by Philippe Denis. The museum also has a Richard bentside spinet from 1690 and a Goujon bentside from 1753. The external differences between the two are striking: in typical seventeenth-century fashion the Richard is finished in natural wood and rests on a simple stand with turned balustrades, while the Goujon is painted gray, with gilt bands, and has a stand in Louis XV style. Both have painted soundboards.

The Flemish builder Simon Hagaerts rates a minor footnote in the history of harpsichord building, since on the death of Ioannes Couchet, his widow, Angela, entered into a partnership agreement with Hagaerts to teach the trade to her son Petrus. As part of the agreement Hagaerts had access to nearly all of Couchet's tools, patterns, and jigs. One of Hagaerts's double-manual instruments is owned by the museum; the date of 1612 is thought to have been added during an eighteenth-century *ravalement*.

Longman & Broderip were dealers rather than builders, reselling instruments made by others under their name. A Longman & Broderip (but signed by Baker Harris) single of 1775 is a standard late English harpsichord, without machine stop or Venetian swell. Aside from it and an anonymous, undated instrument, the rest of the museum's harpsichords

are Italian. A 1543 inner without outer by Dominicus Pisaurensis is at octave pitch, and a full-size Dominicus, dated 1553, still has its outer case.
Another inner-without-outer is an extremely long 1578 Baffo, whose case
interior, including the nameboard, is covered with complex marquetry and
paint. This instrument is disposed 1×8′, 1×4′—a normal disposition for its
time, but one often changed to 2×8′ in the seventeenth century.

The much-copied 1703 Carlo Grimaldi, also very long, is a classic Italian harpsichord whose beauty lies in the elegance of its shape, its architectural features, and its complex moldings. Its naturals are covered with
mother-of-pearl, which, to the modern eye, seems a bit like gilding the
lily. At one time it was turned into a tangent piano, and when we last
saw it, it still had that action.

A 1677 inner-outer by the Bolognese builder Pietro Faby is one of the
most ornate Italians extant. The *faux marbre* outer case, lid exterior, stand,
and even the turned lidstick are eye-catching, with marbling of bluish-
black and red contrasting with rope designs in black-streaked white. A
pastoral scene graces the lid. The interior of the inner case, the jackrail,
and the nameboard are covered with panels of ebonized wood and inlaid
with mother-of-pearl and ivory. Nicely turned ivory studs decorate the
instrument's top molding and jackrail. The tails of the ivory naturals are
etched with intricate designs and filled with ink. The ebony sharps are
inlaid with ivory strips. The endblocks and jackrail holders are architectural in concept and ornately decorated with ebonized wood, inlaid ivory,
complex moldings, ivory studs, and miniature pawn-like ivory devices.
The soundboard has a black and gold geometric rose.

The 1677 Faby is disposed 2×8′; but unlike most seventeenth-century
Italian harpsichords, it has two 8′ nuts. This was probably done to equalize
the string lengths of each pair; hence, when plucked together, each string
would respond with a tone quality as similar as possible to the other's.
Indeed, the 1677 is a fine-sounding Italian harpsichord, but its ornateness
almost adumbrates its function as a musical instrument. The other Faby,
from 1681, is also highly decorated, but not to the extent of the 1677. The
museum also owns an undated octave spinet by Faby.

The museum claims to have a Cristofori harpsichord dated "end of
the seventeenth century"; but Henkel (pp. 1, 2) lists only five genuine
surviving Cristofori plucked keyboards, and this one is not among them.
In a letter to *Early Music* 20/4 (1992), p. 701, Wraight also refutes the
assertion. Hence, it is likely that the Musée joins several other institutions
in having an unauthenticated instrument attributed to Cristofori.

A 1668 Girolamo Zenti and an anonymous seventeenth-century clavicytherium with the normal C/E–c³ compass complete the list of Italian

1677 harpsichord by Pietro Faby. Collection Musée de la musique/Cliché Publimages.

harpsichords. There are, in addition, about a half-dozen anonymous Italian virginals and spinets, and spinets by Irena (1594) and Trasuntino (1601). A 1598 Ruckers spinett-virginal is the earliest full-size rectangular-shaped example of the Ruckers virginal with the keyboard on the left. The gilded rose is made of *papier mâché*. There are also two Ruckers octave virginals, a 1618 Ioannes and a 1634 Andreas, both "motherless children," and a 1738 spinet by Albert Delin.

Although we have not seen most of the pianos in the Musée de la Musique's large collection, its checklists indicate many Parisian instruments among its holdings, including some by Érard, Pleyel, and Pape. Érard is represented by ten grands, four squares, and two uprights, covering a period from 1791 to 1914. Of particular interest are an 1853 and a ca. 1900 with pedal divisions. Six grands, a square, and eight uprights (one with pedal division) bear the Pleyel name. From Pape come four grands, two squares, and an upright. Other instruments by Parisian builders are a 1788 Pascal Taskin grand, elegantly decorated in French harpsichord style, an undated square by Pascal-Joseph Taskin, an undated Hatznbühler grand, and a 1817 Schmidt grand. The only non-Paris French grand is an undated instrument by Boisselet of Marseilles. Parisian squares and uprights abound, by Aury, Beck, Blanchet Fils, Bressler, Caspers, Chartier, Franck, Freudenthaler, Gaidon, Mussard Frères, Peronard, Peters, Roller, Swanen, and Wolber.

The pianos from foreign shores form an eclectic lot. There are two grands attributed to Stein or his school, a Matias Svameyer (Ferrara), a Schmidt-Flohn (Bern), a Broadwood, a Brodman, a Bechstein, and a Steinway. Among the non-French squares are two from Stockholm, by Granfeldt (ca. 1830) and Nordqvist (1823). Aside from two Viennese—one anonymous and the other by Walter—the other squares are English: Astor & Horwood, Érard (London), and Schoene.

Some special instruments deserve mention. With its slightly concave sides, delicate wooden grillework surrounding its lovely brass bas-reliefs, and three painted miniatures framed by molded ovals, a ca. 1820 Austrian pyramid piano is a quiet, elegant piece of furniture, one of the most beautiful pyramids we have seen. Like others of its type, a Christian Dietz harp piano of 1810, combining harp with keyboard, is graceful by virtue of its shape. Somewhat bizarre, and certainly less elegant, is an 1842 "Euphonicon," by John Steward of London. The front of this unusual instrument looks very much like a normal upright console piano. Behind it can be seen the upper end of a harp portion, and behind the strings, in lieu of a soundboard, three large cello-like resonators, graduated in size. Other Euphonicons can be found in Munich's Deutsches Museum,

Anonymous 19th-century pyramid piano. Collection Musée de la musique/Cliché Publimages.

London's Victoria and Albert Museum, and New York's Metropolitan Museum.

The Musée de la Musique has fewer than ten clavichords, mostly anonymous. The earliest is an instrument in polygonal shape attributed to Dominicus Pisaurensis, dated sixteenth century. An ornately decorated four-octave short-octave anonymous instrument, dating from the end of that century, was thought to be Portuguese, but it is now assigned an Italian provenance. Its lid painting portrays the battle of Lepanto. Since this famous 1571 naval engagement between the Christian Holy League and the Ottoman Empire involved almost 500 vessels, one would think its scale would be of a magnitude unsuited for the lid of a small clavichord; it is indeed a busy lid. A 1786 instrument by the German-born Copenhagen builder Otto Joachim Teiffenbrun is one of the few surviving examples of his work. Another eighteenth-century clavichord is thought to be by Johann Heinrich Silbermann, Gottfried's nephew and a prolific builder.

⁂ Musée des Arts et Métiers

Address: 292, rue Saint-Martin, 75003 Paris; mailing address: 292, rue Saint-Martin, 75141 Paris, Cedex 03; hours: 10 A.M.–5:30 P.M. daily; telephone: 4027 2371; fax: 4027 2662.

Museums often shut their doors temporarily in order to refurbish exhibits, make repairs, redecorate, or readjust internal spaces; and for one of these reasons or another, the Museum of Arts and Crafts has been closed every time we have been in Paris. Accordingly, even though we have some knowledge of its early keyboard holdings, we cannot speak to this museum's contents from personal experience.

Its two harpsichords are both intriguing. A 1752 two-manual Richard has four registers, and although neither the museum's checklist nor Boalch (p. 540) say so, the fourth is probably a *peau de buffle*. The museum reports the maker's first name to be Marius, but Boalch claims that Frank Hubbard (in a private communication) doubted that attribution. The instrument may then be by Michel Richard, a Parisian builder active in the second half of the eighteenth century and the maker of the bentside spinet owned by the Musée de la Musique.

The second instrument, dating from 1786 and also a double, is by another Paris builder (albeit another of those born in Germany), Jacques Joachim Swanen. Its EE–a^3 compass is unusual, since it begins one note lower than most eighteenth-century French harpsichords and ends four notes higher. Taskin also used that low EE, incorporating it into five of his extant instruments. Even though it is never called for in the literature, it was probably included as a means of improving the tone of the FF; and it may have been tuned down to CC. The extension at the upper end of the range is less easily explained, since we know of no eighteenth-century harpsichords that went higher than g^3, though some late clavichords did. The Swanen harpsichord is also the only French harpsichord known to have a 16′ register, and it is the only known antique harpsichord of any sort to have a separate two-octave pedal division, although its strings are activated by hammers rather than plectra. We hope to see this fascinating instrument the next time we are in Paris.

The museum's five pianos include three squares, two of which merit some discussion. The first is a 1778 English instrument by Johann Cristoph Zumpe & Gabriel Buntebart. Buntebart was an early partner of Zumpe, and both were Germans—Saxons, to be more specific. They left Saxony at the outbreak of the Seven Years' War, a conflagration that involved North America and India as well as much of Europe. Although it was probably the first "world war," much of the initial fighting took place in Saxony, drastically curbing the careers of these young builders. Like so many other German artisans before them, they and other of their Saxon colleagues emigrated to England and set up shop there. These builders, many of whom had been trained by Gottfried Silbermann in Freiburg, are known as the "twelve apostles." Although there were more than a dozen of them, it is generally conceded that they were the ones who founded London's piano industry.

The second square is from 1770, by Johann Kilian Mercken, another German who emigrated to Paris, perhaps for the same reasons as the apostles, although he was younger than they. It is the earliest extant French piano (the piano came late to France) and has no stand—only four legs— and two hand stops in a box at the lower left corner of the case. Mercken's instrument was no match for the magnificent French harpsichords and spinets still being built. The other two pianos are a small 1849 upright by Pleyel and a ca. 1900 upright console.

CHAPTER VI

$\mathcal{G}$ERMANY

BAD KROZINGEN

The Neumeyer-Junghanns-Tracey Collection

*Address: Am Schlosspark 7, D-79189 Bad Krozingen; hours: Thursday
4 P.M.–5 P.M. or by appointment; telephone: 7633 3700; fax: 7633 15660.*

Bad Krozingen is an elegant little spa city. Though the Neumeyer-Junghanns-Tracey Collection is open to the public, it is a private early-key-
board museum of some four dozen items. It is housed in an upper wing
of Schloss Bad Krozingen, an imposing sixteenth-century château on
beautifully tended grounds. Fritz Neumeyer, a professor of music in Berlin
(1939–44) and Freiburg-Breisgau (1946–68), was devoted to reviving the
sound and touch of early keyboards long before such ideas became popular. He assembled a choice collection of antiques and replicas to show the
instruments' development. Rolf Junghanns, who studied with Neumeyer
and taught at the Schola Cantorum in Basel, and Bradford Tracey, a pupil
of Junghanns and Neumeyer, carried on Neumeyer's work with further
acquisitions and service to the public.

Instruments in this well-maintained collection were selected for their
tonal, and when possible, for their visual appeal as well. Many items have
been restored. The harpsichords and clavichords are a mix of antiques
and recent replicas, the former including some fascinating items, the latter
displaying high quality. In the second group are harpsichords and a
mother-and-child muselar virginal by William Dowd and John Koster,
based on French, German, and Flemish models; a spinet after early Italian
designs by Martin Skowroneck; and a few others.

The oldest of the antiques is an octave virginal, of seventeenth-century
Italian origin, in a painted outer case probably of later date. Its C/E–c^3
keyboard and thin walls are typical, but curiously, the wrestpins are behind

Anonymous undated octave virginal

the jackrail—in the manner of a Neapolitan virginal, which it otherwise does not resemble—rather than on the right side of the case.

A small, square virginal at quint pitch, also seventeenth century and C/E–c^3, with inset keyboard and geometric rose, is a rare Swiss example. Interestingly, its coniferous soundboard is slab-sawn; that is, the boards were cut off the log in slabs, like slicing a loaf of bread lengthwise. Generally, only cypress soundboards were slab-sawn; coniferous boards were made of quarter-sawn wood, where the log was quartered and the boards cut at right angles to the annular rings. Its lid painting and other decor are somewhat naive, but colorfully done.

A big, 2×8′ harpsichord from 1695 by Antonio Francesco Nobili of Rome has the unusually wide compass of GG–f^3. Called a "cembalone," meaning a cembalo (harpsichord) of large proportions, its bold, grandiose tone commands attention and respect.

Clavichords are represented by late eighteenth-century fretted and unfretted types: a 1787 Späth & Schmahl, AA–f^3, and a ca. 1800 anonymous German with a rare six-octave, FF–f^4 compass are both fretted, as is a slightly smaller modern replica (C–f^3) by Scholz. The six-octave example, resting on an elaborately carved, cabriole-legged stand into which two drawers have been built, has a particularly fine tone. There are two unfretted clavichords: a Christian Gottlob Hubert of 1772, and an undated

1801 Tangentenflügel by Carl Friedrich Schmahl.
On loan from Albert Ludwigs Universität, Freiburg

anonyme possibly by Carl Schmahl, one of the brothers of the better-known Johann Matthäus.

The collection's principal weight and significance lies in its many pianos. An 1801 Carl Friedrich Schmahl *Tangentenflügel* (on loan from Albert Ludwigs Universität, Freiburg), with its ebony and ivory keyboard, FF–f³ compass, enclosed bottom, floating-panel lid, and straight-strung string-pairs on a single bridge, holds few surprises for those used to Viennese designs; but its three knee levers (for *una corda*, moderator, and damper) and three hand stops (for split-buff muting) provide a variety of tone colors differing from those of most early pianos or of any clavichord. It is one of the few of these rare hybrids that have been restored to playable condition.

Among some two dozen pianos are three from the Stein-Streicher family. Johann Andreas Stein of Augsburg is represented by an elegant ca. 1780 FF–f³ example, his usual action without back checks, five slender turned and fluted legs, and knee levers for moderator and damper. (This instrument, the Hubert clavichord, and the Späth & Schmahl *Tangentenflügel* are on loan from the University of Freiburg's Musicology Department.) The second, from 1816, is by Stein's talented daughter, Nannette Streicher, with six octaves (FF–f^4) and four pedals (*una corda*, bassoon, moderator, and damper). Like the Stein example, it still has a single bridge and an enclosed bottom, with two gap spacers to brace the frame against tension and internal supports for a dust cover over the string band. The third piano is an 1864 by Nannette's son, Johann Baptist, with an open bottom, two iron tension bars, an AAA–a^4, eighty-five-note compass, and two pedals. It has a Viennese action, albeit by this date one much enlarged, with thick, leather-faced felt hammers; and it still has straight stringing.

A handsome 1810 Michael Rosenberger, with a six-octave, FF–f^4 range, is noteworthy for its six pedals and lyre on a graceful bow connected to the two front legs. To the usual *una corda* and damper are added bassoon, partial and full moderators, and a Janissary stop. Conrad Graf's superb CC–g^4 grand from 1825, probably the most outstanding piano in the collection, should be heard as well as seen. A Johann Gottlieb Fichtl of 1795 extends the treble to c^4 and adds a bassoon-stop knee lever to the usual moderator and damper. Knee levers were replaced by pedals only gradually in the German-speaking countries, as can also be seen in a Heinrich Christian Kisting & Sohn of 1835, whose three levers are *una corda*, moderator, and damper.

English builders are represented by Broadwood grands from 1798 and 1817. Both have his "English" action and two pedals. Those on the 1798 are built into the two front legs, but those of the 1817 are centered, with the damper pedal split for bass and treble. The 1798's compass is FF–c^4, that of the 1817, CC–c^4; and both have enclosed bottoms and straight triple stringing. They are instructive examples of Broadwood's progress in design, as well as an interesting contrast with contemporary Viennese models.

There are fewer small squares than may be seen in some other collections, but a Thomas Green (London, 1785) and a Cammeyer (Mannheim, 1792), the only instruments known by these builders, provide another opportunity to compare English and Austro-German types. Upright instruments include a ca. 1835 lyre piano by Johann Christian Schleip, and a big ca. 1820 upright grand, presumably of Swiss origin, whose cloth-covered doors conceal shelves in the open area to the right, by the bentside. Interestingly, this piano has a vertical dust cover in front of the strings, possibly indicating that the purpose of this frequently found accessory had more to do with homogenizing the sound than with housekeeping. A ca. 1820 Joseph Wachtl pyramid combines severeness of line with filigree work and caryatid legs. Both the upright grand and the Wachtl pyramid have the ubiquitous rising sun motif mounted on the case under the key-

1798 piano by Broadwood & Son

board; but both accessories look more like sections of wagon wheels than heavenly bodies.

An 1845 piano by Jean Henri Pape, with a down-striking action and the unusual compass of DD–g⁴, is shaped like an octagonal table. To play, one lifts a hinged apron of the octagon and pulls the keyboard out of its drawer. When closed, the piano is an attractive and quite useful mahogany tea table.

The collection's German-language checklist by Rolf Junghanns, *Historische Tasteninstrumente: Katalog der Sammlung Fritz Neumeyer, Bad Krozingen* (Waldkircher Verlagsgesellschaft, n.d.), is somewhat out of date but still useful. Also by Junghanns, and from the same period, *Die Sammlung historischer Tasteninstrumente Fritz Neumeyer* is an undated sixteen-page folder in German, French, and English that contains similar information and photos of selected items. It is available only with the purchase of a set of recordings.

BERLIN

▓ Schloss Charlottenburg

Address: Louisplatz 1000, Berlin 19;
telephone: 030 32091 1; fax: 030 32091 200

Charlottenburg was an independent municipality on the outskirts of Berlin until 1920, when it was incorporated into that city. The Schloss, or castle, was built in 1695 by Sophia Charlotte. Her husband became Frederick I of Prussia in 1701 (he was also known as Frederick III of Brandenburg and as the grandfather of Frederick the Great). The Schloss is now a palace-museum housing a fine collection of art, furniture, and other treasures.

Among its holdings are two large unsigned harpsichords now almost universally believed to be the work of Michael Mietke, a respected instrument builder at the court of Frederick I from 1697 to 1713. The more famous one, known as the "white harpsichord," is a ca. 1703 2×8′ single, exquisitely adorned in gold and polychrome chinoiserie on a white ground. The decoration is done in a rare, porcelain-like style; although it is unsigned, it is almost universally accepted as the work of Gerard Dagly, a lacquerer who specialized in this difficult technique. Dagly, ultimately known as the finest japanner in Europe, was a court cabinet maker and interior decorator as well, and undoubtedly one of the cultural adornments of Frederick I. The second instrument, the "black harpsichord," is a 2×8′, 1×4′ double finished in chinoiserie on a black ground. It was probably built a few years later, and the decoration is different in character.

Despite the obvious distinctions between these instruments—one entirely black, the other entirely white, one a single manual, the other a double—they are quite close in execution. Both have short scales, rounded tails, thin cases, knee-like interior framing, box guides, and overlapping sides with bottom moldings. Applied moldings overhang the tops of the sides, and the keywells are done in unpainted wood veneers. The inner-outer suggestion is strong. These characteristics are typical of a German realization of International style, although the instruments are rendered in a manner reminiscent of seventeenth-century French harpsichord building. Given that all things French were fatuously admired at the Berlin court, this is not surprising. In a fascinating parallel to the creation of "old" Ruckers harpsichords by French builders, early in his career Mietke adopted a Frankish façade for his harpsichords, claimed his instruments were French imports, and sold them for two or three times the sums he could otherwise charge. Eventually he was found out and forced to lower his prices.

It is only since the publication of a wide-ranging and penetrating article on these instruments by Sheridan Germann, "The Mietkes, the Margrave and Bach," in *Bach, Handel, Scarlatti: Tercentenary Essays*, edited by Peter Williams (Cambridge: Cambridge University Press, 1985), pp. 119–48, that authorship of the white and black harpsichords has been ascribed to Mietke; prior to that time we knew only his name, not his work. A third Mietke has recently been discovered. In two articles, "A Signed Mietke Harpsichord," in *Fellowship of Makers and Restorers of Historical Instruments Quarterly* 64 (July 1991), pp. 59–62; and "The Hudiksvall Mietke," in *Harpsichord and Fortepiano* 5/1 (October 1994), pp. 15–18, Andreas Kilström describes a single-manual harpsichord in the Hälsinglands Museum in Hudiksvall, Sweden, bearing the words "Michael Mietke Instrument-macher in Berlin Anno 1710" inked on the last treble key lever.

🎵 Staatliches Institut für Musikforschung Preussischer Kulturbesitz

Address: Tiergartenstrasse 1, D-10785 Berlin 30; hours: 9 A.M.–5 P.M., Tuesday to Friday; 10 A.M.–5 P.M. Saturday and Sunday; telephone: 030 254 810; fax: 030 254 81 172.

Established in 1888 as part of the Königliche Hochschule für Musik, Berlin's Musikinstrumenten-Museum (to use its less official name) opened its doors in 1893, mostly with instruments acquired from the Dutch dealer Paul de Wit. The collection, which has grown considerably over the years, was particularly augmented in 1902 by instruments acquired from the Belgian César Snoeck. (Snoeck must have been a formidable collector: aside from the instruments that went to Berlin, another group was consigned to the Brussels Musée Instrumental and a third to St. Petersburg in Russia.) Curt Sachs, the legendary musicologist and organologist, was director from 1919 until 1933, when he was driven out of Germany by the Nazis. World War II was a bad time for the museum; the city was heavily bombed, and many of its instruments were lost or destroyed. Reconstruction was begun after the war, and in 1951 it reopened in the Charlottenburg Palace. It moved into the present facility in 1984, and a more ideal building would be hard to find. It is modern, spacious, and well lit, with a main floor and balconies above. The instruments are beautifully and expansively arrayed, and its collection of early keyboards is large and choice.

The Musikinstrumenten-Museum has some important German harpsichords: a 1740 Silbermann, a 1710 Fleischer, a 1792 Oesterlein, and the notorious "Bach" harpsichord. It also has four Ruckerses, including one of the three extant harpsichord-virginal combinations; three Delins; a rare Swiss harpsichord-piano combination; and nine instruments from the early twentieth-century harpsichord revival. Almost all the rest of its plucked keyboards are Italian, some of which are interesting for one reason or another.

On the basis of its rose, the dimensions of the keyboards and keys, and features of its construction, the two-manual ca. 1740 Silbermann is believed to have been built by Gottfried himself. There is little reason to doubt this attribution; if it is true, this is the only harpsichord extant by the Freiburg master. Its natural-wood finish, floating-panel lid, and mitered tail are typically Central German. The bridge is neither mitered nor bent in the bass, but continues straight. The geometric rose of paper or cardboard, based on an equilateral triangle with an *S* in the middle, is similar to those found on other Silbermann instruments. In fact, except for the right-side-up wrestplank, it looks almost exactly like one of his pianos.

The 1710 single by Johann Christoph Fleischer is the only surviving harpsichord by this Hamburg builder, although his extant clavichords are in the Ringve Museum in Trondheim and in the Drottningholm Theater and the Stiftelsen Musikkulturens främjande in Stockholm. Like his father before him, Fleischer built lutes as well as harpsichords and clavichords, and it may have been this uncalled-for versatility that got him in trouble with the joiners guild in 1708. His brother Carl Conrad, also a builder, stuck to harpsichords, clavichords, and organs. The Berlin single has three sets of jacks, but is strung 1×8′, 1×4′; thus, the 8′ strings are plucked by either of the 8′ jacks, assuring some tonal variety. Still, the instrument is incapable of the full 2×8′, 1×4′ sound, and one wonders why

1710 harpsichord by Johann Christoph Fleischer

the builder made this choice. It is so lightly braced that, in attempting a lutelike delicacy of construction, Fleischer may have felt that another set of 8′ strings would strain the instrument unduly.

This harpsichord has been reworked many times—the first, according to some writing on the underside of the soundboard, by Fleischer himself in 1724. At some point its square cheeks were cut down in a graceful, but non-Hamburgian ogee curve, leaving the painted borders on the case to extend into nothingness. The lid was lost years ago, while the harpsichord was in New York, where it resided for over a hundred years before going to Berlin. Nevertheless, with its shallow case, polychrome chinoisery on a red ground, painted soundboard with a bucolic vignette in back of the gap, and an exquisite upside-down wedding-cake rose, it represents a more elegant side of the Hamburg harpsichord tradition.

Dated 1792, a double-manual harpsichord by Johann Christoph Oesterlein of Berlin must be one of the very last harpsichords built in Germany. Relatively plain and unadorned, with a natural-wood finish, it begs to be considered as furniture rather than as a decorative object. Superficially, it resembles earlier instruments from Central Germany, although it is not unlikely that the Classical German piano also influenced its look; still, the grain on the case runs horizontally rather than vertically, and the rather Baroque-looking scroll-sawn cheek ornaments and jackrail holders hark back to the harpsichord's earlier inner-outer tradition. As in many earlier eighteenth-century German instruments, the register levers on the wrestplank do not protrude through the nameboard. It sits on a shallow apron-stand whose large, square, tapered legs almost belong to the next century. This instrument is the property of the famous Berlin Sing-Akademie and is on loan to the Musikinstrumenten-Museum.

The ca. 1700 "Bach" harpsichord has had an interesting and negative influence on twentieth-century building practices. When Paul de Wit sold this five-octave double to Berlin in 1890, he claimed that it had been the personal harpsichord of J. S. Bach. There was scant evidence for this assertion, but even the possibility that the Cantor of Leipzig had owned it was too seductive to be resisted. As often happens in such cases, opinion became "fact," and the museum's 1892 catalog identified it as a harpsichord by Gottfried Silbermann, formerly owned by J. S. Bach. Curt Sachs disputed the attribution to Silbermann but accepted Bach's ownership, and with the weight of his authority, everyone else accepted it too. It also came with the disposition 1×16', 2×8', 1×4', with the 16' and an 8' on the lower manual and the other 8' and the 4' on the upper.

German builders in particular seemed determined to copy this organ-like layout, and until the 1960s, revival instruments with the "Bach disposition," with the 4' on the upper manual, were to be found everywhere. In the light of subsequent scholarship it is clear that Bach never owned the instrument, and the 4' was on the lower, not the upper manual. The museum now attributes the instrument to the workshop of Johann Heinrich Harrass of Gross-Breitenbach. The story of the "Bach" harpsichord is told in several places, but nowhere so trenchantly as in Russell, pp. 107–108.

Berlin has two South German virginals—a square from around 1600, and a polygonal from a century later. Extant German virginals are rare, so these instruments, a hundred years apart, are important documents. The earlier instrument has the C/E–a² range found in sixteenth-century Flemish virginals (although this one lacks the high g-sharp). It is a small instrument, designed to sound about a fourth above normal pitch. As in the rarest of the three types of Flemish virginals, its keyboard is centrally placed, with plucking points more like a harpsichord's. Also like a Flemish instrument, it has a Latin motto, "Sic transit gloria mundi," but it is on the jackrail rather than on the lid. It is highly ornate, with a complex polychrome marquetry covering the outside and gold filigrees on a brown ground on the interior of the case. The soundboard is nicely painted, and it has a complex geometric rose. The nameboard is divided into two panels by an applied molding, reminiscent of the exterior case moldings on some seventeenth-century South German harpsichords. At one time it was part of a claviorganum—a harpsichord-organ combination.

The ca. 1700 virginal invites comparison with the 1591 Hans Ruckers polygonal virginal in Bruges's Gruuthuse Museum. The C–c³ range of the ca. 1700 is almost the same as the Ruckers's C/E–c³. Both are polygonal in shape, with inset keyboards, and with sides heavy enough to support a lid. In both, the lid is rather precariously hinged to the short section in the middle of the back. In both, the keyboard is placed at the left; in the ca. 1700 that placement is extreme, with plucking points quite close to the bridge. This virginal must have made a pungent, nasal sound, much like the lute stops on some English, seventeenth-century South German, eighteenth-century North German, and late Flemish harpsichords. The exterior is painted a light reddish-brown marble, and the interior case walls, above the soundboard, are red with tiny lone chinoiserie figures every three to six inches or so. Similar figures are found on the soundboard. The geometric rose and the soundboard moldings are gilded.

The Musikinstrumenten-Museum has a late instrument seemingly Germanic in style: a 1779 single-manual combined harpsichord-piano attributed to the Bern builder Johann Ludwig Hellen. Finished in natural wood, with veneered panels and cross-banding, it is vaguely reminiscent of the work of both Hubert and the London builders. It also mixes paint and natural wood: the lid painting and the floral designs of the lid border and the case interior above the soundboard are contrasted with the natural wood on the case exterior. The lid painting, a rural scene with a *Dudelsackpfeifer* (bagpiper) playing for four dancing monkeys, is said to illustrate one of the animal fables from the *Panchatantra*. The soundboard is painted and has a geometric rose descending into the case, from which appears to be growing a budding flower. The effect of this instrument is quite rich, and it is evident that its construction was given much thought and great care.

Of Berlin's four Ruckers harpsichords, two (Andreas, 1618; Ioannes, 1627) are *ravalement* singles originally disposed 1×8′, 1×4′, with the usual C/E–c³ range. The 1618 was at some point turned into a 2×8′, a common conversion; but it has since been restored to its original disposition. Its outer decoration—white, with geometric snowflake patterns placed at regular intervals—is certainly not original, but it still has its lid papers with a "Soli Deo gloria" motto. The case of the 1627 was widened during

1628 harpsichord/virginal by Ioannes Ruckers

rebuilding to accommodate the new range of C–e³, but the octave span remained the same. O'Brien (pp. 248–49) reports that neither the sound-board, its un-Ruckers-like cross-barring, nor its soundboard painting are original. Its exterior is painted in a strapwork design that is similar in concept to the Ruckers strapwork cases but is obviously a later accretion.

The third Ruckers, an Andreas of 1620, was originally a non-aligned double, but like almost all similar instruments was turned into an aligned double during its *ravalement*. At first it was disposed 1×8′, 1×4′; but a second set of 8′ strings was added, the case was widened, the range was enlarged to GG/BB–f³, and it was given an entirely new bracing system and soundboard barring. Non-aligned harpsichords had 8′ and 4′ jacks for each keyboard, making a total of four register guides. In the usual *ravalement* these registers were discarded and replaced by three wider ones for a 2×8′, 1×4′ disposition; in this instrument, however, the four registers were retained and the instrument was disposed so that it could play 2×8′, 1×4′ on the lower manual and 1×8′, 1×4′ on the upper (the 4′ is doglegged in order to be available on both keyboards). The instrument has been refinished in an attractive *grisaille*.

The Musikinstrumenten-Museum's fourth Ruckers is one of the three extant Ruckers harpsichord-virginal combinations (the others are in Schloss Köpenick in Berlin and the Musée Instrumental in Brussels). Much of it is no longer original, but it has fared better than its two sister instruments in this regard. The lid painting, a "Conversion of St. Paul," is on a canvas glued to the lid. The instrument has lost its original exterior finish, but now, in an amusing *trompe-l'oeil*, is made to resemble a large block of grey stone in which are embedded enormous jewels. It is possible that this was intended as a pun on the Ruckers's strapwork finish, in which jewels appeared at the intersections of the dark iron straps. The instrument is undated, but O'Brien (pp. 244–45) believes it to have been built ca. 1628.

The Belgian builder Albert Delin made harpsichords, clavicytheria, and bentside spinets, and Berlin has one of each. With its single manual, short-octave bass (but now chromatic), 2×8′ disposition, and registers projecting through the cheek as in the Flemish models of a century earlier, Delin's 1750 harpsichord seems hopelessly old-fashioned. Perhaps it was, compared with the resources of those of Paris, London, and Hamburg; but it speaks to the inherent conservatism of instrument builders, most of whom were content to apply what they learned in their apprenticeships, build as well as they could, and leave innovation and invention to others. And it also speaks to the inherent conservatism of harpsichord buyers.

The resources of Delin's 1752 clavicytherium are similar to those of his two other surviving uprights, the 1750 in Brussels, in the Musée Instrumental, and the ca. 1760 in The Hague, in the Gemeentemuseum. All three are disposed 2×8′ with ranges just short of five octaves. And all have endblocks of ebony sandwiched between two layers of ivory. The 1765 bentside spinet, undoubtedly intended as a workaday instrument, is painted a bluish-green with a natural-wood lid interior.

A 1560 2×8′ Italian inner harpsichord by the Venetian Vito Trasuntino, C/E–f³, was originally disposed 1×8′, 1×4′; and signs of the 4′ bridge and hitchpins can still be seen on its cypress soundboard. But even without that clue, the position of the rose indicates the earlier disposition: had it been built 2×8′ the rose would be placed midway between the 8′ bridge and the spine; instead, it is centered between the missing 4′ bridge and spine. The eye-catching feature of this instrument is not its disposition,

Ca. 1560 harpsichord by Vito Trasuntino

however, but its extraordinary decoration. Contrary to the normal Italian practice of avoiding illusionistic decoration on inner cases, the exterior is painted in a spectacular repeating design in red, green, black, and gold. It was originally owned by Alfonso d'Este II, the last of the art-loving dukes of Ferrara.

Two Italian polygonal virginals are interesting for their attributions. Wraight (pp. 20, 21) discusses the first instrument, a rather plain ca. 1550 by Dominicus Pisaurensis, at some length. He notes that the signature on the nameboard is suspect for a number of reasons and concludes that the instrument cannot be attributed to Dominicus on that basis. Wraight suspected that a crude attempt was made to increase a seemingly anonymous virginal's value by using a nameboard from another instrument to attribute it to a known builder. But in comparing the moldings on this instrument to others by Dominicus, Wraight comes to the inescapable and ironic conclusion that it was indeed a Dominicus instrument all the time!

The second virginal, unsigned but ascribed to Benedetto Floriani, is a handsome instrument with black-dyed sides and both nameboard and inner surfaces enhanced by gold patterns. The nameboard is divided into three sections, each containing a portrait: on the left is Francesco de' Medici; in the center, Phillip II of Spain; and on the right Joanna of Austria, first wife of Francesco. Leipzig's Musikinstrumenten-Museum owns a 1571 virginal strikingly similar to Berlin's anonymous instrument in construction and decoration, and signed Benedetto Floriani. It also has a tripartite nameboard, although with designs in the left and right panels, and "Benedicti Floriani MDLXXI" in the center. Further, its molding patterns indicate that both virginals probably came from the same workshop. Thus, it would seem that the Berlin catalog is correct in attributing its virginal to Benedetto. Another virginal, which resembles the Berlin instrument even more, is in the M. I. Glinka Museum of Musical Culture in Moscow. It also has nameboard portraits of Francesco on the left and Joanna on the right, although the central portrait is of Charles V of France. It is signed, also on the nameboard (or more precisly, on the name batten) by Marco Jadra ("Marci Iadrae MDLXV"). All three virginals almost certainly passed through the hands of the same decorator, and it is within the realm of possibility, although far less likely, that all three may be by Jadra *or* Benedetto.

Berlin owns two large English harpsichords, one a 1761 single-manual Jacob Kirkman, 2×8', 1×4' with lute stop, machine, and a pedal. The other, a 1787 by Jacob and his son Abraham, has the same disposition, but with two manuals, a Venetian swell, and two pedals. Both are handsome instruments, covered with hardwood veneers and cross banding, and stringing of contrasting woods.

An early eighteenth-century *clavecin brisé* by Jean Marius is the very instrument Frederick the Great took with him on his military campaigns, although it was owned by his grandmother Sophie Charlotte (a gift from her cousin Liselotte von der Pfalz, wife of the Duke of Orleans). With a 2×8', 1×4' disposition and a range of GG/BB–c³, it is probably as fancy and complete as these folding harpsichords became; it even includes a device to give a tuning note. Its unusual soundboard painting consists not only of flowers and insects, but also wrought-iron patterns on which stand fanciful figures from the *commedia dell'arte*. Even more curious than a folding harpsichord is an octave virginal in the shape of a box. On this anonymous eighteenth-century instrument, probably French, the bridges, strings, pins, jacks, and guides are divided among three separate soundboards in front, rear, and top. This forms a case roughly 6 inches deep, 9 inches high, and 30 inches long, from which a normal-sized c–c⁴ keyboard projects. It seems like the ultimate way of folding a harpsichord.

The Berlin museum is fortunate in having nine harpsichords dating from 1889 to 1933, from the beginning of the harpsichord revival to its approximate mid-point. Interestingly, the earliest of these—Tomasini's and Érard's, both built for the 1889 Paris Exposition—look more like tra-

1700–04 clavecin brisé by Jean Marius

ditional harpsichords than those that followed. Tomasini's even has a bottom, although its exterior is painted with bucolic scenes in a romanticized style reminiscent of Watteau. The Érard is heavily framed, has no bottom, and has a soundboard barred in piano style, but it too has a painted finish and at least looks like an eighteenth-century harpsichord. Both instruments are disposed 2×8′, 1×4′, and both have hand stops protruding through the nameboard.

The 1891–93 harpsichord by Pleyel, Wolff, Lyon & Cie is also painted (again, in a romanticized Watteau style), but departures from eighteenth-century practice are obvious. Ostensibly a copy of a French instrument, it has a lute stop and the case has a *bombé* contour quite out of character for a French harpsichord. Most jarring, however, is the lyre with six pedals. Another Érard, from 1896, also with a lute stop and a pedal lyre, is neatly finished in natural wood and inlaid with modern versions of eighteenth-century English motifs.

The 1921 Gaveau has a painted case, a keyboard with black naturals, a rounded tail, and slanted cheeks. It sits on a quasi-Louis XV stand with a pedal lyre. It also has a 16′ set of strings, although they are much shorter than in the eighteenth-century instruments so disposed. Under the influence of the handful of Hamburg instruments that had 16′ choirs, and with the conviction that Bach's harpsichord had one, that stop was found on nearly every revival harpsichord that professed to be worthy of the name. The 1927 Pleyel harpsichord, the *Grand Modèle de Concert* known to every fan of the great Wanda Landowska, is the ultimate in modern plucking machines. It has a 16′ stop, a lute stop, overhead dampers, an iron frame, and a lyre with seven pedals. It is a thoroughly piano-ized version of the harpsichord, and taken on its own terms, as all these instruments must be, it is a fairly handsome piece of furniture; and if what was desired was a plucked sound, maximum variety, and the ability to make quick changes of timbre, it certainly delivered.

A free copy of the "Bach" harpsichord, the 1930 Steingraeber is an enormous and impressive-looking instrument. It has no pedal lyre, but the four hand stops protruding through the nameboard are supplemented by two knee levers. The 1933 Neupert, also in the "Bach disposition," also relies on hand stops and a knee lever. With its vertical-grain natural finish and floating-panel lid, it might have been inspired by an eighteenth-century Viennese fortepiano. Although the 1932 Maendler-Schramm also has a vertical-grain natural finish, it looks more like a modern piano than anything else, and an enormously strong one, at that. It has some twenty ribs running across the bottom of the soundboard.

Berlin has one more revival harpsichord, one that experiments with the combination of acoustic sound and amplification. The Wittmayer *Modell Bach Elektronik* was built in 1970, just when such instruments were giving way to the modern harpsichord based on a return to antique practices. In an effort to give this huge but relatively quiet instrument some of the resonance the antiques had, it was equipped with an amplifier, and two speakers were built into the soundboard.

Berlin's Musikinstrumenten-Museum has some nice clavichords. A C/E–c^3 Dutch instrument from ca. 1700 is typical of its time. It differs from the German clavichords of that period only in its decoration, a green exterior with some yellow acanthus leaves and a nondescript soundboard painting, both of which may well have been applied by the owner. A print of a monochromatic winter panorama, perhaps inspired by similar scenes by Pieter Bruegel, is glued to the interior of the lid. These small clavichords were meant to be played on a table and stored in a closet or under a bed when not in use.

The 1728 clavichord by Hieronymus Hass is one of the earliest examples we have of the "new" German clavichord of the eighteenth century. Its soundboard area is much larger than the Dutch instrument's, it has a wider range—C–f^3 chromatic, and is important enough as a musical instrument to have its own gracefully turned legs. Although its outside is painted a plain brown, its colorful interior includes a lid decorated with gold arabesques on a red ground and a centered painting of a dolphin rescuing Arion. With tortoise shell naturals and ivory arcades, and sharps topped with tortoise shell and ivory chevrons, the keywell is a lively burst of exotically covered surfaces.

Although sedate in comparison to the colorful, energetic instruments of Hass, the 1775 J. H. Silbermann and the 1784 Hubert clavichords, with their veneers, natural wood finishes, and floating-panel lids, have a quiet elegance. The clavichords of both these builders were highly respected and sought after. Johann Heinrich Silbermann achieved at least as much fame as his uncle Gottfried, in whose shop in Freiburg he was trained,

1784 clavichord by Christian Gottlob Hubert

1776 piano by Johann Heinrich Silbermann

and Hubert's instruments, known for their tonal superiority, were found throughout Europe.

No doubt the most historically interesting piano in the Berlin collection is the 1776 J. H. Silbermann. Like those built by his uncle, it has a Cristofori action with an intermediate lever, leather-covered hollow hammer heads, and an inverted wrestplank. With its horizontal-grain book-matched veneers, floating-panel lid, and gently curved cabriole legs with carved knees, it closely resembles the harpsichords and pianos made by Gottfried. Other than the style of the legs—the tapered square ones on the earlier instrument looking more "modern" than the cabrioles on the later—there is little indication that this 1776 piano and Gottfried's ca. 1740 harpsichord could not have been built in the same shop in the same year.

Possibly because the Musikinstrumenten-Museum was started with purchases from de Wit, a Netherlander, and Snoeck, a Belgian, there are comparatively few Berlin pianos in the collection. A ca. 1837 Heinrich Kisting & Sohn has a Viennese action, but its decor is perhaps more English-inspired, with book-matched mahogany burl veneers, cross-banding, and stringing. It is a rugged, handsome instrument, with three sturdy turned legs and a plain lyre with two pedals. There are two verticals by Berlin builders. A particularly lovely ca. 1840 burl-wood lyre piano by Johann Christian Schleip has brass lion's-paw feet and yellow silk hiding the strings; and a mid-nineteenth-century Johann Müller giraffe has candlestick holders and a small platform for a vase or statue at the deepest part of the bentside. A ca. 1860 piano by Kisting's student Theodor Stöcker, with its down-striking action, iron frame, heavy case, and massive legs, looks thoroughly modern.

The museum has many Viennese pianos, beginning with a 1775 example by Johann Andreas Stein. With its floating-panel lid, vertical-grain case veneer, fluted slanted cheeks, and four slender turned legs, it is the classic fortepiano of Mozart's early days. It was built only two years before Mozart's famous visit to Augsburg in 1777 and the letter to his father praising Stein's pianos. A Joseph Brodmann grand from 1810 is in the Stein tradition of lightly built fortepianos. Although it is triple-strung, it has thin case walls, slim tapered square legs, delicate-looking music rack, and an unpretentious lyre supported by a slender bow attached to the two front legs. These features lend a lightness in contrast to the more substantial-looking instruments of Walter, Graf, and other Viennese builders. It has pedals for *due corde*, bassoon, buff stop, and dampers and has a knee lever for the moderator. This piano is said to have belonged to Carl Maria von Weber, and his son claimed that the opera *Der Freis-chütz* was composed on it. Other Viennese grands are by Walter & Son (ca. 1800), Graf (1838), and Bösendorfer (1845).

A modernistic—one might even say futuristic—piano from the turn of the twentieth century was the result of a collaboration between Carl

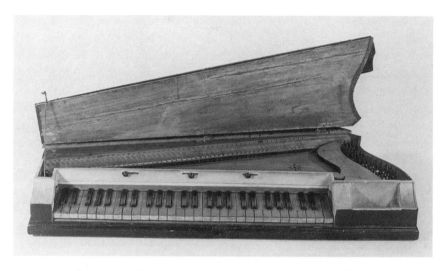

Ca. 1770 "lying harp" piano by Johann Matthäus Schmahl

Mand, a builder from Koblenz, and an architect, Joseph Maria Olbrich. With no bentside (or any other curves, for that matter) and with a two-piece lid hinged across its middle, the instrument is a succession of planes and angles—more an interesting sculptural object than a conventional piano.

Johann Matthaüs Schmahl's little table pianos with a "bentside" at the wrestplank—the "lying harp" form appropriated by that Ulm builder—all seem to have their individual differences. A 1770 model, painted a brownish green, has boxwood naturals, sharps of a dark wood, and three stop levers exiting the nameboard. In contrast, another from around the same time is painted a bluish grey, with ebony naturals, bone-covered sharps, and five stop levers.

Johann Gottlob Wagner built conventional squares and usually supplied them with legs, such as those found on Berlin's 1788. In common with many other builders of *Tafelklaviere*, he provided dust covers for the keyboard and soundboard areas. On many of his instruments a touch of a pedal or knee lever opened the soundboard cover, allowing it to function as a swell. The same sort of device is found on a 1775 Adam Beyer of London, where a large pedal on the right side of the instrument activates the swell lid. Three smaller pedals on the left control the more usual functions of dampers and buff.

A 1791 square piano-organ combination by Samuel Kühlewind of Volkstedt in Saxony also has a combined swell-dust cover over the sound-board, and its two pedals (one for the swell) are augmented by six hand stops controling harp, buff, dampers, and the organ's flute register. Dating from ca. 1800, an anonymous German square with a diminutive sound-board area is lovingly decorated with marquetry, inlays, and *appliqués*. With veneers, crossbanding, and a satinwood keywell, an 1815 square by John Broadwood is truly elegant. Its six graceful reeded legs obscure the presence of a seventh, which supports the instrument's single damper pedal.

A beautifully preserved 1793 *Tangentenflügel* by Späth und Schmahl is a fine example of the high quality of late eighteenth-century German instrument building. The burl-wood panels, stringing, veneered cross-banding, elegant bottom molding, and six slender legs all embody grace and proportion. Tangent pianos were remarkable instruments; their special qualities explored the softer side of stringed keyboard instruments. Al-though capable of a respectable *forte*, like clavichords, they could also be played at an almost inaudible *pianissimo*.

The Musikinstrumenten-Museum has had several catalogs, but three current ones are of greatest interest. Gesine Haase and Dieter Krickeberg's *Tasteninstrumente des Museums: Kielklaviere, Clavichorde, Hammerklaviere* (Berlin: Staatliches Institut für Musikforschung, 1981) is a narrative ac-count of the most important harpsichords, clavichords, and pianos in the collection, with color photos and occasional black-and-white pictures of details such as roses and nameplates. Not exactly a catalog, *100 Jahre Ber-liner Musikinstrumenten-Museum, 1888–1988* (Berlin, Staatliches Institut für Musikforschung, 1988) is a series of essays dealing with the history of the museum, with some wonderful pictures and close-up photos of details. John Henry van der Meer et al., *Kielklaviere: Cembali, Spinette, Virginale* (Berlin: Staatliches Institut für Musikforschung, 1991), is a catalog of all the plucked instruments owned by the museum. It is one of the finest examples of its kind, with photos, drawings, descriptions, molding profiles, and tables. It also contains important essays on the history of the harp-sichord and the harpsichord revival.

EISENACH

Bach-Haus

Address: Bach-Haus, 99817 Eisenach, Frauenplan 21; hours: October through March, 9 A.M.–4:45 P.M. Tuesday to Sunday, 1 P.M.–4:45 P.M. Monday;

April through September, 9-A.M.–5:45 P.M. Tuesday to Sunday,
Noon-5:45 P.M. Monday; telephone: 03691 203714; fax: 03691 76437.

Part of the province of Thuringia, Eisenach is a central German city with a distinguished past. Martin Luther lived there for three years while in his teens, electors and dukes held court in Eisenach, the German Social Democratic party was founded there, and Johann Sebastian Bach was born and lived in Eisenach for his first ten years—reason enough for a museum in his honor. The Bach-Haus is a modest establishment, with fewer than twenty early keyboards: three plucked, four clavichords, and ten pianos. Neither the instruments nor the building are connected with Bach or his family.

The three plucked instruments are a ca. 1765 Johann Heinrich Silbermann bentside spinet; a two-manual Jacob Hartman 2×8', 1×4' harpsichord from 1765; and a one-manual anonymous Thuringian harpsichord from ca. 1715. The spinet is typical of Silbermann's understated craftsmanship: book-matched burl-walnut sides, a floating-panel lid, and graceful cabriole legs with carved knees. The Hartman at one time was attributed to Gottfried Silbermann and was strung 1×16', 1×8', 1×4'. It now has the proper attribution and disposition. Transposing keyboards are found on harpsichords from time to time, but the one on the Thuringian instrument, spanning four semitones, is unusual. It was possibly intended to function at the various pitch levels then current for church and chamber performances.

Of the four clavichords, all anonymous, the most commanding is one with a pedal division, perhaps built by Johann Georg Marckert in the second decade of the nineteenth century. This large, unfretted clavichord rests atop an even larger instrument with 16' and 8', all supported by a stand from which projects a pedalboard spanning two octaves plus two notes. Intended to serve as an organist's practice instrument, it is imposing in appearance for a clavichord, exceeded only by Johann David Gerstenberg's 1760 double clavichord with pedal division in Leipzig's Musikinstrumenten-Museum.

Six of the pianos are squares: a 1774 Friedrich Beck (London), an anonymous English instrument from ca. 1775, a 1788 Johann Gottlob Wagner (Dresden), an 1817 Johann Georg Schenck (Weimar), an 1820 "portable" piano by Johann Schiebe and Anton Walter & Sohn (Vienna), and a ca. 1835 Johann Schneider (Berlin). There are two grands, a ca. 1820 by Franz Lautterer (Vienna) and a J. B. Streicher with down-striking action. Two other instruments of interest are a ca. 1790 Späth & Schmahl tangent-piano with five different tone-altering devices and a handsome her-

Ca. 1815 pedal clavichord by Johann Georg Marckert

ringbone veneered claviorganum with tangent action, probably by C. F. Schmahl, ca. 1805.

The catalog for the collection is Herbert Heyde, *Historische Musikinstrumente im Bachhaus Eisenach* (Eisenach, 1976).

HALLE

✹ Händel-Haus

Address: Händel-Haus Halle, 06108 Grosse Nikolaistrasse, Halle 5; hours: 9:30 A.M.–5:30 P.M. Friday to Wednesay, 9 A.M.–7 P.M. Thursday; telephone: 0345 500 900; fax: 0345 500 904 11.

Both Germans and English have legitimate claims on Georg Friedrich Händel, or George Frideric Handel, as he later called himself. He was born in 1685 (the same year as Bach and Scarlatti) in Halle, a bustling city near Leipzig, and received a basic musical education there. He even attended law school at the University of Halle for a year, intending to honor his father's wish that he train for a legal career; but music was really his first and only love. It was not until 1714, when Handel was twenty-nine years old, that he decided to make England his permanent home, and thirteen years later that he became a British citizen.

The Händel-Haus museum was established with the purchase of the building in 1937, but World War II intervened, and it was not until 1948 that the East German government opened it to the public. Instruments now in the museum were bought from the Neupert collection in Bamberg and the Rück collection in Erlangen, two large private collections broken up and dispersed during and after the war. The Händel-Haus has an interesting group of harpsichords and a nice assortment of pianos. A significant number of the latter, mostly nineteenth-century squares and upright consoles, were built by Halle makers, and there are also a few clavichords from the area.

Several plucked keyboards are of particular interest. Pride of place goes to the earliest extant double-manual harpsichord, a 1599 Ruckers ascribed to Hans because of the presence of an HR rose, but, according to O'Brien (pp. 240–41), almost certainly by Ioannes, since Hans had died just before that date. It is now a five-octave instrument, but originally the upper manual (the one at normal pitch) began with a short-octave C/E and went only to a², the range of the earliest Flemish harpsichords. Its *ravalement* took place in several stages and has been comprehensive, extending even to cutting the instrument's square cheeks on a slant in the manner of a Viennese fortepiano. The excellent lid painting is claimed to be original, but the pseudo-Rococo ornamentation with which the case is encrusted and the cabriole stand are later additions.

A small spinet virginal, probably sounding a fourth higher when new, is ascribed on the jackrail to Hans Ruckers in 1610; but as noted above, Hans was long dead by that time. The museum appropriately calls it an Antwerp virginal built between 1595 and 1620. Its Flemish papers are in good condition and may be original. Its lid motto is one of our favorites: "Dulci sonum reficit trista corda melos" (A sweet-sounding melody refreshes the saddest heart). Although extensively rebuilt, it remains an attractive-looking instrument.

An anonymous seventeenth-century Italian inner-outer is claimed by the catalog to be in Florentine style, resembling the work of Antonio Migliai and Bartolomeo Cristofori. That could well be correct; at least the instrument has the relative simplicity of decoration typical of late seventeenth-century Italians. Although by that time those builders were making integral-case harpsichords—either false inner-outers or instruments that ignored that convention altogether—there were still many craftsmen who clung to what must have been a lingering inner-outer tradition. It is disposed in the manner of a Northern harpsichord: 2×8′, 1×4′, with buff. There are examples of that sort of disposition in seventeenth-century Italy, and this is probably original (although the buff is not). Perhaps the most unusual thing about the instrument is its lid painting, a home concert in which the harpsichord depicted is the very harpsichord upon which the scene is painted, and is also the harpsichord painted on the lid of the instrument painted on the lid.

In view of the number of spurious harpsichords bearing his name, Giovanni Battista Giusti must have been one of Franciolini's favorite builders; however, the Händel-Haus instrument, an inner-outer dated 1677, seems genuine. At one time the six lowest notes had pulldowns to a pedalboard.

The Händel-Haus also has a polygonal virginal ascribed to the Venetian Alessandro Trasuntino. It may be genuine, but its date of 1604 poses something of a problem, since Trasuntino's other instruments fall between 1531 and 1538. If this date is correct, Alessandro would have been in his nineties when this virginal was built—certainly not beyond the realm of possibility; but if the date is true, one wonders why we do not have instruments from 1538 to 1604. That there were possibly as many as four other Venetian makers with the surname Trasuntino, all building in the sixteenth century, does little to clarify the situation. That it was listed in one of Franciolini's catalogs (the Trasuntino name was one of his favorites) is a further argument against its authenticity.

Other plucked keyboards in the Händel-Haus museum include an Italian harpsichord at octave pitch, signed by Giovanni Chianei of Venice, 1766, but considered to be a forgery; an unsigned seventeenth-century Italian harpsichord, and another from Florence, dated 1695; an Italian virginal from the early eighteenth century; and an eighteenth-century harpsichord turned into a clavicytherium around 1900. The museum also has a revival harpsichord, a 1939 Maendler-Schramm.

The Händel-Haus has seven clavichords, but only one is signed, a fretted one from 1784 by Christian Gottlob Hubert. Three unsigned, dating from ca. 1720, ca. 1780, and ca. 1790, are products of Saxony, the state that includes Halle. The others are also eighteenth-century German.

Nine of the museum's impressive collection of pianos are from Vienna: Both the ca. 1805 Joseph Brodman and the ca. 1810 Caspar Katholnik are in the Stein tradition, with knee levers. Two somewhat later and much heavier pianos, from 1825 and 1835, are by Conrad Graf, who belongs to the not-inconsiderable ranks of makers who married their deceased masters' widows. Although a conservative builder, Graf was well thought of, and some of the best nineteenth-century German pianists preferred his instruments. In 1824 he was awarded the title of Royal Piano and Keyboard

Maker to the Viennese court. The newest Viennese instrument, by A. Parttart, dates from the end of the nineteenth century. Though it is a modern piano in almost all respects, it still contains a Viennese action, albeit a much heavier version than those found earlier in the century.

The Händel-Haus has four pianos bearing the name Stein or Streicher. Two are by Nannette Streicher, the daughter of piano maker Johann Andreas Stein and one of the finest builders of her day. The first is from 1820, when she was still signing her instruments "née Stein" (after marrying Johann Andreas Streicher in 1794, she signed her instruments "Nannette Streicher," but was obviously aware of the publicity value of the Stein name). The second instrument, from 1828, signed Nannette Streicher & Son, was built after she took her son Johann Baptist as a partner in 1823. From 1827 is a piano by Matthäus Andreas Stein, Nannette's younger brother and Stein père's twelfth child (Matthäus seemed to prefer to use his middle name, Andreas, which, in 1803, he changed to the French version, André). He and Nannette were partners for ten years, first in Augsburg, after old Stein died in 1792, and then in Vienna, after Nannette married. Their partnership was dissolved in 1802, after which each built independently. Finally, there is an 1870 piano by Johann Baptist Streicher & Son, Nannette's son and grandson. By this time the Streicher firm was building pianos in "American" style, with cast-iron plates, cross-stringing, repetition actions and felt-covered hammers; but they also continued to make pianos with bolted-on tension bars, straight stringing, Viennese actions, and leather-covered hammers. This instrument is an example of the latter type.

Franz Jacob Späth and Christoph Friedrich Schmahl were another well-known pair in piano making. Schmahl married Späth's daughter, and the two became partners in Regensburg. They concentrated on producing *Tangentenflügeln*, and the museum has one such instrument from 1790. An unsigned square, perhaps a Schmahl, is dated 1780, and a Schmahl fortepiano is from 1804. Johann Caspar Schlimbach of Königshofen specialized in *Querflügeln*—transverse pianos looking very much like bentside spinets. The Händel-Haus has one dated ca. 1815.

Other German pianos in the Händel-Haus include a ca. 1789 by the Salzburg builder Johann Schmid (some of whose instruments are in Salzburg's Museum Carolino Augusteum), a ca. 1790 instrument by Edmund Ignaz Quernbach of Mainz (his only extant piano), a 1794 by Johann Gottfried and Johann Wilhelm Gräbner of Dresden (sons of harpsichord maker Johann Heinrich Gräbner and brothers of harpsichord maker Karl August Gräbner), a ca. 1820 lyre-piano by Johann Christian Schleip of

Ca. 1820 lyre-piano by Johann Christian Schleip

Berlin, and two giraffes—an 1817 by Christoph Ehrlich of Bamberg and an 1838 by Anton Biber of Nuremberg.

According to the catalog, an 1800s South German grand began life as a harpsichord but was converted to a piano ca. 1770–80. Many harpsichords suffered such a fate, although we suspect that this one may have always been a piano. That aside, the unusual thing about this instrument is its FF/C, GG–AA–BB-flat/D, BB–C/E short octave, with split keys for D/F-sharp and E/G-sharp.

The Händel-Haus holds a 1785 square attributed to the Worms builder Johann Christoph Jeckel, an anonymous ca. 1820 upright grand, and several foreign pianos: from Paris, an 1845 Pleyel and an 1844 Pape console; and from London, squares from 1773 by Zumpe and 1777 by Buntebart and Adam Beyer. The Händel-Haus also has a ca. 1870 Gustave Baudet *piano-violon*, an instrument resembling an upright console piano but capable of producing sustained tones. It is an earlier version of Baudet's *piano-quatuor*, described below in the section on Stuttgart's Württembergisches Landesmuseum.

The Händel-Haus has published a compact but informative catalog of its collection, which includes organs, winds, strings, and percussion as well as stringed keyboards: Herbert Heyde, *Historische Musikinstrumente des Händel-Hauses: Führer durch die Ausstellungen* (Halle an der Saale, 1983).

HAMBURG

Museum für Kunst und Gewerbe

Address: Steintorplatz, D-2099 Hamburg 1; hours: 10 A.M.–6 P.M. Tuesday, Wednesday, Friday, Saturday, and Sunday; 10 A.M.–9 P.M. Thursday; telephone: 040 2486 2830; fax: 040 2686 2834.

The Museum for Art and Industry has only a handful of early keyboards, but among them is the famous 1728 two-manual harpsichord by Christian Zell of Hamburg, with 2×8′, 1×4′ plus buff. It is one of the three known instruments by Zell (the second, in Aurich's Ostfriesische Landschaft, is not far from Hamburg, but the third is in Barcelona's Museu de la Música). The 1728 is indeed a magnificent instrument, much copied in construction if not in decoration. In the manner of many Hamburg instruments, it is eclectically and colorfully embellished. The exterior of the case and lid display a phantasmagoric raised polychrome chinoiserie on green *faux* tortoise shell. The interior of the case above the soundboard and the jackrail are painted a light red with gilded moldings. The keywell

1728 harpsichord by Christian Zell

is veneered and cross-banded in natural wood, with four-point stars of ebony and ivory inlaid in the cheeks and the nameboard. The naturals are topped with ivory, the arcades are ebony, and the sharps are tortoise shell. The three parts of the lid each have paintings (done later than the instrument) dealing with mythological subjects in which gods, goddesses, nymphs, angels, mortals, and *putti* engage in a whirl of activity in forests and gardens, with impressive castles and buildings in the background, the whole surrounded by red *faux* tortoise shell borders. The soundboard is painted with flowers and birds; in place of a rose there is a vignette of the goddess Minerva flanked by two women playing lute and violin. The instrument sits on an elaborate stand with eight ornately carved and painted legs. The 1728 is a breathtaking sight, and must have been even more so when the paint and decoration were fresh.

In typical International-derived North German style, the rounded-tail case is built with the sides overlapping the bottom, internal knees, a thin bentside, and a heavier spine. The bridges and nuts are tall, with molded tops. The instrument is strung in brass and has a somewhat dry, powerful sound with a pronounced attack that seems to lend itself to almost any harpsichord music. It has been recorded.

During World War II the museum's two polygonal Italian virginals—a 1569 by the Milanese builder Annibale dei Rossi and a 1594 by the Venetian Giovanni Celestini—were sent to locations near Dresden for safe keeping. After the war that area became part of East Germany, but with reunification the instruments were returned to the Museum für Kunst und Gewerbe. It is unfortunate that the Celestini suffered serious damage in storage, because both it and the Rossi are among the very few virginals, Italian or otherwise, that have two sets of 8′ strings. Unlike Cristofori's instrument in Leipzig, neither of these virginals combines the plans of two normal virginals in mirror image; instead, the jacks for the unison pairs all protrude through the soundboards in the usual fashion. Nevertheless, with twice as many strings and jacks as normal, the instruments are quite deep. The case of the Celestini is elaborately decorated in gold, blue, and red arabesques and cartouches on a black ground. Both virginals have half-inset keyboards.

Another Celestini is a harpsichord in grand form, an inner-outer dated 1608. The ornate outer case sits on a pair of fanciful table stands.

The museum has three five-octave FF–f^3 clavichords bearing the Hass name: a 1732 by Hieronymus Albrecht, a 1760 by Johann Adolph, and a 1796 by Dietrich Christopher. The first two were father and son, but the last, although also a Hamburger, does not seem to be related. The 1760 is a lovely unfretted instrument, with a set of 4′ strings in the bass, a black exterior, and a glowing red interior. A classical scene is painted in a cartouche on the underside of the lid.

Five square pianos, a lyre-piano, and a grand complete the collection. The squares make a nice variety: a Schoene & Co. (London, 1789), an Érard Frères (Paris, 1805), a Johann Wilhelm Freudenthaler (Paris, 1815), a C. Gerlach (Germany, 1825), and a G. Kühnst (Darmstadt, ca. 1850–55). The tone-altering mechanisms on these instruments are interesting: the Schoene has only a knee lever, for raising the dampers; the Érard and the Freudenthaler both have four pedals, for *una corda*, dampers, moderator, and bassoon. The Érard's pedals are affixed in the simplest manner, projecting from a low, slender stretcher connected to the rear legs; but the Freudenthaler's are mounted on a large block, supported from the bottom of the case by four sizeable columns. Clearly, the first instrument deals with the aesthetics of pedals by minimizing their appearance, while the second makes them into a design feature. Both the Gerlach and the Kühnst have traditional lyres centered between the legs, the former with two pedals (*una corda* and dampers) and the latter, like the Schoene built sixty-five years earlier, with only one, for dampers. These squares are all nicely done, avoiding the bizarre and the overdecorated. The legs of the Érard are capped with brass Nikes, and a small brass frieze on the case depicts a winged Apollo playing a lyre while mounted on a centaur playing a double aulos (thus reconciling the Apollonian and Dionysian); this instrument reflects early nineteenth-century society's strong desire to connect the piano with classical antiquity.

That connection is even more forcibly expressed by a ca. 1840 Johann Christian Schleip lyre piano, with its shape reflected in miniature by the pedal lyre below and seven rods representing the strings of the lyre. A small grand by Theodor Steinweg of Braunschweig, dated 1896, has an elaborate painted, carved, and inlaid decoration. Elaborate pianos such as this were made on special order for rich architectural surroundings. The museum calls this a "salon piano," and it seems an apt name.

Museum für Hamburgische Geschichte

*Address: Holstenwall 24, D-2000 Hamburg 36; hours: 10 A.M.–4 P.M.
Sunday, Tuesday, and Friday; 10 A.M.–1 P.M. Saturday;
telephone: 0411 34 1091.*

Like its sister museum, the Museum for Hamburg History has only a few stringed keyboards among its fascinating collection of artifacts. Nevertheless, it takes great pride in a 1716 single with 2×8', 1×4' and buff, by Carl Conrad Fleischer, brother of Johann Christoph. Only two of his instruments survive—the other is in Barcelona's Museu de la Música (although a third has been reported to be in Italy). The 1716, like the Zell in the Kunst und Gewerbe, is a colorfully decorated instrument. The case is painted with scenes involving sailors, nymphs, and *putti*; a seascape graces the spine; and Orpheus charms the beasts on the nameboard. The exterior of the lid is painted with a profusion of flowers, with a violin and some sheet music at the front. The lid painting is said to be a concert scene depicting or inspired by Handel's *Messiah*. None of this decoration is original, and it is really not very well executed; but the effect is nonetheless captivating. The nice soundboard painting, with a large red bird above the rose, is probably original, as is the gilded parchment upside-down wedding-cake rose. The long and unusually wide naturals are covered with ivory, and the sharps are tortoise shell. A gilded or bronzed Louis XV stand with carved floral designs completes the ensemble.

In sound, the Fleischer belongs to the same tonal world as the 1728 Zell. Its *tutti* is impressively majestic, with a pronounced attack, and its single 8's are warm, though somewhat dry. It is a lovely sounding instrument.

Another harpsichord, an undated anonymous single-manual 1×8', 1×4' with the plain appearance typical of eighteenth-century Italians, is unusual in that both 4' and 8' bridges are mitered. One expects to see a miter on an 8' bridge, since most harpsichords are not long enough to allow that bridge to continue straight; but it must be considered an affectation on a 4' bridge. The soundboard has been replaced, but the old one has been preserved and shows clear signs of the bridge miters.

The Museum für Hamburgische Geschichte has two clavichords, a 1742 Hieronymus Hass and a 1769 Johann Christian Gerlach. The Hass's exterior is a plain brownish-black, probably from a later redecoration; but the interior is a blaze of color, with red case walls, a natural wood keywell, a painted soundboard, ivory-covered naturals, and tortoise shell sharps. The lid paintings of Hass clavichords are usually quite well done, but this one—an outdoor musical scene—is unusual in that the characters are almost like cartoons in their demeanor. One of the instruments portrayed is a clavichord, making this the only clavichord we know of to depict a clavichord in its lid painting. The Gerlach, undoubtedly repainted at some time, is now black on the outside with a somewhat garish red and green interior. Both instruments have the Hamburg trademark, an additional set of 4' strings in the bass; and both are fine-sounding clavichords.

LEIPZIG

Musikinstrumenten-Museum der Universität Leipzig

Address: Täubchenweg 2 e (mailing address, 2 c), 04103 Leipzig;
hours: 10 A.M.–5 P.M. Tuesday to Saturday, 10 A.M.–1 P.M. Sunday;
telephone: 2142–120; fax: 2142–135.

Leipzig University's Musical Instrument Museum was formed in 1927 from the private holdings of Wilhelm Heyer of Cologne, a factory owner and amateur musician. Heyer's enormous collection was twice augmented through purchases: in 1905, from the dealer Paul de Wit, a Dutchman who lived in Leipzig; and in 1908, from Alessandro Krauss, another inveterate collector who was born in Frankfurt but lived in Florence. For a while Heyer had his own museum, established in 1906 in Cologne, with over 2,600 instruments, but it was all transferred to the University. Consequently, with about fifty plucked instruments, more than thirty-five clavichords, and at least 140 pianos, the University of Leipzig has one of the world's great collections of early keyboards.

Recent history has not been kind to this collection. During World War II over twenty harpsichords, clavichords, and pianos—not to mention other instruments—were bombed into oblivion, and many more were damaged. For forty years after the war Leipzig was part of East Germany, and the institution to which the collection was attached was known as Karl Marx University; but since the reunification of Germany it has once again become the University of Leipzig.

Even without its sheer bulk, this collection would be exceptional, since five of its instruments—four plucked keyboards and a piano—were made by one of the greatest and most inventive of builders, Bartolomeo Cristofori. Cristofori, of course, was the inventor of the piano, or, as it was called, the *gravicembalo col piano e forte*—large harpsichord with soft and loud, or the *cembalo a martellini* (or *martelletti*)—hammer harpsichord. Henkel estimates that Cristofori built between twenty-five and thirty pianos, but only three remain: in New York's Metropolitan Museum (1720), Rome's Museo Nazionale di Strumenti Musicali (1722), and Leipzig (1726). This last instrument, therefore, is an exceedingly valuable document. It looks very much like one of the master's harpsichords, except for the so-called inverted wrestplank. Actually, it is not the wrestplank that Cristofori inverted, but the nut, which he placed on the underside of the plank. Thus, the strings, which go *under* the wrestplank, when struck, were driven *into* rather than *off* the nut. With this invention, and with his use of a stronger case with heavier strings, hollow hammer heads, checks, intermediate levers, and escapement, Cristofori brilliantly demonstrated both his understanding of the problems inherent in hitting a string with a hammer and his ability to provide solutions for them.

Cristofori added a further refinement—a stroke of sheer genius—that provided the piano with a "soul," and which may have been the element most responsible for assuring it a secure place in the world of keyboard instruments. His hammer heads are made from rings of glued, rolled parchment, covered with pieces of leather. In comparison with the sophistication of the rest of the action, these "hollow" hammer heads at first seem rather crude, but they are actually highly efficient. Subdued playing compresses the leather only slightly. Exciting a string with this relatively soft material tends to suppress high-frequency sounds and pro-

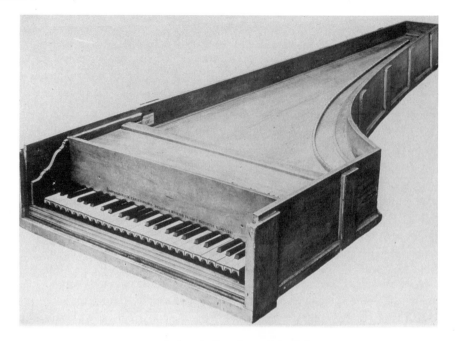

1726 piano by Bartolomeo Cristofori

duces a quiet tone consisting mainly of lower partials. But when the velocity of the hammer increases, and the string is struck with increasing force, the leather is compressed more and more, bringing the harder parchment into play. The hollow head has some give to it, but the greater the force of the blow, the "harder" the mass of the hammer seems to the string. Exciting the string with this relatively dense material tends to generate more higher-frequency components, so that at a *fortissimo* the sound fairly crackles with acoustical energy. Exactly the same principle is used in the modern hammer head; though it is made of solid wood, it is covered with an inner layer of hard felt and outer layers of softer felt. Thus, from the beginning the piano allowed gradations not only of dynamics but also of tone quality.

Of the museum's two Cristofori harpsichords, the 1722 looks very much like a standard early eighteenth-century Italian model, with its thick case, long, graceful lines, and 2×8' disposition. The keyboard is inset rather than projecting. The 1726, bearing only an external resemblance to its sister, is a unique instrument with three choirs of strings, at 8', 4', and 2' pitch. Through an ingenious combination of register extensions protrud-

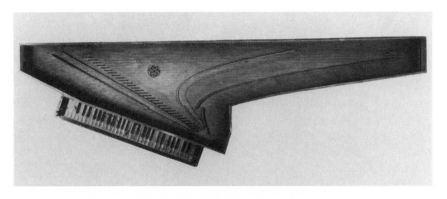

1693 virginal by Bartolomeo Cristofori

ing from cheek *and* spine, and stop levers mounted on the wrestplank, six registrations are possible: 8′, 8′+4′, 4′, 4′+2′, 2′, and 8′+4′+2′. In addition, the 8′ register is split at middle C, allowing the 4′, 2′, or both together to sound with the 8′ in the bass only. This instrument could be thought to combine a harpsichord strung at normal pitch with an octave spinet and a double-octave spinet, and it is the only known Italian harpsichord with a 2′ choir. Furthermore, by Cristofori's time the normal Italian disposition was two sets of 8′ strings, so even a 4′ choir could be considered something of a rarity.

The other two Cristofori instruments in Leipzig are also unique. The first is an extraordinary symmetrically shaped 2×8′ virginal built in 1693, looking like an oblong with half-ovals projecting from each end, and having a mechanism for playing either set of strings or both together. If a line were drawn through its center from one side to the other, the upper half would contain what looked like the two bridges of a normal virginal, while the lower half would bear the mirror image of those bridges. Thus, each of the two normal virginal bridges is symmetrically duplicated.

Presumably, all this was done so that the instrument could accommodate its two sets of unison strings. The longest pair of strings runs down the middle, from left to right. The next longest pair goes alongside, the next on the other side and so on. The two shortest pairs are the most widely separated, one at the back, the other at the front. The slots in the soundboard from which the jacks protrude are close to the left bridges and mirror their configuration. The keyboard projects from the front of the case, from left of center, with the key levers essentially extending under the left bridges. The key levers are of two sizes: from bass to treble, levers one, three, five, seven, etc., *decrease* in length, operating the jacks that pluck the strings on the lower part of the instrument. But levers two, four, six, eight, etc., *increase* in length, activating the jacks that pluck the strings in the upper half. Thus, from the bass up, every long key is a little longer, every short key a little shorter. This is a rare disposition for a virginal. Normal Italian virginals—in fact, virginals of all kinds—were either square or polygonal and had only one set of strings and were rather simple instruments. Cristofori's work is an elegantly engineered *tour de force*.

The second instrument, built about 1700, looks somewhat like an elongated bentside spinet. It has two sets of strings, 1×8′, 1×4′, with a mechanism to play either of the stops alone as well as both together. This instrument was called a *spinettone da teatro,* or theater spinet. Perhaps Cristofori created this new, space-saving design because his orchestra pit could not accommodate a normal harpsichord. Washington's Smithsonian Institution has a similar spinettone, which is neither signed nor dated but is nevertheless believed to be by Cristofori.

More information about these fascinating instruments can be found in Henkel. Two recent books that deal with Cristofori and his instruments are Konstantin Restle, *Bartolomeo Cristofori und die Anfänge des Hammerclaviers* (Munich: Editio Maris, 1991), and Stuart Pollens, *The Early Pianoforte* (Cambridge: Cambridge University Press, 1995).

Most of the other plucked strings are either anonymous Italian harpsichords or polygonal and rectangular virginals. Among them is the simple but elegant single-strung 1533 C/E–f^3 Dominicus Pisaurensis, a "classical" early sixteenth-century Italian harpsichord and the earliest recorded instrument by this builder. A 1612 Vincentius Pratensis is elaborately decorated. The interior surfaces of the case have been stained black, gold acanthus leaves grace the nameboard and the jackrail, vine patterns adorn the case walls above the soundboard, and the cheeks are carved cornucopias.

An anonymous harpsichord from the second half of the seventeenth century, disposed 1×8′, 1×4′, still has its 4′ bridge, nut, and strings. Most of these instruments were later changed to a 2×8′ disposition. At one time six or seven inches were cut off the tail, so now, when this harpsichord is placed in its outer case, a neat little tool compartment is formed between the outside of the inner and the inside of the outer. Also unusual is its lid painting, a panorama of the city of Pisa.

Home instruments, as much furniture as music-making devices, were frequently elaborately decorated. Leipzig's 1571 Benedetto Floriani virginal (discussed above in connection with the Berlin Musikinstrumenten-Museum's ca. 1570 anonymous Italian virginal) has case walls made of ebony or some black-stained wood and covered with gold borders and various designs. The ebony sharps also have gold designs picked out on them, and ivory studs set into the cap molding outline the plan view of the instrument. The Benedetto is the earliest virginal in the collection; one by Alessandro Riva of Bergamo, dated 1839, is the latest. Riva's instrument is entirely outside the old Italian practice and resembles a square piano. Another of his curious instruments, dated 1836, is in Milan's Museo degli Strumenti Musicali. An anonymous nineteenth-century virginal in Copenhagen and another in a private collection in Italy, both looking like square pianos, evidently came out of the same tradition, although neither resembles Riva's instruments.

Leipzig has many more Italian harpsichords, most anonymous but a few signed. A 1676 Giovanni Battista Giusti is a "classic" four-octave long-tailed Italian. Girolamo Zenti is represented by a harpsichord with the spurious date of 1683. Since Zenti died in 1668, 1653 is more likely for this instrument; however, in 1653 Zenti was in Stockholm working for the court of Queen Christina, so even that date could be questioned. A 1689 with the classical Italian disposition of 2×8′ is the only extant work of the Florentine builder Lorenzo Magniai. A 1702 harpsichord, one of the three extant by another Florentine, Antonio Migliai, has an unusual split FF/GG-natural key, with the FF in the back. Looking stubbier than the usual Italian harpsichord, a 1757 Giovanni Francesco Franco has three sets of 8′ strings but only one 8′ nut. This arrangement is somewhat enigmatic, since a harpsichord can have only two strings on the same level, and a lower level requires a second, lower nut. Nevertheless, it does have a splendid elephant portrayed in its "Orpheus charming the beasts" lid painting.

Most of the other plucked keyboards are of seventeenth-century German origin. The museum has two rather nice anonymous virginals, one with the bridge layouts of a Flemish spinett, with the keyboard to the extreme left, designed to produce a close-plucking nasal quality. Although its exterior is painted a crude black, its soundboard is densely decorated, the case walls above the soundboard are papered, and the lid painting is yet another "Orpheus charming the beasts." The second virginal more resembles a small Italian in design, but with an inset keyboard. It has no soundboard painting but does have papers on the interior case walls and a humorous lid painting in which two trumpeters bedecked in seventeenth-century finery serenade a captive audience, and each other, in the middle of a field.

An anonymous South German square octave virginal, while of minimum musical value, is nevertheless finely made, with inlay veneers, a painted soundboard, and a landscape-and-peasants lid painting represent-

Anonymous 17th-century Italian harpsichord

Anonymous 18th-century German virginal

ing spring and summer. When the instrument is closed it becomes a sew-ing box, with a pin cushion on the lid and drawers for thread and tools. At one time this instrument was attributed to Hans Ruckers.

Double-manual bentside spinets are rare, but Leipzig has two. The first, built by Israel Gellinger of Frankfurt am Main in 1677, at 4′ pitch,

Anonymous 17th-century South German octave virginal

has two sets of strings and a three-octave range—really little more than a toy. The second, a small instrument (although at or near 8′ pitch), was made in 1713 (the date is in question) by Christoph Bohr of Dresden; it has a 4′ in addition to two 8′ sets of strings. The museum also owns a large, elegant bentside spinet with floating-panel lid and book-matched veneers by Johann Heinrich Silbermann, built between 1760 and 1775.

Johann Heinrich Gräbner (the younger) from Dresden was one of a long line of organ- and harpsichord-building Gräbners, but only one of his instruments has survived, a two-manual harpsichord dated 1744. Its natural-wood finish, undecorated soundboard, cut-down nameboard, and unpretentiousness are typical of eighteenth-century Central German instruments. Before the turn of the twentieth century one of its 8′ choirs was replaced with a 16′, and the instrument was re-disposed so that the

1543 clavichord by Dominicus Pisaurensis

4' was on the upper manual and an 8' and 16' were on the lower. It has since been restored to its original 2×8', 1×4' disposition, and the 4' has been returned to the lower manual. At one time it was thought to have been built by Gottfried Silbermann.

A 1633 Andreas Ruckers harpsichord, originally a nonaligned double, was transformed into a single, the reverse of the usual *ravalement* procedure. The case exterior has been redecorated, but the instrument still has its Flemish papers. The well-preserved soundboard painting shows a couple playing a violin and a lute. An anonymous Dutch single-manual harpsichord, a 1767 Kirkman, a 1713 *clavecin brisé* by Marius, and two bentside spinets—a 1687 Charles Haward and an early seventeenth-century French—complete the list of instruments from outside Italy and Germany.

The museum has some early twentieth-century harpsichords: a 1909, by the Leipzig restorer Hermann Seyffarth, has a 16' and three manuals; and a 1911 by Otto Marx, another Leipzig restorer, is a copy of the museum's 1744 Gräbner.

Three of the earliest-known clavichords are in this museum, exemplifying two of the earliest forms of the instrument. The first is a 1543 by Dominicus Pisaurensis, the earliest surviving signed and dated clavichord. The other two are anonymous instruments from about the same time, also almost certainly of Italian origin (although the Henkel clavichord catalog cited at the end of this section ascribes them to a German maker). About two-thirds of the soundboard of the Dominicus slopes down to the wrestplank on the right-hand side of the polygonal case, and the strings bear on three separate straight bridges of different heights. A so-called second soundboard runs underneath the keys. It is an elegant clavichord, resembling the virginals built at that time, with its polygonal shape, handsome moldings, and projecting keyboard. The strings are parallel to the spine, in contrast to later examples, in which they run at a shallow angle from lower right to upper left.

The two anonymous instruments, known as Leipzig Numbers Two and Three because of their position in the Henkel catalog, are similar to the Dominicus, although they are square rather than polygonal. However, their soundboards do not slope (although they both have second soundboards); instead, two pressure bars behind the two (on Number Two) or three (on Number Three) straight bridges control the downbearing. While it is thought that the instruments were made by different builders, the exposed key levers of both are shaped to form interesting semicircular designs. These patterns seem to be unique to these two clavichords, so it is not unlikely that the builders were known to one other. All three clavichords are inner-outers; the Dominicus and Number Two still have what are presumed to be their original outer cases.

The center of clavichord building shifted to Germany in the seventeenth century, and the museum's first example from that region is an anonymous instrument from after 1650. Of a later type than the Dominicus and Leipzig Numbers Two and Three, the soundboard is flat, there is no second soundboard, there are no pressure bars, the keyboard is inset, and the strings angle up to the left from the single curved bridge. Clavichords of this type were almost always integral-case instruments, and this one is no exception. The lid painting is of a rather naive St. Cecilia.

Polygonal clavichords were built for the same reason as polygonal virginals: eliminating the superfluous segments of the upper right- and left-hand corners of the case. The Italians favored the polygonal form, but now and then it was found in other traditions as well. A 1692 clavichord by Georg Haase of Bautzen is a case in point. This particular instrument also has a broken short octave; otherwise, it is typically seventeenth-century German, with an applied bottom molding, a top molding cut into the edge of the case, papers on the nameboard and interior of the case, and a plain, unpainted wood finish.

North German clavichords became much more ornate in the eighteenth century, but in Central Germany, like harpsichords, they tended to plainness. Typical of such instruments, the 1787 Christian Gottlob Hubert has little more than top and bottom moldings to relieve that simplicity. However, it is considerably larger than the earlier models, with more soundboard area and a range expanded to almost five octaves. Despite its late date it is partially fretted. A ca. 1775 unfretted Hubert is finished in a striking Rococo decoration that was done in the late nineteenth century; in fact, little of the instrument is original.

The 1760 Johann David Gerstenberg double clavichord with pedal division is an imposing structure. It is really three instruments in one: the two clavichords—the second in a drawer beneath the first—sit atop a long pedal clavichord, which in turn is mounted on a chest containing the stickers linking the pedals to the key levers. A full pedalboard projects from the chest. The manuals each have a range of four and a third octaves unfretted, while the pedal division has a range of two octaves, with 16' and 8' strings. Obviously, such an ensemble was created for an organist as a practice instrument; but it makes a powerful statement in its own right.

In seeming contradiction to our remark about the ornateness of eighteenth-century northern clavichords, a 1748 Johann Adolph Hass has a bare wood exterior and lid interior, even though its soundboard is painted and the keyboard has tortoise shell sharps. The exterior finish and perhaps the lid painting may have been removed at some time. Like most Hasses, this one has a choir of 4' strings to brighten the bass.

Another nonstandard shape, the 1787 Friedrich Carl Wilhelm Lemme clavichord, has rounded rather than squared ends. It provides for a graceful plan view, and the instrument is nicely appointed, with moldings applied to the case exterior, and square, tapered legs. Only in the 4' set of bass strings and the presence of tortoise shell naturals does the appearance of this instrument betray its Northern origins. Lemme claimed that this design produced a superior tone; he also claimed to have invented the laminated (e.g., what we would call plywood) soundboard, which he contended was superior to the normal plank board. Deserved or not, Lemme had an excellent reputation.

One of the first of four generations of keyboard instrument builders, almost all of whom had the same first name, Christian Gottlob Friederici was the brother of Christian Ernst Friederici, the maker of the elegantly marquetried 1745 pyramid piano in the Brussels Musée Instrumental. C. P. E. Bach preferred Friederici clavichords to those of Hass and his Hamburg colleagues, mainly, it seems, because they did *not* have a 4' set of strings in the bass! The Mozarts also owned Friederici instruments. Leipzig's example is a large five-octave instrument from 1765.

We have already discussed in some detail the most famous of Leipzig's pianos, the 1726 Cristofori; otherwise, most of Leipzig's pianos are in storage, and we have not seen them. The museum kindly sent us a copy of a checklist developed for internal use, and some of the names listed— Beyer, Broadwood, Friederici, Gräbner, Schleip, Schmahl, Steinway, and Wachtl—are familiar; others are more obscure. Johann Andreas Stein is represented by a 1773 instrument; his daughter Nannette by four, dated ca. 1810, 1816, and 1829 and one undated; and Nannette's son, J. B. Streicher, by an undated example. The mid-nineteenth-century Leipzig builder Alfred Dolge has a few instruments in this collection, but he moved to New York and is better remembered today as a supplier of piano components and for his book, *Pianos and Their Makers* (Covina, CA: Covina Publishing Co., 1911; 1972 paperback edition by Dover Publications, Inc.). In all, thirty-two of the museum's pianos are by Leipzig builders, and of these, fourteen are grands.

The Musikinstrumenten-Museum has two organized pianos: a ca. 1800 square by Johannes Pohlmann, London, one of the "Twelve Apostles"; and a grand from ca. 1800 by Christian Gottlob Friederici. Two other instruments of interest are a Späth & Schmahl *Tangentenflügel*, and a J. C. Dietz harp piano. There is also a *piano quatuor* by Baudet, similar to the one described in the Württembergisches Landesmuseum.

The Musikinstrumenten-Museum published two catalogs of its keyboard instruments, one on the plucked instruments, the other on the clavichords (this volume also includes *hackbretts*, or hammer dulcimers). They are informative, with elaborate descriptions of each instrument and black and white pictures of many, drawings of molding profiles, details of roses and builders' signatures, and color illustrations of some of the more interesting features. Even the instruments destroyed during the war are reported. The catalogs are Hubert Henkel, *Kiel-Instrumente, Musikinstrumenten-Museum der Karl-Marx-Universität, Leipzig Katalog, Band 2* (Leipzig: Veb Deutscher Verlag für Musik, 1979); and Hubert Henkel, *Clavichorde, Musikinstrumenten-Museum der Karl-Marx-Universität, Leipzig Katalog, Band 4* (Frankfurt am Main: Verlag das Musikinstrument, 1981).

MUNICH

Deutsches Museum

Address: Museumsinsel 1, D-80538, Munich; hours: daily, 9 A.M.–5 P.M.; telephone: 089 2179 1; fax: 089 2179 324.

The capital of Bavaria and the second largest city in Germany, Munich is one of that country's most important cities, with a deep and rich cultural history. It was heavily damaged during the strategic bombing of World War II; nevertheless, many old buildings remained standing, including some dating back to the fifteenth century. Hence, like so many of Germany's great cities, Munich now blends old with new. Built in the first decades of the twentieth century, the large, attractive Deutsches Museum is to Munich what the Smithsonian's National Museum of American History is to Washington, DC: a repository of technology, science, and industry, and, as such, contains musical instruments.

There are many curiosities among the keyboards, and, in fact, it is in these that this museum finds its niche. Rather than one more seventeenth-century Italian harpsichord or another eighteenth-century English double, its less-familiar assets lead us to consider some instruments that do not fit so neatly into standard categories. Our discussion of its fourteen plucked keyboards, twelve clavichords, nearly fifty pianos, and a harp piano will focus on those unusual items. It should be noted, however, that the display area is limited, and many of the instruments are kept in an inaccessible storage facility some distance from the Museum.

Its earliest harpsichord, a 1561 Italian inner (no outer case) by Franciscus Patavinus (also known as "Il Hongaro," the Hungarian), disposed 1×8′, 1×4′, has an extremely long case and three roses. It is an ornate instrument, with an ebony case, cheeks sandwiching ivory between ebony, and black and white marquetry of flowers, petals, and vines above the soundboard. The naturals are covered with mother-of-pearl. Taken as a whole, the instrument is a study in black and white. Its range, now GG/ BB–c³, was originally the typical sixteenth-century Italian C/E–f³.

The museum owns a 1617 Andreas Ruckers virginal, one of the few surviving full-size spinett-virginals with keyboard to the left. Although its compass has been enlarged from the usual C/E–c³ to C–f³, many of its parts have been replaced, and its decoration bears little resemblance to its original appearance, it is nevertheless an important instrument. On the other hand, a "1573 Hans Ruckers" single-manual harpsichord represents yet another attempt to increase the value of a small and probably not very notable instrument of uncertain provenance. The rose is genuine, although it is not from Hans Ruckers; the initials were originally A R, but the top of the *A* was pried open to make it an *H*. Its decor is thoroughly inappropriate Rococo.

Chronologically, the Deutsches Museum's next plucked keyboard is a bentside spinet with some strange characteristics. It is in natural wood; the cheeks of its projecting keyboard are *L*-shaped, similar to that on many modern pianos; its geometric rose, while competently made, refers to no traditional school; there is a unique carved grille in the left-hand corner of the soundboard; the front of the nameboard is carved in a shallow relief; its lid painting is reminiscent of *Sturm und Drang* motifs. It is a mystery instrument, and may well have been made by a competent woodworker—say a joiner or a cabinetmaker—but not a harpsichord builder. The date of 1659 on the front of the nameboard is suspicious.

An early seventeenth-century inner-outer Italian virginal with a rare shape—an oblong with the upper right corner "cut off"—is noteworthy for its enharmonic keyboard. It has a broken short-octave compass of C/E–f³, and its E-flats and G-sharps are also split in the second and third octaves.

One of the Deutsches Museum's more bizarre instruments is a three-manual Italian harpsichord, now disposed 1×16′, 1×8′, 1×4′, with a nameboard ascribing it to "Bartolomeo Cristofari [*sic*] . . . MDCCII." Needless to say, it is neither a genuine Cristofori nor a genuine three-manual instrument, but the work of Franciolini, who sold it to the collector Georg Steingräber around the turn of the twentieth century. It is very long, almost nine feet, with three geometric roses on the soundboard. The catalog reports that Denzil Wraight, who examined it in 1991, believes it was originally an instrument by Zenti. Regardless, it is an imposing-looking instrument, with "genuine" Franciolini decoration; it joins similar three-manual Italians in Edinburgh's *Russell Collection* and the University of Michigan's *Stearns Collection*.

An anonymous 2×8′ C/E–c³ Italian clavicytherium bearing the date 1709 was probably built in that year, but as a normal horizontal harpsichord. It was transformed into an upright in 1910, and many of its parts, including a buff stop, the door, and its painting, also date from that year. The builder of another Italian harpsichord had been known only by the initials G. S., and the date 1729, found inked on the highest and lowest keys; but it was recently determined that the maker is Giuseppe Solfanelli from Pisa. This instrument has two buff stops, one for each 8′; even a single buff is rare on Italian harpsichords.

The museum has three anonymous octave instruments: a harpsichord and a spinet from Italy and a virginal from Germany. The first is a rather rare type, which is usually ungainly looking because of the strong curve of the bentside. But this false inner-outer example from ca. 1700 is quite graceful in shape; its lid painting depicts circle-dancing women, and its outlandish blue-and-gold three-legged stand must be seen to be appreciated. The second anonymous instrument is a triangular octave spinet, which was a common type; however, the decoration on the outer case of this example was done in Franciolini's shop, through which this instrument obviously passed. The ca. 1700 German virginal, with a natural wood exterior and a flowered soundboard, is of a high order of workmanship.

The jacks are placed so that they pluck extremely close to the left bridge, a feature seen on some other German virginals, such as the anonymous 8′ example in Berlin's Staatliches Institut. The tone color would be quite nasal. The museum has yet a fourth octave spinet, a Franciolini fabrication of little musical value. Franciolini advertised it in one of his catalogs as a spinettina by "Petrus Semanni," 1750.

Two eighteenth-century harpsichords are from England, the first of which is a 1771 two-manual Jacob Kirkman with machine, nags-head swell, and one pedal (the other is missing). The second is an example of a much rarer type, a single-manual combination harpsichord-piano with down-striking action built by Joseph Merlin, London, 1780. Merlin, sometimes called "the ingenious mechanic," was born in France, but he came to London at the age of twenty-five to seek fame and fortune. He patented a combination harpsichord and piano with down-striking action and began to build instruments for such worthies as Charles Burney. He is also known as the inventor of roller skates, and was reported to have shown up at a party on a pair, while playing the violin. His demonstration came to an end when he crashed into a wall, destroying a valuable mirror and his violin. The Museum's Merlin is disposed 1×16′ in leather (it is the only English harpsichord to have a 16′ set of strings), 1×8′ (plus a second 8′ when the piano is engaged), 1×4′, buff, celestial harp (a device that allows a set of 8′ strings to vibrate sympathetically), three pedals (for 16′, piano on and piano off), and a device for recording improvisations. The last is a frame placed inside the instrument, over the soundboard. A small clockwork attached to one corner of the frame controls a roller that holds a long sheet of paper. Pencils attached to trackers are, in turn, attached to the jacks; when the paper moves, an imprint of the jack movement in time—the notes played and the exact duration of each—is recorded on the paper. Merlin also worked out a way of deciphering and transcribing these markings. This instrument is indeed amazing, one of the great oddities of the stringed keyboard world.

The museum also has two early twentieth-century revival harpsichords, a 1909 Carl Pfeiffer, with the "Bach disposition" discussed in connection with the ca. 1700 "Bach" harpsichord in Berlin's Staatliches Institut; and a 1925 Maendler-Schramm.

The Deutsches Museum's twelve clavichords include an anonymous seventeenth-century example, eight mainly from the latter part of the eighteenth century, and three from the first part of the nineteenth century. A C–f³ fretted instrument by Friedrich Carl Wilhelm Lemme of Braunschweig, 1766, though small, includes an octave of 4′ strings in the bass. Although Lemme's clavichords seemed well-thought-of during his time, only two survive, this one and the 1787 with the oval ends in Leipzig's Musikinstrumenten-Museum. A 1782 partially fretted Christian Gottlob Hubert, C–g³, is typical of the Ansbach master's careful work, with herringbone veneers on the exterior of the case and a floating-panel lid. The Schmahl family of Regensburg is represented by two instruments, both unfretted and quite plain looking, a 1790 by Christoph Friedrich, and a big FF–c³ ca. 1812–15 by Christoph Friedrich's two sons, Jacob Friedrich and Christian Carl. The latter is built into a cabinet, as a drawer.

Roses are less common in clavichords than in harpsichords, but an otherwise unadorned FF–g³ Gottfried Joseph Horn, 1796, has two. Johann Paul Krämer is another famous name in clavichords, but the museum's 1806 unfretted instrument with an octave of 4′ strings was made by his sons, Johann Christian Friedrich and Georg Adam. Perhaps the Deutsches Museum's most unusual clavichord, both for its late date and its disposition, is an 1844 pedal instrument by Carl Ludwig Glück. While clavichords fitted with pulldowns and a small pedalboard were not uncommon, instruments with separate pedal divisions are rare; the 1760 Gerstenberg in Leipzig's Musikinstrumenten-Museum, with two manuals and pedals, is perhaps the best known and certainly the most elaborate. This one is actually two separate instruments, a C–f³ clavichord under which sits a two-octave (CC–d) instrument at 16′ pitch. Trackers lead down to the pedalboard, which is a modern replacement. Glück cleverly constructed the 16′ clavichord with the keys and strings under the soundboard, thus making the tracker action more direct.

Most of the pianos come from the latter half of the nineteenth century, and most are German. There are some eye-catching specimens among them, and some interesting earlier ones as well. The museum's earliest example, from ca. 1770–80, is an anonymous fortepiano with many of the characteristics of Silbermann instruments. The case looks more Viennese than Saxon, but it has a Cristofori-like action and an inverted wrestplank, with the nut underneath, both features found in Silbermanns. Unique, however, is the soundboard, which slopes down at a shallow angle from tail to gap, in order to allow the strings room to pass under the fairly thick wrestplank.

Although not properly a piano, the *Tangentenflügel* was, for a short time, a viable competitor. While it did not have the inherent flexibility of the piano, neither did it have that instrument's finicky action. The museum's example was made in 1800, by Christoph Friedrich Schmahl of Regensburg.

Four of the grands are from Munich: a ca. 1820 Ludwig Dulcken & Sohn, a ca. 1840 Johann Klüh, an 1866 Christian Then, and an 1867 Alois Biber, the last two with full seven-octave compasses (Biber is also represented by an 1858 square). Surprisingly at this late date, the Then has mother-of-pearl naturals and tortoise shell sharps. An 1834 Johann Baptist Streicher (Vienna) and an 1860 Theodor Stöcker (Berlin) both have down-striking actions.

The Deutsches Museum piano holdings include nine verticals. The two earliest, both German, anonymous, and from ca. 1750–70, are pyramid upright grands. Like most such instruments, the strings run from lower left to upper right (the photograph of the first, on p. 181 of the catalog, is reversed). Although similar under the skin, these pianos look quite different from each other. The first, with compass C–g^3, develops its pyramid shape with gentle concave curves on each side, while the second, FF–f^3, though starting the same way, bulges out at the top. Both have upper and lower doors, one at eye height when seated, the other at the top of the pyramid. While the second instrument is taller and its more interesting shape appears to be more elegant, the first seems more carefully made, with floating-panel doors and inlay designs.

An anonymous ca. 1820 five-octave vertical is one of those rare giraffes lacking the animal's "head"—the semicircle projecting to the left from the tail of the case; but it does have fours bars above the keyboard, to suggest strings, and a rising sun above its three pedals. A ca. 1830 Anton Biber, Nuremburg, has the more traditional shape, although it eschews both the string metaphor and the rising-sun motif; instead, the upper panel is covered with cloth while the lower is not covered at all (although surely it once was), exposing the mechanism of the Janissary stop controlled by one of its six pedals. A third giraffe, an anonymous ca. 1830, range FF–c^4, has all the amenities, with nine "strings," a rising sun, five pedals, and a Janissary stop.

Two small instruments—an 1813 by Brettschneider and an anonymous from ca. 1850—might be called reverse giraffes, since they slant to the right, placing their "heads" over to that side, rather than over the left of the case. But as in a similar piano, by Peter Christian Uldahl, ca. 1810–20, in Copenhagen's Musikhistorisk Museum, the bass strings run up the long left side of the case. As might be expected, the earlier instrument, with a range of FF–c^4 as opposed to the later one's CC–g^4 compass, is the more petite of the two; but the shapes are surprisingly elegant.

A ca. 1830 lyre-piano is a charming instrument, with a mahogany case, lion's-paw feet, and a bronzed lyre with seven bars representing its strings dominating the front of the case. Johann Christian Schleip of Berlin invented this form of the pyramid and was almost the only one to build them, but this instrument was made by another Berliner, F. A. Klein, who copied one of Schleip's models.

A ca. 1845 John Steward Euphonicon resembles a cross between an upright piano and a console, with the strings rising vertically on an exposed cast-iron harplike frame. Behind the console there are three sound-boxes instead of a soundboard. Because it has an exposed vertical iron frame, a Christian Dietz harp-piano bears a superficial similarity to the Euphonicon; but the Dietz is a harp played from a piano keyboard, while the Euphonicon is a piano looking something like a harp.

The Deutsches Museum's *Tafelklaviere* are mainly from Germany. They include two 1770 instruments by Johann Matthäus Schmahl: a C–f^3 square, and a "lying harp" model with a larger, FF–g^3 compass. A small, five-octave ca. 1780 anonyme is nicely decorated with inlay bandings. A ca. 1810 five-octave square by Jacob Pfister cleverly allows the keywell flap to be turned into a music desk, on which is mounted a cartouche containing Pfister's portrait. An 1810 instrument by Martin Lautenhammer, a Munich builder, can hardly be called square, since the builder slanted the sides of the case from the keyboard cheeks almost to the spine, creating a six-sided shape that would fit against a wall as neatly as a square and take up even less room.

The museum also has upright consoles, including three "dog-house" pianos, so-called because the bottom of the console has an opening shaped either like a C with the opening facing downward, an inverted V, or an inverted U, like the entrance to a dog house. The Richard Lipp, Stuttgart, 1830–31, has a C opening, that on the Leonhard May & Söhne, Mannheim, ca. 1835 is best described as an inverted V, and an inverted U is under the anonymous ca. 1850 instrument.

An opulent catalog of the museum's stringed keyboards has recently appeared: Hubert Henkel, *Deutsches Museum Kataloge der Sammlungen, Musikinstrumenten-Sammlung: Besaitete Tasteninstrumente* (Frankfurt am Main: Erwin Bochinsky, 1994). Almost every instrument is pictured in black and white, and information on the builder, building practices, materials used, dimensions, scales, plucking and striking points, finishes, decoration, history, and other technicalities are given in full detail, with an informative essay preceding each type of instrument discussed.

Städtische Instrumentensammlung der Stadt München

Address: St. Jacobs-Platz 1, D-8000 Munich; hours: 9:30 A.M.–4:30 P.M. Tuesday to Sunday; telephone: 0811 224 844 46.

Few cities are fortunate enough to have two public collections of early keyboard instruments, but Munich has both the Deutsches Museum, with its emphasis on the technological and scientific, and the Stadt Museum, which focuses primarily on artifacts from the city's past. The musical instrument section of the latter is based on the collection of Georg Neuner, and it now also houses part of the private collection of C. F. Colt.

The Stadt Museum has a small but interesting collection of harpsichords, with an anonymous ca. 1700 2×8′ Italian probably the earliest one. It has a buff stop—rare on Italians, and possibly not original. It sits on a simple three-legged stand, beautified by some gold rope that serves as an apron. There are two instruments by Joseph Mahoon, the smaller of which is a lovely looking 1742 bentside spinet with a five-octave range and skunk-tail sharps. Like almost all London builders except for Kirkman and Shudi, Mahoon specialized in spinets; but the museum also has a 1738 double-manual harpsichord of his, 2×8′, 1×4′ with buff. While it is not as fancy as some other English instruments, its burl veneers and delicate herringbone and chevron stringing on case, nameboard, and jackrails are wonderfully effective.

Two Kirkmans are also in evidence. The earlier one is a 1750 single with 2×8′, by Jacob—another of those 2×8′ English instruments perhaps built with continuo service in mind. One of the 8's is controlled by a rodlike knee lever. The other, a double, was built by Jacob's grand-nephew Joseph, fifty years later, in 1800. Disposed 2×8′, 1×4′, lute, machine, Venetian swell, and pedals, it has all the resources of the late English harpsichord; and with its rich veneers and panels it is a sumptuous piece of natural wood furniture. Although there is some evidence that the Kirkman firm continued to make harpsichords for the next nine years, this is the last dated harpsichord to come from an English builder. As such, it is an instrument of importance beyond its own considerable antique value.

An anonymous ca. 1700 fretted clavichord with a C/E–f³ range exploits some favorite German contrasts. The exterior is painted in *faux* tortoise shell, while parts of the interior are left in natural wood. The ebony sharps and the tortoise shell box lid are edged with ivory. Ebony is also used for the top and bottom case moldings, and for little feet that raise the case off the table. The soundboard, while not decorated, carries a geometric rose. The lid painting, an "Abraham and the Angels," is extremely well done. It is a clavichord of extraordinarily high quality for its date.

Two Broadwood & Sons pianos make an interesting contrast. The earlier, from 1800, looks very much like a late English harpsichord, with its mahogany-veneered bentside divided into panels by borders and stringing. The tapered square legs of its stand support two rather ungainly pedals. Nevertheless, it is obviously a piano, and anything other than a casual look reveals iron gap stretchers, a divided bridge and nut, and a five-and-a-half-octave range (FF–c⁴). The later instrument, dated 1819, makes a virtue of its increased heaviness; there is little of the harpsichord about it. The natural wood case is simple and unpaneled; its nameboard is decorated with applied brass ornaments, but it has no borders, stringing, or moldings. It sits on its own turned legs, and its two pedals (with the right split for bass and treble dampers) project from a graceful lyre. With a six-octave compass, it is a true Beethoven piano. Another English instrument is a tall, refined-looking 1816 cabinet piano by Clementi & Co., with reeded legs and silked doors.

An elegant 1805 Viennese fortepiano by Pfister is the earliest of the Austro-Germans. The builder was a student of Walter, and the graceful lines of this instrument, with its half-bent, half-straight tail, reveal the mark of that master. Johan-Lodewijk Dulcken was the grandson of Johann Daniel Dulcken, the famous harpsichord builder. His nicely decorated ca. 1815 piano, built in Munich, has its lyre and four pedals supported by a graceful bow attached to the front legs.

As a piece of furniture, an 1820 giraffe by Gregory Deiss is worth examining. It is done in mahogany and contrasting lighter woods, and its design elements are reinforced and decorated in brass. Its upright form is accentuated by large vertical brass or brass-painted bars representing the strings of some classical instrument. A decorative wooden plate across the case at eye level is embellished by a griffin at either side guarding a central head—perhaps Apollo—encircled by a wreath, all in brass. Rather than the more usual caryatids, brass busts top the tapered square legs. The bottom of the case features a rising sun, again in brass, and on the right, in the curve of the bentside, is a cast-brass statue of a half-draped reclining woman. The overall impression is one of solidity and the most refined bourgeois taste.

Two other pianos are by Munich builders. A ca. 1835 Alois Behringer has legs topped with atlantes, and an Alois Biber from 1857 has several tension bars.

NUREMBERG

Germanisches Nationalmuseum

Address: Kartäusergasse 12, 90402 Nuremberg; Postfach 9580, 90105 Nuremberg; hours: Tuesday and Thursday to Sunday, 10 A.M.–5 P.M.; Wednesday, 10 A.M.–9 P.M.; telephone: 09 11 1331–0; fax: 09 11 1331 200.

In his 1868 music drama, Richard Wagner immortalized fifteenth- and sixteenth-century Nuremberg as the home of Hans Sachs and his fellow

Meistersinger, but the city was also known for its painting, sculpture, printing, watchmaking, science, and scholarship, as well as for the purity of its drawn wire and the superiority of its trumpets and trombones. By the nineteenth century Nuremberg had become a center of heavy industry as well, and its production of armament during World War II made it a target for Allied bombing. The city was largely destroyed, along with many of the museum's keyboard holdings.

The current collection was formed after the war from the holdings of Ulrich Rück (in 1962) and Hanns Neupert (in 1968). The present building, modern and spacious, now houses one of the most impressive collections of early keyboards in Europe. The instruments on exhibit are but a small fraction of the holdings, and the enormous basement storage area contains an impressive number of instruments on roll-out pallets. Its well-equipped restoration *atelier* is equally imposing.

The museum holds approximately fifty plucked keyboards, sixty clavichords, and more than 270 pianos of various types. Although we have visited this collection a number of times, we have seen few of the clavichords; thus we can say little about them, other than that the museum's checklist claims sixty-one fretted and twenty-nine unfretted. Sadly, six of the latter were destroyed in the bombing, among them a 1760 Hass, a 1765 Hubert, and four from after 1780, one with pedals.

The collection of Flemish instruments includes a 1580 mother-and-child virginal by Marten van der Biest of Antwerp. He was one of the group of ten harpsichord-making members of the Guild of St. Luke who, in 1557, successfully petitioned the Guild for permission to regulate harpsichord building in Antwerp. In 1575 he was an official witness to the marriage of Hans Ruckers and Adriana Knaeps, and about ten years later he moved to Amsterdam.

This double virginal is one of the few surviving non-Ruckers Antwerp instruments. It and the ca. 1600 Ruckers mother-and-child spinett-virginal in Milan's Museo degli Strumenti Musicali are the two extant mother-and-child combinations in which the larger instrument's keyboard is on the left, with the child's compartment on the right. Rich and expensive looking, it reminds one of the opulent 1581 Hans Ruckers muselar-and-child in New York's Metropolitan Museum. Both have strongly balanced Renaissance-style lid paintings showing a garden party in progress, with courtiers diverting themselves in a variety of pleasurable pastimes; both have embossed medallions and cases painted in the style later found on Flemish papers; and both have two geometric parchment roses on the mother's soundboard. Most Flemish virginals have a fallboard hinged to the bottom of the case, to be raised when the instrument is closed; but

1580 mother-and-child spinett-virginal by Martin van der Biest. Sammlung Ulrich Rück.

the van der Biest's flap is hinged to the front of the lid, and is lowered when closed. This flap also carries a painting, but from the next century, a "David playing his harp for Saul" flanked by panels with depictions of musical instruments. Although the original compass was probably C/E–c³, it now has a chromatic bass. This stunning instrument is still in playing condition and has been recorded.

Another early (1605) Flemish spinett-virginal, with keyboard at the left, is by the little-known Amsterdam builder Artus Gheerdinck. The bottoms of its lowest keys show evidence of former pulldowns for about an octave of pedals. Its somewhat tasteless case overpainting probably dates from a much later time, perhaps as late as the Victorian era, and might even have been done in Franciolini's shop. However inappropriate in a strict sense, the redecoration documents the dawning of the appreciation of antique keyboards. The lid painting is said to be from the same redecoration. The case has handles on the sides, an unusual but undeniably useful accoutrement for a virginal.

Two Ruckers harpsichords from 1637 and 1654 offer an interesting contrast. Initially virtually identical, each began its life as a 1×8′, 1×4′ single, with a range of C/E–c³. The 1637 still has that range and disposition; indeed, it is one of the least-altered Ruckers extant. Even the case decoration, black-gray strap work on a red ground, with large semiprecious jewels painted where the bands cross, is original. At one point the cheeks were cut on a slant, in eighteenth-century fortepiano style. The 1654, on the other hand, was subjected to a typical drastic eighteenth-century conversion into a 2×8′, 1×4′ double, with a compass of GG/BB–f³. Based on writing found on the jacks and keys, O'Brien (p. 271) suggests that the *ravalement* was done in Flanders; this hypothesis is further supported by the positioning of the 4′ jacks farthest from the player—a common placement in the Low Countries at that time—rather than between the two 8′s, as in French practice. Interestingly, after the rebuilding, the harpsichord was repainted to imitate its original exterior.

A 1658 double bearing the name of Hans Ruckers is probably of Flemish (or at least of Netherlands) origin, but since Hans died some sixty years before the date of this instrument it obviously cannot be his. Originally built with a C/E–c³ compass, it is now C–c³ chromatic. Another harpsichord, a five-octave single dated 1689, is signed "Johannes Dulcken"; but it was probably built by the Antwerp builder Johann Daniel Dulcken around 1750. It has a fine Italianate "Apollo and the Muses" lid painting with Pegasus, the winged horse, hovering overhead. The 4′ is placed between the two 8′ in French fashion, but that was not necessarily its original position. In any event, this is a superb example of late-Baroque Flemish harpsichord making.

A description of the instruments just mentioned can be found in John Henry van der Meer's "Flämische Kielklaviere im Germanischen Nationalmuseum, Nürnberg," *Colloquium: Restauratieproblemen van Antwerpse klavecimbels, Museum Vleeshuis 10 tot 12 mei, 1970* (Antwerp: Ruckers Genootschap, 1971), pp. 63–76. They are also discussed in O'Brien.

A 1566 inner-outer polygonal virginal was built by Dominicus Pisaurensis, or "Dominicus of Pesaro"; but when he made this instrument he was working in Venice, so he signed it "Domenicus Venetus." The cypress inner case has the usual C/E–f³ short-octave keyboard with boxwood naturals, and an especially fine geometric rose. The rectangular outer case, decorated with inlays of wood and metal, bears yet another "Apollo and the Muses" on the interior of its lid. The name of the Duke of Bologna, the virginal's first owner, appears in the nameboard motto: *Unicuiq(e) probo patet praeclara Bentivoli domus*— (to all honest men Bentivoglio's house is open). The museum also has a two-manual 2×8′, 1×4′ harpsichord attributed to Dominicus and dated 1590, but both the date and the attribution are suspect. It is, however, a genuine two-manual Italian harpsichord, and thus a *rara avis*. The 4′ is on the upper manual and there is no coupler.

"1590" harpsichord attributed to Dominicus Pisaurensis. Sammlung Ulrich Rück.

1697 harpsichord by Carlo Grimaldi. Sammlung Ulrich Rück.

Although only two harpsichords by Carlo Grimaldi are extant, a 1703 now in the Paris Musée de la Musique and the 1697 here in Nuremberg, he has had an excellent reputation among modern builders, many of whom have built copies "after" him. The museum's rather plain but elegantly shaped 2×8′ instrument is enclosed in a sumptuous outer case of black lacquer and indented gold. It rests on a carved and gilded stand whose sinuous shape defies description and visually overwhelms the harpsichord itself.

Other Italians in the Germanisches Nationalmuseum include a 1681 2×8′ false inner-outer by Giovanni Battista Giusti of Lucca, a fine-toned instrument by one of the many builders known to have built lutes as well as harpsichords. A 1662 Giacomo Ridolfi is one of four (possibly five) of his that survives and apparently, the only one in Europe; the others are in the United States. An anonymous late seventeenth-century Italian was attributed to "Johannus Antonius Baffo," 1581, by Franciolini, who often pre-dated instruments as much as a century, since earlier examples were considered more valuable. There are many other Italians in this collection—harpsichords, virginals, and octave spinets, all anonymous. That so many instruments from south of the Alps are found in this museum, which is dedicated to German interests and artifacts, underscores their widespread popularity and influence.

As might be expected, the Germanisches Nationalmuseum has some important German harpsichords. The earliest, an anonymous single-manual clavicytherium from ca. 1620, deserves serious attention, both because it is a rare seventeenth-century German harpsichord and because of its unique features. It is disposed 2×8′, 1×4′, with lute and buff, with an unusual four-octave FF–f² range. In commmon with contemporaneous German organs, the stops are divided, making it possible to operate the bass and treble of each independently. Its four registers are covered with an imposing expanding jackrail, of solid wood framed by moldings, that grows to about nine or ten inches at the bass end. The harpsichord's tail has the same double miter seen on the anonymous South German harpsichord in Budapest's Hungarian National Museum. The soundboard has three rose holes in the area bounded by a 4′ bridge, spine, and gap, but the roses themselves are missing. The soundboard decoration is confined to three large black-inked filigrees surrounding the rose holes, with two small areas of similar design near the top and bottom of the 4′ bridge. The prominent cheeks are made of carved, fret-sawn ebony. The naturals are of ivory, and the sharps of ebony with narrow inlaid ivory borders and a small ivory lozenge laid in the center of each. In typical International style, the spine is fairly thick, while the bentside, tail, and cheek are of thinner wood, and the sides are topped with a narrow molding overhanging the interior. Despite the detail on the keys and elsewhere, this instrument gives the impression not of sumptuousness but of workaday utility, an opinion fortified by the presence of iron handles on the sides of the case for easy transporting.

A ca. 1640 automatic 2′ spinet by Samuel Biderman of Augsburg is another German instrument, but its intent is entirely different from the clavicytherium just described. The three-octave Biderman, in a black case so small it could easily sit on a night table or dresser, contains a barrel with projections and a wind-up clockwork that play six tunes. Although it is really little more than a music box with a keyboard, its soundboard is gracefully flowered, and its lid is ornamented with a central silvered

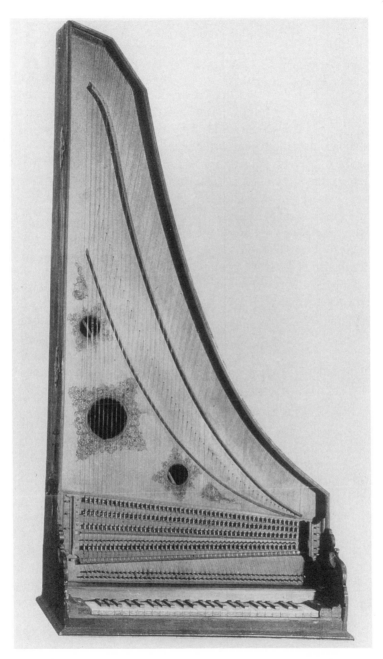

Ca. 1620 anonymous German clavicytherium. Sammlung Ulrich Rück.

plaque flanked by delicately colored miniature paintings. A photo of the internal workings of this spinet can be found on p. 30 of the *Wegweiser* noted at the conclusion of this section. A similar, though larger Bidermann instrument, also with barrel and clockwork, is in Vienna's Kunsthistorisches Museum.

A brass-strung 2×8′ double-bentside 1738 single with a range of GG/BB–e³, the only extant harpsichord by the Hannover builder Christian Vater, has an appealing tonal response. Its clear sound, full of variety as it goes from bass to tenor, alto, and treble, is easily characterized as Italianate; but it speaks to the strong influence of the seventeenth-century International School on eighteenth-century German harpsichord building. The soundboard has a gilded rose but is not distinguished by other decoration. A few large gold designs relieve the plain black lacquered case.

The Gräbners, a family of keyboard makers almost all of whom were named Johann, lived in Dresden in the late seventeenth and eighteenth centuries. A 1782 double by Karl August, the last of the Gräbner line, is disposed 2×8′, 1×4′ plus buff, with a five-octave compass. Its natural wood finish is typically Central German in appearance, although its fortepiano-like walnut case and floating-panel lid look a bit incongruous atop a stand with six graceful cabriole legs. It is certainly among the last of the full-sized harpsichords made in Central Germany, where clavichords, and by then, fortepianos, were more popular. Nevertheless, it is worth pointing out that keyboard players knew all three instruments equally well. It is a matter of record, for example, that Clementi, born four years before Mozart, often chose a harpsichord rather than a fortepiano for solo performances; so despite its late date, this Gräbner remains relevant to its time. It is interesting to note that the instrument has no knee or pedal assists for register changing, such as were often found on contemporaneous French and English harpsichords.

In the transition from Rococo to Classic in Germany, the large five-octave bentside spinet, with its attractive and space-saving asymmetrical shape combining economy with good sound, found public favor. The museum's 1767 example by Johann Heinrich Silbermann, nephew and student of Gottfried Silbermann, with its book-matched veneers, floating-panel lid, and cabriole legs with carved knees, is typical of that genre. Interestingly, by that time the Silbermanns had already been making fortepianos for some two decades.

The Germanisches Nationalmuseum has an unusual replica harpsichord, a copy of one of the marvels of the early keyboard world. The original is a 1606 instrument (now in Bologna's Museo Civico) by Vito

Trasuntino, a Venetian builder who had been influenced by the work of Nicola Vicentino, a sixteenth-century organist, theorist, and *maestro de capella* to Cardinal D'Este. Vicentino was convinced that he could revive the diatonic, chromatic, and enharmonic genera of ancient Greek theory; and he actually wrote some madrigals that specify what we would now call quarter tones. In 1555 he also wrote a book, *L'antica musica ridotta alla moderna pratica* (Ancient Music Adjusted for Modern Practice), in which he described his idea for a harpsichord with thirty-one notes to the octave. It was essentially this instrument that Trasuntino built in 1606, and it belongs to the class of harpsichords called *archicembali*, or harpsichords with more than twelve notes to the octave, although its builder called it a *clavemusicum omnitonum*. It is single-strung, with three roses, an extremely deep bentside, and a four-octave range. Its incredible keyboard of thirty-one notes to the octave has the naturals and accidentals arranged as tiers upon tiers. Such an instrument comes close to playing every chord in just intonation, with all intervals as nearly pure as possible. While playing in anything but meantone temperament could present formidable difficulties, at least one player, Luzzasco Luzzaschi, court organist at Ferrara and the teacher of Frescobaldi, was said to have mastered it. A picture of the original keyboard can be seen in the 1991 catalog of Berlin's Staatliches Institut für Musikforschung, *Kielklaviere: Cembali, Spinette, Virginale*, p. 58.

The checklist of the Germanisches Nationalmuseum inventories five tangent-pianos, including a 1794 by Christoph Friedrich Schmahl, cousin of the better-known Johann Matthäus. It also catalogs some ninety grands; more than thirty giraffes, pyramids, and lyre-pianos; two dozen upright consoles, including some by Jean-Henri Pape; about 120 squares; and sundry miscellany. Only a few of these can be described here.

A ca. 1790 Anton Walter fortepiano, veneered in walnut, with dust cover, has dampers operated by hand stops rather than knee levers, and is papered on its interior. The museum has other Walters, including one much like the instrument once owned by Mozart and now in Salzburg. Two Johann Andreas Steins from the 1770s, two Johan Jacob Könnickes (1796 and 1810), and others by German makers demonstrate the extent to which the still-new piano was accepted by South German and Austrian musicians.

Early Romantic grands also abound. Three of the six examples by Nannette Streicher are dated ca. 1803, ca. 1807, and 1808. A fourth, now believed to be ca. 1830, is dated 1811 in the museum's checklist, although Clinkscale (pp. 293, 294) reports the recent discovery of a soundboard label listing the makers as Nannette and her son, Johann Baptist; all pianos built by these two date from after 1820. The fifth and sixth instruments are both 1814, by Nannette or her brother, Matthäus Andreas Streicher.

There are three Johan Lodewijk Dulckens, one ca. 1815 and two ca. 1830. An 1805 Conrad Graf is one of that maker's earliest instruments. A ca. 1826 Graf, with decorated keywell and elegant veneer, rests on three gold-banded legs ending in square pads below. Its four pedals extend from a lyre connected to the left-most leg pad. Large for its time, this piano shows almost no twisting or deformation, a tribute to the solid joinery and the good design of its maker. With a smooth feel and a superb tone, it is a joy to play.

Most unusual is a ca. 1800 Johann Schmid piano with a built-in pedal-board. The front of the piano is supported by the pedal case, and only the tail is braced by individual legs. Hammers operated by the pedals strike strings mounted on a second soundboard on the bottom of the case. Other than its slightly wider range (FF–a^3), this piano appears to be quite similar to the five-octave ca. 1790 Schmid pedal piano in Salzburg's Carolino Augusteum Museum. A third extant Schmid pedal instrument, in New York's Metropolitan Museum, resembles its two sisters in other respects but has no separate under soundboard.

Christian Gottlob Hubert was famous for the high quality of his clavichords, but contemporary accounts indicate that he was highly regarded as a piano maker as well. Many of his clavichords are extant but only two of his hammered instruments survive, a bentside spinet-shaped piano from 1785 and a 1787 square, both in Nuremberg. The spinet-piano's lid has three segments that can be raised separately for a rudimentary sort of volume control. Its handsome natural wood case is decorated with book-matched burl veneers, the nameboard is graced with inlaid marquetry, and its three cabriole legs are delicately carved.

Late Romantic grands are here too, with their full seven-octave AAA–a^4 compass: Bösendorfer, J. B. Streicher, and Henri Herz, to name only three.

The museum has nearly twenty giraffes and pyramids dating from 1812 to 1845. In Germany, these designs far outnumbered the large upright grands made mainly in England. A ca. 1825 combination instrument, a "giraffe-harmonium," by Johann Kaspar Schlimbach, is a marvel of mechanical ingenuity. Two large pedals work the air supply for the "Aeoline" (harmonium), and five others, below them, are for damping and the customary Viennese timbre mutations. Hand stops controlling the change from piano to harmonium are divided for treble and bass. The case is

1785 bentside piano by Christian Gottlob Hubert. Sammlung Ulrich Rück.

richly veneered in walnut, the string band hidden behind green silk. Whatever its sound might have been, its appearance is spectacular.

The vast number of square pianos owned by the museum makes it impossible to survey them all. However, the earliest known dated square is here, a 1742 Johann Socher. Its most interesting trait other than provenance is an elaborate lid painting in three panels—a central one of St. Cecilia, flanked by two harbor scenes. An underdamping mechanism is controlled by a hand stop (pedals were added to such simple instruments somewhat later). The museum has an especially elaborate 1840 Pape upright console with rosewood and mother-of-pearl inlays and remarkable curving sculpted legs joined in pairs by intricately carved braces.

Also worthy of attention are the many non-keyboard instruments, displayed in glass cases; but the presence of the former Rück and Neupert keyboard holdings make this museum's music space a magic experience.

Its magnificent row of stringed keyboards, on a raised platform against one long wall, is an inspirational sight to be cherished in memory forever. The museum's other divisions exhibit many artifacts pertaining to German history, including particularly fine displays of armor and heraldry. A visitor might do well to allow time for a stroll through other areas after sampling the treasures of the instrument collection.

John Henry van der Meer's 128-page *Wegweiser durch die Sammlung historischer Musikinstrumente* (Nürnberg, Germanisches National Museum, 1982) is a guide to the collection. In German, it deals only with a small number of the museums's instruments, discussing them as representatives of their types from the sixteenth through the nineteenth centuries. There is also an informative checklist: Renate Huber, *Verzeichnis Sämtlicher Musikinstrumente im Germanischen Nationalmuseum Nürnberg* (Wilhelmshaven: Florian Noetzel Verlag, 1989).

STUTTGART

Württembergisches Landesmuseum

Address: Schillerplatz 1, 70173 Stuttgart 1; hours: 10 A.M.–5 P.M. Wednesday to Sunday, 10 A.M.–1 P.M. Tuesday; telephone: 0711 279 3400; fax: 0711 279 3499.

Stuttgart is the capital of Württemberg, a state with a long and complex history. It has seen many battles, and the oldest part of the city was almost completely destroyed in World War II. However, its ancient castle—a number of buildings constructed over a period of five centuries—has survived, and it houses the collection of musical instruments.

Although we have not visited this museum we had reference to two published guide books, illustrations from other sources, and a set of slides from a colleague. According to the 1993 guide, Stuttgart has five antique plucked keyboards, a revival harpsichord, six clavichords, thirty-two pianos, a *Tangentenflügel*, a harp-piano, and an operating *Streichklavier*.

The museum has two early virginals, a 1586 Francesco Poggio (Florence) inner-outer, and a 1623 mother-and-child muselar by Ioannes Ruckers. The last, purchased from Chicago's Harding Museum, is one of the few such instruments that might look as it did when it was new. It still has its papers, and the exterior paint, though not original, copies the green porphyry marble finish the Ruckerses seemed to have put on all their virginals. The soundboard paintings have been extensively but competently retouched, and the instrument was recently restored.

A large, 1772 Joseph & Abraham Kirkman double has a nags-head swell, a machine stop, and two pedals. As is typical of so many eighteenth-century English harpsichords, despite the exquisite veneers and the beautiful casework, its appearance is marred by a badly cocked cheek.

There are two anonymous seventeenth-century harpsichords. One, a large, lovely 2×8' inner-outer Italian, with nicely carved cheeks, looks perfectly normal except for its four-octave FF–f² range, rather than the more normal C–c³. Since we have not seen the instrument it is impossible to tell, but original or not, the keyboard may be transposing the pitch down by a fourth.

The other anonymous instrument is even more of a mystery. A large 2×8', 1×4' double with a natural walnut case, it has a first-rate lid painting, after a work now in the Louvre by the Italian painter Albani. On first glance the harpsichord looks to be seventeenth-century French, and was so identified during most of its recent history in Hubbard, pp. 100–104, in the 1993 guidebook, and in a picture postcard of the instrument sold by the museum. However, in a descriptive article, "A Seventeenth-Century French Harpsichord?" in *Fellowship of Makers and Restorers of Historical Instruments Quarterly* 63 (April, 1991), pp. 65–72, Christopher Nobbs, who recently restored the instrument, gives convincing arguments for a German origin. He suggests that it was built around the middle of the seventeenth century, then went to France, where it was modified to suit local taste. The lid painting, probably dating from that time, could not have been done before 1680, when the Albani painting came to France. Nobbs has examined the instrument more thoroughly than anyone in recent times, and we cannot help but be heavily swayed by the evidence he presents; nevertheless, the fact that controversy surrounds this harpsichord's provenance demonstrates how widespread were the characteristics of the International School in seventeenth-century France and Germany.

A 1909 revival instrument by the Stuttgart piano builder Carl Pfeiffer is not an antique but may be of interest to those concerned with the harpsichord in the early twentieth century.

The earliest clavichord in the collection is a typical small fretted, C/E–c³ South German instrument, ca. 1687, with colored papers glued to its lid, fallboard, nameboard, and wrestplank. Three of the remaining clavichords are large late unfretted instruments by members of the Schiedmayer family: Adam Achatius (ca. 1785), Johann Christoph Georg (ca. 1790), and Johann David (1791). The Schiedmayers were an important dynasty first in Erlangen, then in Stuttgart. The patriarch of the family, Balthasar, the son of a baker, became a joiner and then an organ and clavichord builder. None of his instruments have survived, but those of his three sons have. Johann David, the youngest, moved to Stuttgart and established a piano-making partnership with Carl Dieudonné, who had trained under Nannette Streicher.

With eighteen grands, two verticals, three squares, eight upright consoles, and a tea-table instrument, the pianos make an interesting group. Four of the eight German grands are from Stuttgart, and three of them bear the Schiedmayer label: two Dieudonné & Schiedmayers are from ca. 1820, and an 1840 is signed Schiedmayer & Soehne. The Dieudonné & Schiedmayer grands are ornate. One, with *bombé* sides, has an inlay pattern on top of the lid apparently representing peacock feathers. The second grand is decorated with inlays of brass, mother-of-pearl, ebony, ivory, and other materials, in repetitive patterns with classical allusions. It is indeed an awe-inspiring instrument, proving that even in the nineteenth century it was possible for decoration to overwhelm the musical function of a keyboard instrument. The fourth Stuttgart grand is by Richard Lipp, ca. 1870. The other German grands are by Johan Lodewijk Dulcken (Munich, ca. 1800), Theodor Stöcker (Berlin, ca. 1865), Carl Bechstein (Berlin, ca. 1870), and Julius Blüthner (Leipzig, 1904–1905).

A 1778 Johann Andreas Stein fortepiano, indistinguishable from most other instruments by this master, has a five-octave range, vertical-grain veneers on the case, slanted cheeks, a floating-panel lid, and simple but well-proportioned turned legs. The case of a second Stein, from ca. 1780, looks exactly the same; but the lid is of solid stock, veneered in a checkerboard pattern on top and covered with colored paper underneath. An 1814 piano by Stein's daughter, Nannette Streicher, has a graceful lyre with four pedals supported by a bow under the front legs. It shows the same high-quality workmanship and careful attention to detail as the father's instrument, although it is more heavily built, no doubt in part to accommodate a sixth octave in the treble. A ca. 1810 Anton Walter has the same range in the treble but extends the bass down another half octave. Aside from that, these last two pianos are strikingly similar in external design and appearance. The Streicher, however, is content to take its beauty from the quiet dignity of its woods and the grace of its form. To these, the Walter adds gilded caryatids and grillework and medallions in brass. A massive Conrad Graf from ca. 1825 and an ornate anonymous grand with six pedals complete the Viennese pianos in the collection.

The four remaining grands are a 1794 Broadwood, with the usual beautiful English veneers and a badly cocked cheek; a 1927 Steinway; a Sébastian Érard (Paris, ca. 1840); and an 1898 Pleyel, Wolff & Cie *tête-à-tête*, a sister instrument to the 1899 in Antwerp's Vleeshuis Museum.

A ca. 1840 piano by Walter Klinckerfuss is shaped like an octagonal table. When a flap is raised the keyboard can be pulled out, like a drawer; but when one is ready for tea, the keyboard is pushed back into its recess, the flap is lowered, and the piano once again becomes a table.

Another flamboyantly adorned piano is a ca. 1820 giraffe by Christoph Erlich of Bamberg. Its keyboard is supported by golden statuettes, the nameboard is graced by two gilded bas reliefs, and the grillework below the keyboard bears a large medallion. The upper part of the case is divided into a narrow panel on the left containing vines, leaves, and panpipes, and a larger panel on the right that might be imagined to represent a sunburst. Instead of the universal giraffe's head, this piano is surmounted by a pedestal and a classic urn. Despite all this eye-catching decoration, the real center of attention is a platform at the crook of the bentside on which is mounted a classical lyre, with five brass rods for strings and a clock in its center. Six pedals, two of which operate bassoon and Janissary stops, provide a musical analog to the visual variety. Despite all this, the effect is fairly harmonious. A lyre piano from around the same time, by G. Perau, Berlin, is much plainer.

A nineteenth-century Parisian upright console by Pretot has eye-popping *bombé* surfaces, herringbone veneers, brass or gold mounts, ebony inlays, rope-pattern stringing, and golden angels supporting the keyboard. It is an impressive and not inelegant piece of cabinetry. Other upright consoles are by one or another of the Schiedmayer firms (1860–70, 1865 and 1910); Carl Pfeiffer (ca. 1930 and 1939, the first with a Janko keyboard); an anonymous English from the early nineteenth century; and a 1917 Steinway. The three squares are by Zumpe (London, 1766) and Schiedmayer (Erlangen, 1785, and Stuttgart, 1845).

An 1809 Viennese sewing-box piano is more gracious looking than the usual members of its genre. The exterior is black with brass mounts; and painted on the inside of the lid, on either side of a mirror, are two soldiers in Napoleonic garb. The Württembergisches Landesmuseum also has what is identified as a "tuning-fork piano"—a nice-looking cabinet with a four-octave range.

Stuttgart also had a late eighteenth-century *Tangentenflügel* by Späth & Schmahl and a ca. 1891 harp-piano by Ignaz Lutz. Another unusual instrument, a *piano-quatuor* (literally a piano-quartet, because the inventor claimed that the instrument sounded like a string quartet), or bowed piano, by Gustave Baudet of Paris, probably dates from about 1870. Its action is not easily described. Although the instrument resembles an upright console piano, its sound is produced when a key raises a jack, which presses a small bundle of vegetable fibers tied at right angles to the string against a pedal-operated rotating cylinder. The vibrations generated in the fibers

Ca. 1810 piano by Anton Walter

Ca. 1825 piano by Conrad Graf

Ca. 1820 giraffe piano by Christoph Erlich

Anonymous 1809 sewing-box piano

are transferred to the string, which sounds as long as the cylinder is in contact with the fibers and continues to turn. Thus, like a mechanically operated violin, the *piano-quatuor* is capable of producing sustained tones; in fact, the inventor maintained that the instrument could achieve all the bowing effects of string instruments and was capable of playing the chamber works of the masters. This Baudet was recently restored, and we believe it to be the only operating antique *Streichklavier*.

The museum publishes an excellent guidebook, with thumbnail descriptions of instruments and many pictures, written by Christian Väterlein: *Musikinstrumentensammlung im Fruchtkasten: Württembergisches Landesmuseum Stuttgart* (Stuttgart, 1993). There is an earlier guidebook, *Württembergisches Landesmuseum Stuttgart* (Braunschweig: Georg Westermann Verlag, 1982), but musical instruments occupy only one page, and only half of that deals with keyboards.

CHAPTER VII

ℋUNGARY

BUDAPEST

🏛 Hungarian National Museum

Address: 1088 Budapest Múzeum körut 14–16, Budapest;
mailing address: H-1370 Pf. 364, Budapest; hours: 10 A.M.–6 P.M.
Tuesday to Sunday; telephone: 138 2122; fax: 117 7806.

Few European cities have the Old World charm of Budapest, with its broad avenues, winding streets, pedestrian malls, parks, museums, and gracious old buildings. The city is split by the Danube, with Buda on the right bank and Pest on the left, connected by many bridges. Ensconced on the Pest side, the Hungarian National Museum, an enormous, imposing structure, houses much Hungarian memorabilia, including the crown jewels. Its early keyboard holdings are small—four plucked instruments, five clavichords, and forty-five pianos—but two pieces—an 1817 Broadwood piano owned by Beethoven and a seventeenth-century South German harpsichord—are important organological documents.

Beethoven may never have had to buy a piano; hoping to win his endorsement, builders were only too happy to supply him with instruments. Conrad Graf, for example, presented him with one of his quadruple-strung models in 1824. Earlier, in 1803, Sébastian Érard had sent a piano with English action over from Paris. Beethoven played the Érard for years but evidently was not happy with it. On two occasions he had the action worked on, perhaps hoping to make it feel more like the Grafs and Streichers he was used to playing. The question of Beethoven's preferences in pianos was dealt with by William Newman in his seminal article, "Beethoven's Pianos versus his Piano Ideals," *Journal of the American Musicological Society* 23/3 (Fall, 1970), pp. 484–504.

The 1817 piano, a gift from John Broadwood and Son, was shipped to

1817 piano by John Broadwood

Beethoven from England (via Trieste, then over the Alps by horse-drawn cart!) at considerable expense to the builder. The composer undoubtedly appreciated its power and particularly its singing sound, a quality he prized above all else. He wanted a vocal-like response from the piano and, according to contemporary accounts, produced a singing tone in his own playing that amazed his listeners; but by 1817 he was almost totally deaf.

The six-octave-plus, triple-strung Broadwood has five iron gap-stretchers. A common feature of English pianos of the time, they were intended to resist the pull of the strings, which, if powerful enough could, and often did, rotate the wrestplank up and into the gap, and at the same time twist up the cheek. The piano has two pedals, one a real *una corda*, able to sound one, two, or all three strings of a unison, and thus capable of producing the distinctions of tone color Beethoven called for on several occasions. The other pedal is a split damper, allowing free resonance to the notes on either side of c^1, or raising all the dampers when both parts of the pedal were pressed at once. After Beethoven's death the piano was purchased from his estate, at auction, by the publisher Anton Spina, who gave it to Liszt, who willed it to the museum in 1887. Restored in 1991, it has also been recorded.

The 2×8' single-manual seventeenth-century South German harpsichord, once part of a claviorganum, is said to have an illustrious history. According to the museum it was acquired in 1875, when a Hungarian antiques collector procured it from an Ursuline convent, which in turn had gotten it from Vienna with the claim that it had been the boyhood harpsichord of the Hapsburg Emperor Joseph II. Whether the story is true or not, the instrument is important because of the relative rarity of seventeenth-century South German harpsichords. It has been recorded at least once.

Two conspicuous features immediately strike the eye. The first is its expanding jackrail, with one rank of jacks plucking a set of strings close to the nut and the other plucking the second set at some distance. The same system is found on the 1619 Meyer harpsichord in Salzburg's Carolino Augusteum, and in a more complex manner, on the anonymous 1620 clavicytherium in Nuremberg's Germanisches Nationalmuseum. On the Budapest instrument, however, the jackrail is in two parts, each covering its own set of jacks. The two parts are mitered together on the treble end and joined with a crosspiece on the bass end, the whole forming an open triangle. The second prominent attribute is its amazing gilt double upside-down-wedding-cake rose: two roses joined at the hip, so to speak. It is the most ornate rose known to us.

Like most German harpsichords of that time it is rather small—slightly less than six feet long. It has a double-mitered tail, similar to the one found on Nuremberg's 1620 clavicytherium. The natural wood case shows typical International School characteristics of heavy spine and thin tail, bentside, and cheeks. Applied top moldings overlap the inside of the case. At present there is no lid, but markings on the spine could indicate where hinges were once located. The jacks are held in two box guides, shifted by brass knobs protruding from the cheek. There is a double buff stop—also

Anonymous 17th-century South German harpsichord

operated by a brass knob protruding from the cheek—capable of damping either set of strings, although that feature does not appear to be original. The nasal register—the one with the jacks plucking close to the nut— is quilled with thin brass plectra, a feature seen on the Nuremberg 1620 instrument and found on some other seventeenth-century instruments as well. The soundboard is painted, and the keywell is spectacularly decorated. Etched, inked, and colored ivory tiles, depicting women singing and playing a variety of keyboard, stringed, and wind instruments, are set into a nameboard covered in tortoise shell. The naturals are topped with mother-of-pearl and the ebony sharps are partially covered with delicate ivory tracings.

A small ornate three-octave 4' virginal with a pin-cushion lid, dated 1617, is said to have been owned by Catherine of Brandenburg. It contains the cryptic initials LKF and IKF, provoking much speculation about possible builders and decorators. The collection also includes an anonymous 2×8' Italian harpsichord. Both external and internal decoration are reminiscent of seventeenth-century South German–North Hungarian painted-marble church decoration. The soundboard is painted with enormous flowers, far out of normal scale and almost certainly not original. The nameboard bears the name of the former owner, Stephanus Thököly, a Hungarian nobleman who led a revolt against Leopold I. A 1571 Italian harpsichord by Nicola Fontana completes the collection of plucked instruments.

Of the three clavichords, two are anonymous, of German origin, and date from ca. 1700 and ca. 1750. The third is of interest both because of its maker, Johann Andreas Stein, and its owner, Wolfgang Amadeus Mozart. This small 1762 instrument, with a four-and-a-half-octave range and a tiny soundboard, was undoubtedly intended for travel. If it is indeed the clavichord given to Mozart by his father when he was only seven years old, it would have been a practice keyboard for the young virtuoso, who began his famed tours of European capitals about that time. The instrument and its history are described in detail in Eszter Fontana, "Mozarts 'Reiseclavier' " in *Das Klangwelt Mozarts* (Vienna: Kunsthistorischen Museums, 1991), pp. 73–78.

The museum owns an 1820 grand piano by Johann Schanz of Vienna. Well-thought-of during his lifetime, Schanz was particularly praised by Haydn as a maker of "quiet" instruments; that is, pianos perhaps more suited to the salon than to the concert hall. A Conrad Graf from ca. 1820 would not have been built with a quiet tone in mind, although its single and double moderators indicate that Viennese builders were still concerned with the more delicate aspects of piano tone. This six-and-half-octave instrument is triple-strung after the first five notes.

Two upright pianos are owned by the museum, a pyramid by Wilhelm Schwab, a builder from what was then Pest, and a giraffe by the Viennese Joseph Saufert, both from ca. 1820. The Schwab is an attractive instrument, painted with yellow on black in what we might call folk motives. The Saufert is a beautiful giraffe, with the ubiquitous rising-sun motif under the keyboard and gilded bronze friezes representing mythological figures mounted on the front surfaces. An ornate gilded candle holder perches in the crook of the bentside. This instrument is kept in Györ, a city in western Hungary.

Three square pianos round out the National Museum's collection: an anonymous late eighteenth-century instrument, perhaps from Liège (kept in Budapest's Museum of Applied Arts); an 1801 Jean Godefroy Wolff, Paris; and a ca. 1800 Caspar Katholnik, Vienna.

There are more pianos in Budapest's Museum of Applied Arts, and some are kept in the Museum of Music History (Institute for Musicology of the Hungarian Academy of Sciences): H-1014 Budapest, TÁNCSICS Mihály u. 7; postal address: H-1250 Budapest Pf. 28; telephone: 156 6858; fax: 157 9282.

An English-language catalog of this collection contains a checklist, with descriptions and photos of selected instruments: György Gábry, *Old Musical Instruments*, 2nd, rev. ed. (Budapest: Corvina Press, 1976). The original, in Hungarian, is entitled *Régi hangszerek* and was published in 1969.

CHAPTER VIII

*I*RELAND

DUBLIN

National Museum of Ireland

Address: Kildare Street, Dublin 2; telephone: 667–6569.

Ireland was invaded by the English in the twelfth century. An 800-year armed and political struggle ensued, and independence was finally achieved in 1948, though the six Northern Ireland counties remain within the United Kingdom. Despite constant friction between the two islands, particularly during the eighteenth century, they maintained considerable economic and artistic exchange. For example, Handel's *Messiah* was premiered in Dublin in 1742; and Handel, who came to Dublin on more than one occasion, became friendly with that city's best-known organ and harpsichord maker, Ferdinand Weber. With a large percentage of its country's total population, Dublin has long had a flourishing cultural life. The city houses an outstanding art collection in its National Gallery, and the eighth-century Book of Kells, one of the most famous illuminated manuscripts in the world, is in the Trinity College Library.

Dublin's collection of musical instruments is part of the National Museum's Department of Arts and Industry; unfortunately, we visited while the collection was in storage, pending a move to new quarters. Still, we did manage to see almost all the plucked keyboards—an early Italian, and five late eighteenth-century Dublin instruments—even if not under ideal conditions. Our description is based on these observations, plus information from a partially annotated checklist shared with us by a colleague.

An Italian antique with case and soundboard of cypress was previously thought to have been made by Domenico da Pesaro (Dominicus Pisaurensis) in 1590, since that is the signature on its nameboard; but it is now attributed to the Brescian maker Giovanni Francesco Antegnato, 1564. Its

C/E–f³ compass is presumably genuine. First disposed 1×8', 1×4', it is now 2×8'; nevertheless, the 4' bridge and nut are still in place, as is the original 8' nut, with holes through which the 4' strings formerly passed. The instrument's decor seems to have been enhanced with slips of ivory on the keys and some elaborate marquetry on the case; that work is thought to be eighteenth-century.

Henry Rother, Ferdinand Weber, and Robert Woffington are the three Dublin builders of the collection's Rococo-era plucked keyboards. The first is represented by an impressive-looking single-manual 2×8', 1×4' plus buff pyramid clavicytherium, dated 1774. As in most harpsichords and pianos of this type, the string band angles from lower left to upper right. Its range, FF, GG–g³, is found on other Irish instruments and seems to have been something of a Dublin specialty. Upper and lower double doors enclose its string band and, reinforcing the organlike appearance of the pyramid shape, is a set of *faux* pipes carved into the upper set. The registers are controlled by hand stops although there is some evidence that pedals may once have existed. Like contemporary English harpsichords, it is a large and heavily built instrument, with no soundboard decoration. Its solid case woods are attractive.

A 1775 Weber bentside spinet differs little from its London counterparts; but that builder (a German expatriate) is also represented by a large FF, GG–g³ single-manual harpsichord of uncertain date, but probably ca. 1780. With 2×8', 1×4', lute register, machine stop, and Venetian swell (slightly different from Shudi's), it is well equipped; however, it has knee levers rather than pedals. Its light-colored wood is handsome, but there is no effort to dress it up in expensive, exotic veneers. Such is not the case with all of Weber's instruments, however; his ca. 1775 single in London's Royal College of Music, while not sumptuous, is veneered and cross-banded.

Boalch (p. 677) lists another Weber instrument in the National Museum, a 1764 pyramid clavicytherium like Rother's; we did not see it, but it is pictured and described in Russell, plates 77 and 78 (the disposition is 3×8', not 2×8', 1×4', as Russell states).

The 1780 Woffington is a rarity—a single-manual clavicytherium-claviorganum. *Faux* pipes on the front of the rectangular case give it the appearance of a chamber organ, but opening the doors reveals an upright 2×8', 1×4' harpsichord with the "Dublin" FF, GG–g³ compass. The pipes, doubtless behind the harpsichord, were not visible.

According to our information, the remainder of the collection consists of about a dozen early pianos, from ca. 1775 to ca. 1825, most of which come from Dublin.

During our visit our host kindly showed us part of the museum's collection of Irish harps, one dating back to the fifteenth century. Some of them had brays—little devices that produce a buzzing sound when they lightly contact the vibrating strings. It might well have been this effect that prompted the muselar's arpichordium stop. As the national instrument of Ireland, the harp appears on coinage and other symbolic representations.

CHAPTER IX

*I*TALY

FLORENCE

Museo degli Strumenti Musicali
del Conservatorio di Musica Luigi Cherubini

Address: Piazza delle Belle Arti, 2, 50122 Florence;
hours: at present closed to the public;
telephone: 055 210 502 or 055 292 180; fax: 055 239 6785.

The composer Luigi Cherubini, a contemporary of Beethoven, was known chiefly for his operas. Although he was abroad for most of his career, particularly in Paris, he was born in Florence and thus is claimed as one of that city's illustrious sons. The Conservatorio is noted for its superb collection of string instruments and bows by Gabbrielli, Stradivari, the Amatis, and others. It even has a bass attributed to Cristofori. It has only five early keyboards, but among them is a 1739 upright piano by the Gagliano priest and builder Domenico del Mela, which is generally conceded to be the earliest-known grand in upright form.

This instrument, with a primitive action and no escapement, is perhaps best classified as an early form of the pyramid piano; but that term does not begin to describe the sinuous in-curving spine, the outward-bulging bentside, the centered bridge, the rounded tail, and the scrolls at the sides echoing the ancient Greek kithara. It is truly a "baroque" instrument, in the sense of something exaggerated, although it is not unattractive. In any event, it is a shape never seen again. The piano sits on a bench of an entirely different character; it may be that the instrument never had a stand of its own.

Aside from a small *Tafelklavier* of uncertain date and provenance, the other instruments are in the harpsichord family. A 1785 one-manual harpsichord with a lute register, Venetian swell, machine stop, and two pedals bears the names Longman & Broderip on the ornate nameboard, but the real builder was Thomas Culliford, who signed his name on one of the keys. In fact, Culliford supplied Longman & Broderip with many instruments. The firms of Kirkman and Shudi controlled the London market for grand harpsichords, leaving others to build bentside spinets and the occasional harpsichord. Culliford's association with Longman & Broderip undoubtedly gave him the opportunity to build some larger instruments.

A 1568 C/E–f³ polygonal virginal by the Venetian builder Benedetto Floriani and an anonymous eighteenth-century Italian harpsichord complete the collection. The museum attributes the latter instrument to Cristofori, but Henkel does not list it as the work of the Florentine master.

The museum has a catalog of all its musical holdings: *Conservatorio di Musica Luigi Cherubini: Antichi Strumenti* (Florence: Palazzo Pitti, 1980). Although it does not give a great deal of information about the instruments, it includes at least one picture of each, in color. An earlier and more technical catalog is Vinicio Gai's *Gli strumenti musicali della corte medicea e il Museo del Conservatorio "Luigi Cherubini" di Firenze* (Florence: Licosa, 1969).

MILAN

Museo degli Strumenti Musicali, Castello Sforzesco

Address: Piazza Castello, I-20121 Milan; hours: 9:30 A.M.–5:30 P.M. Tuesday to Sunday; telephone: 33–2–869 3071; fax: 33–2–869 3071.

Museums are often imposing structures, but the Castello Sforzesco *really* commands respect! Approached by a long, wide walkway lined with vendors hawking mementos, the former castle of the Sforza family houses an immense agglomeration of art and artifacts. Occupying only a small part of the museum, the musical instrument collection is nevertheless spaciously laid out. Founded in 1958 from the private holdings of Natale Gallini, the keyboard holdings form a moderately sized group: thirty-five in the harpsichord family, about thirty pianos, and a Dolmetsch clavichord (number 3, from 1894). As we might expect, it contains a fair number of harpsichords and pianos by Milanese builders: from the sixteenth century, Annibale dei Rossi; from the eighteenth, Antonio Scotti and Antonio Battaglia; from the nineteenth, Gaetano Scappa, Francesco Barbanti, Giuseppe Prestinari, and Fratelli Colombo; and from the twentieth, Luigi Erba.

The smaller plucked instruments consist of six polygonal and four

1600 mother-and-child spinett-virginal by Ioannes Ruckers

square virginals, five bentside spinets, and a triangular octave spinet, all but one of Italian origin. The exception, the only extant mother-and-child spinett-virginal by a Ruckers (it has a Hans Ruckers rose, but is signed by Ioannes), dated ca. 1600, is one of the more important instruments in the collection. Its keyboard is to the left, with the child housed on the right; all the other extant Ruckers mother-and-child virginals are muselars, with the keyboard to the right and the child to the left. Although the instrument no longer has its green porphyry exterior—the original finish evidently given to all Ruckers virginals—its papers, soundboard painting, and lid painting are intact. The subject matter and style of the lid painting—courtiers amusing themselves with dancing, music, and sports—is similar to that found on the 1581 Hans Ruckers mother-and-child muselar in New York's Metropolitan Museum and on the 1580 Martin van der Biest mother-and-child spinett-virginal in Nuremberg's Germanisches Nationalmuseum.

A handsome ca. 1549 polygonal virginal had been attributed to Annibale dei Rossi, a sixteenth-century Milanese builder known only by a handful of instruments; but the museum now thinks it may be by some other builder, perhaps the Venetian Benedetto Floriani. Another of the virginals, from 1562, has been attributed to Floriani and, in fact, bears his name on the nameboard. But Wraight (p. 80) convincingly demonstrates that despite the inscription, a crucial case molding is identical with one found on Rossi's but not Floriani's virginals. Wraight further points out that the half-inset keyboard and the heptagonal shape of this virginal are characteristics of instruments made in the Milan-Brescia area (where Rossi worked) not Venice. Taken together, the evidence that the virginal was built in Milan by Rossi, rather than in Venice by Floriani, is quite persuasive. The museum is changing the attribution.

The "Apollo flaying Marsyas" lid painting of an anonymous seventeenth-century Italian square virginal is ascribed to a Flanders provenance. The instrument itself bears a superficial resemblance to a Flemish virginal by virtue of its fully inset keyboard; but even though inset keyboards are rare on Italian virginals, they are not unheard-of. A 1556 Venetian instrument by Dominicus Pisaurensis, in the Yale Collection, also has this configuration.

The only other signed virginal is by Matteo Cardinali, 1659. The museum has a 1692 triangular octave spinet with outer case by Giovanni Andrea Menegoni of Venice. An 1836 virginal is by Alessandro Riva, the same late virginal builder whose 1839 instrument shaped like a square piano is found in Leipzig.

Only two of the bentside spinets are signed, a 1690 by a Pentorisi, from Murano, and a 1735 by "F. B. F. Mediolani," probably Francesco Battaglia of Milan. The outer-case decoration of the first was probably applied by Franciolini or some other dealer in an effort to make the instrument appear more authentic. The lid painting on the second, a classical "Apollo and the Muses" with Christian overtones, is particularly interesting. Another otherwise uninteresting eighteenth-century bentside has an exterior decoration of *découpage*, or, as the Italians call it, *arte povera* (poor man's art). It is probably not the original decoration, and the instrument itself may be a Franciolini concoction.

One of the most important of Milan's grand harpsichords is a 1780 (or 1788; there is confusion over the date) black-and-red two-manual instrument attributed to the Parisian master Pascal Taskin. It has an Andreas Ruckers rose, and Taskin may have passed it off as a *ravalement* Ruckers.

Another significant harpsichord is a 1753 2×8′ single by Antonio Scotti of Milan. The exterior is covered with an eye-dazzling herringbone pattern of contrasting maple and walnut, and the interior uses the same materials in a slanted formation banded with ebony. A complex ebony and ivory molding tops the case rim, and the nameboard is inlaid with a con-

1735 bentside spinet by Francesco Battaglia

trasting wood and mother-of-pearl. The naturals are covered with a dark
wood and inlaid with ivory patterns. The cheek blocks and the sharps, of
a darker wood, are also inlaid with ivory filigrees; and a geometric parchment rose, ringed with ebony and ivory, graces the otherwise undecorated
soundboard. Interestingly, note names are inlaid into each of the naturals,
reminiscent of the practice in Italy and elsewhere more than a century
earlier. It is an ornate instrument, although modern taste might consider
it a little garish. The Scotti's greatest claim to fame is that it was supposedly given to Mozart, when he was in Milan in 1770 to produce his
opera seria *Mitridate rè di Ponto*. A complete account of the event and
a detailed description of the instrument is given in Francesco Augelli,
"Indagini Conoscitive sul Clavicembalo Mozartiano di Antonio Scotti,"
in *Strumente per Mozart* (Milan: Longo Editore, 1991), pp. 193–208.

Authentic Italian harpsichords with two keyboards are rare, although
Franciolini and his colleagues sometimes rebuilt single-manual Italians
into doubles and even triples. A 1675 two-manual instrument with 4′, by
Pietro Todini of Rome, was indeed advertised in one of Franciolini's catalogs; nevertheless, the counterfeiter often sold genuine instruments, and

1753 harpsichord by Antonio Scotti

this may have been one of them. The 4′ is available only from the upper manual and, in fact, 4′ and 8′ sounds cannot be combined. The exterior case decoration is undoubtedly nineteenth-century, with an impressive and perhaps original lid painting of a naval scene.

Domenico Traeri was born in Brescia, near Milan, but worked in Bologna. His 1700 harpsichord looks like a standard Italian instrument, although the ebony sharps are decorated in ivory.

At least five sixteenth- and early seventeenth-century builders, perhaps

1675 harpsichord by Pietro Todini

related, share the name Trasuntino. The museum has a 1571 1×8′, 1×4′ harpsichord by Vito Trasuntino that may have been built for Alfonso II, Duke of Ferrara. As befits an instrument intended for a highly placed patron, the case walls above the soundboard, the jackrail, and the nameboard are inlaid in geometric patterns with contrasting woods, ebony, and ivory. The ebony naturals are edged with ivory. Vito was also the maker of an *archicembalo*, a four-octave harpsichord with thirty-one notes to the octave, which he called a *clavemusicum omnitonum*. That instrument is now in the Museo Civico in Bologna, but several years ago it underwent a restoration in Nuremberg's Germanisches Nationalmuseum, where a copy now resides.

An anonymous 2×8′ inner-outer harpsichord was identified as sixteenth-century English by Arnold Dolmetsch, when he restored it in 1895. The next earliest extant English harpsichord we have (the Haward, or Hasard, in Knole Park) is dated 1622, and it and the few other surviving seventeenth-century English instruments bear no resemblance to this one. Although it does have some inexplicably crude features, we see no reason to consider it anything but another anonymous Italian harpsichord.

At some time in the past an unnamed and undated Italian harpsichord was turned into a clavichord by setting tangents into the key ends. If the catalog date of 1503 is true, it would be the oldest extant harpsichord in the world. There seems to be little evidence for this attribution; the instrument was probably made at least fifty years later. The museum is reassessing its date and provenance.

The Museo Civico has three miniature instruments: a false inner-outer single-manual harpsichord, an inner-outer square virginal, and a false inner-outer spinet with a mirrored lid. Jacks are apparent in the virginal, so it, and perhaps the others, may be working models.

Five of the fourteen square pianos are from Milan: an Antonio Battaglia of 1778, a Gaetano Scappa of 1804, an anonymous instrument from the late eighteenth century, and two undated early nineteenth-century instruments, by Francesco Barbanti and Giuseppe Prestinari. Most of them are finished in natural woods. The Scappa has flowers painted on the case and a fifteen-note pedalboard with pulldowns. An undated eighteenth-century square is by Peter Aquilinus from Varese, near Milan. London squares are well represented: Zumpe & Meyer, 1778; William Rock, 1782; John Broadwood & Son, ca. 1807; William Stodart, ca. 1800; and Muzio Clementi, ca. 1810.

Milan has a strange-looking anonymous nineteenth-century Viennese giraffe. Normally, these instruments have scrolled tops; but this one's looks like a snail shell. Upright grands include a John Broadwood and

Sons from ca. 1850; two undated, from Paris, by Érard and Bardies; and an eighteenth-century example with cabinet doors, tentatively assigned to Domenico del Mela. The last is a curious attribution, since aside from its primitive action there appears to be no similarity between the slender, sinuous 1739 del Mela piano in Florence's Museo degli Strumenti Musicali and this ponderous, four-square instrument in Milan. Two cabinet pianos are French: a ca. 1860 by G. Maurer, and an 1844 by Henri Herz. A small upright console by Luigi Erba, a late nineteenth-century Milanese builder, was once owned by Giuseppe Verdi.

One of the grand pianos is a late eighteenth-century unsigned Italian example, and another, from the nineteenth century, is by Fratelli Colombo of Milan. Two are Viennese: an early nineteenth-century Michael Rosenberger, with six pedals and a Janissary stop; and a Benjamin Teichmann from the early 1800s. The remaining grand is an 1858 by Érard. Milan also owns a hexagonal table piano by Jean-Henri Pape of Paris. Closed, this instrument becomes a six-sided table, but when the appropriate side is opened, it reveals itself to be a piano. Pape may have specialized in this sort of configuration; a similar one is in Stuttgart's Württembergisches Landesmuseum.

The museum published a catalog when it opened in 1958: Natale Gallini, *Civico Museo di Antichi Strumente Musicale* (Milan: Comune di Milano, 1958). Five years later a revised catalog was issued: Natale and Franco Gallini, *Museo degli Strumente Musicale* (Milan: Castello Sforzesco, 1963). All the instruments are described, even if not in great detail, and there are pictures, some in color.

ROME

﷽ Museo Nazionale degli Strumenti Musicali

Address: Piazza Santa Croce in Gerusalemme, 9a, 00185 Rome;
hours: 9 A.M.–2P.M.; telephone: 757 5936, fax: 702 9862.

The instrument collection in Rome was founded by the Italian government after World War II, with the purchase of most of the holdings of Evan Gorga, a well-known early twentieth-century tenor. Our report is based on what was exhibited when we visited in 1988: three pianos, a glassichord, ten virginals and spinets, and seven harpsichords. Among the collection's riches are some instruments extremely important to the history of early keyboards. Rome has one of the earliest pianos, the earliest-known German harpsichord, one of the two earliest Flemish virginals, one of the two Ruckers non-aligned doubles still with original keyboards, a rare Italian pyramid clavicytherium, and more.

Bartolomeo Cristofori may have built as many as thirty pianos, but only three have survived: the 1720 in New York's Metropolitan Museum, the 1726 in Leipzig's Musikinstrumenten-Museum (see discussion in that section), and the 1722 here in Rome. They share many obvious similarities although they are by no means identical, since the Florentine master always seemed to be experimenting. For example, while the hammers on the Leipzig instrument were made of hollow parchment rings, on the Rome piano they are of solid wood. But both sets of hammers were covered with leather, and the same phenomenon of tonal distinctions with loud and soft playing, discussed earlier, would also be characteristic of the Rome instrument.

Like the Leipzig example (but not the New York instrument), this piano has an inverted wrestplank. In all three instruments the tension of the strings is taken by a hitchpin rail attached to the case but not to the soundboard; in fact, the soundboard is glued to thin inner walls, independent of the case exterior. This not only isolates the soundboard from the tension of the case but also serves to extend its vibrating area. Since there is a great deal of curiosity about Cristofori's pianos that cannot be satisfied here, we recommend an article by Stewart Pollens, "The Pianos of Bartolomeo Cristofori," in *Journal of the American Musical Instrument Society*, 10 (1984), pp. 32–68; as well as his *The Early Pianoforte* (Cambridge: Cambridge University Press, 1995).

The earliest surviving dated harpsichord was built in 1515–16 by Vincentius and is now in Siena; but Rome owns one of the earliest harpsichords by a non-Italian builder, Hans Müller of Leipzig, dated 1537. It is now double-strung in brass and is at 8′ pitch, but it is obvious that the bridge has been moved closer to the bentside, suggesting that the pitch had been considerably higher. With iron stringing it could have been at 4′. The instrument has three sets of jacks—one for each set of strings and for the lute stop. This insistence on a variety of timbres seems to have been a specifically Germanic trait, but several of its other characteristics are not. The soundboard extends over the wrestplank, with cutouts for the jacks and lower guides rather than box guides, an International concept. The sides sit on the bottom, and the case uses upper and lower braces, the archetypical Flemish bracing scheme. The thin-case inner-outer construction with top and bottom moldings is both Italianate and International. Interestingly, the instrument has a mechanism to transpose the keyboard by a whole step, which is a rarity at any time.

Another instrument of more than passing interest is the second-oldest extant Flemish virginal, made in 1550 by the Antwerp builder Ioes Karest. We have partially described it and its sister, Karest's 1548 virginal, in the section on the Musée Instrumental in Brussels. It is obvious that both represent a tradition that differs in many ways from the heavy-case square virginals built later in the century. Both instruments are polygonal in shape, with inset keyboards, and both are thin-case inner-outers. The Rome example is the larger of the two and has, for its time, the exceptional compass of C–f^3. Although this range was also found on contemporaneous Italian instruments, here it is chromatic in the bass (less a C-sharp) rather than short-octave. The Rome instrument also has a "bentside" to make the polygonal shape somewhat more elegant, but the gesture may be more aesthetic than acoustical, since it is "bent" at the wrestplank side. Both are spinett-virginals, with keyboard to the left and with the left bridge closely following the line of the jacks.

For some fifty years the Ruckers family made two-manual harpsichords with non-aligned keyboards. Most often, the upper manual sounded at normal pitch while the lower was offset in a downward direction by a fourth, but other schemes were also tried. During eighteenth-century *ravalements* almost all of these instruments were turned into aligned doubles by giving them new keyboards. Only two Ruckers non-aligned doubles have their original keyboards, a 1638 in Edinburgh and the 1637 in Rome, both by Ioannes. The Rome instrument has been restored, although it is not now in playing condition. The question of why a transposition of a fourth needed to be built into an instrument has vexed the harpsichord world for many years. One view is that the Flemish delighted in combining two instruments into one case, as in the mother-and-child virginal and the harpsichord-virginal combination. Here, the combination is two harpsichords at pitch levels a fourth apart. Whatever the reason for their existence, non-aligned Flemish harpsichords were really two separate instruments sharing one case. Disposed 1×8′, 1×4′ with buff, they had four sets of jacks, two for each keyboard. It was impossible to use both keyboards at once, since in order to play on the upper the jacks of the lower had to be withdrawn and those of the upper advanced. The process was reversed with the lower manual. The registers were controlled by extensions of the upper guides, which came through a wide slot in the cheek.

Clavicytheria usually look like normal harpsichords set on end, but some examples adapted a pyramid shape with double bentside, perhaps because symmetry was more of an issue when the instrument was viewed in an upright position. In most pyramid clavicytheria the strings slant upward from left to right, as they do in pyramid pianos. However, in two of these instruments, the 1675 Kaiser clavicytherium in Vienna's Kunsthistorisches Museum and the anonymous seventeenth-century example here in Rome, the strings are dealt with in an entirely different manner. The soundboard is given two bridges, and the longest bass strings run straight up the middle. The next longest are positioned on one side of the center strings, the next on the other side, and so on, until the penultimate highest note comes from one side of the instrument and the highest from the other. The problem of matching key to string is solved by supplying a roller-board such as is commonly found on organs. On the basis of its ingenuity and fine workmanship, it is thought that the Rome instrument may well have been made by Cristofori.

Another eighteenth-century harpsichord deserves special mention, not because of its likely builder, but for its rarity. It is a folding harpsichord for traveling—a *clavecin brisé*, of the type claimed to have been invented by the Frenchman Jean Marius. Only five of Marius's traveling instruments have survived, and a few by other makers are extant. Two versions not by Marius are in New York's Metropolitan Museum: a 1757 by Christian Nonnemaker and an eighteenth-century anonymous instrument of Italian construction. A third example is in the Rome collection. In his article "Folding Harpsichords," *Early Music* 15/3 (August, 1987), pp. 378–383, Lawrence Libin attributes this instrument to Carlo Grimaldi of Messina and offers circumstantial evidence that questions Marius's claim to have invented the idea.

An anonymous inner-outer harpsichord in Rome still has its split-sharp keyboard. Italian instruments with split sharps were not uncommon in the seventeenth century, since in meantone tuning accidentals are not enharmonic. An A-flat, for example, is not the same pitch as the G-sharp to which that key is normally tuned. If the former is required there would normally be only two choices: retune the note, or obtain a harpsichord where that accidental has been split into two keys, each with its own set of strings and jacks. As was usual in such cases, sharps were not split in the upper octave, which, one assumes, was most often used for rapid passagework and would not require the nicety of tuning needed in the middle and low registers where the tone is more sustained. Since most instruments with split-sharp keyboards have been rebuilt into normal chromatic versions, few examples are still to be found.

At least some virginal building in Naples differed from the practices of the rest of Italy. Honofrio Guarracino, who is particularly associated with a type of virginal we now refer to as Neapolitan, is represented here by 1677 and 1692 square inner-outers with half-projecting keyboards mounted on the extreme left. The wrestplanks are not in their usual place, on the right side of the instruments, but behind the jacks, and the left bridges sit above them. This scheme differs from that of the normal virginal in that only one bridge—the right one—is mounted on free soundboard. The left bridge is also fairly close to the jacks and does not curve away in the bass, as in most Italian virginals. This gives these instruments a rather pungent sound, not unlike the Flemish spinett with keyboard to the left. A 1668 Guarracino virginal is in the Finchcocks collection in Edinburgh.

Rome's other keyboard offerings are more pedestrian. Plucked instruments include two octave virginals and an octave spinet, all seventeenth-century and all nicely decorated; two sixteenth-century inner-outer polygonal virginals with outer cases, one anonymous, the other, ca. 1550, by Giovanni Francesco Antegnati of Brescia; an anonymous undated false inner-outer bentside spinet; an anonymous eighteenth-century false inner-outer harpsichord; and a large 1780 harpsichord by Ignazio Mucciardi.

A Sebastian Érard square piano is the subject of a minor controversy: the museum dates it 1781, but Clinkscale (p. 97) puts it in the 1790s, maintaining that the address on the nameboard was not Érard's address in 1781, and that the five-and-a-half-octave compass and four pedals suggest a later instrument. The remaining piano is a handsome five-octave grand from the late eighteenth century by the Viennese builder Johann Jacob Könnicke. The only other non-plucked instrument is a charming sewing-box glassichord of uncertain date and provenance.

Rome has a "mystery instrument," a 2×8′, 1×4′ two-manual harpsichord with many unusual features. It is a false inner-outer, but with none of the interior moldings usually associated with that technique, and without the expected scrolled or carved cheeks in the keywell. Its lid painting has a mythological subject, and there is no decoration on the soundboard. The bentside is deeply in-curved. The tail is mitered, as are both the 8′ and 4′ bridges. The gilded and painted *vernis martin* exterior, which appears to be eighteenth-century and not necessarily original, is heavily laden with applied ropelike moldings. The Louis XV stand is also gilded and is even more encrusted with carvings, probably of *gesso*. Where did this harpsichord come from, and when was it built?

The Museo Nazionale degli Strumenti Musicali has yet another treasure, one involving a story. The crowning glory of the instrument collection of the Metropolitan Museum in New York is a ca. 1675 Italian keyboard, known as "the golden harpsichord," whose gilt outer case is completely carved in bas relief. But it is only part of a larger panorama: its base is an ocean from which creatures of the sea arise to support the case, and it is flanked front and rear by free-standing statues representing the cyclops Polyphemus and the sea nymph Galatea. This fantastic ensemble was once owned, and may have been built, by Michele Todini (b. 1625), an ingenious Piedmontese entrepreneur, and probably the father of the Pietro Todini whose two-manual harpsichord is in Milan's Museo degli Strumenti Musicali. Todini made and exhibited all sorts of mechanical instruments in a *galleria armonica.*

The rest of the story is told by Emanuel Winternitz, *Musical Instruments and Their Symbolism in Western Art* (New Haven: Yale University Press, 1979), pp. 10–15. Winternitz was for many years curator of the instrument collection at the Metropolitan Museum of Art in New York. In 1949 he visited Gorga, the tenor who first amassed the present collection, at his home in Rome. Gorga showed Winternitz many pictures of Rome's instruments, which he no longer owned, and which the museum had not yet displayed. Among them, Winternitz was fascinated to see a photograph of a model of the golden harpsichord and the attendant statues. Shortly thereafter, Winternitz was at the Palazzo Venezia in Rome, which was storing fragments of art works from places in Italy bombed during the war. Rooting through the boxes, he came across a tiny version of the bagpipe played by Polyphemus in the Metropolitan's full-sized version. Recognizing the object, he continued his search until the entire ensemble was uncovered. That model is now displayed in Rome's Museo Nazionale degli Strumenti Musicali.

Rome has a new catalog: Luisa Cervelli, *La Galleria Armonica: Catalogo del Museo degli strumenti musicali de Roma* (Rome: Istituto Poligrafico e Zecca dello Stato, 1994).

CHAPTER X

THE $\mathcal{N}$ETHERLANDS

THE HAGUE

Gemeentemuseum

Address: Stadhouderslaan 41, 2517 HV 's-Gravenhage; Postbus 72, 2501;
hours: 11 A.M.–5 P.M. Tuesday to Sunday;
telephone: 070–3381–111; fax: 070–3557–360.

Amsterdam is the official capital of the Netherlands, but its government's administrative offices are in The Hague. With a long history of arbitration, the city was known earlier in the twentieth century as the site of international peace conferences, and after World War II, for the International Court of Justice. It is also a city of museums, among them one of the world's great repositories of European and non-European art, the Gemeentemuseum. That institution's collection of musical instruments was started in 1933, when it purchased the impressive private holdings (which also included music, books, and iconographic material) of a local banker, D. F. Scheurleer. Since then many accessions have expanded the holdings. Its interesting plucked keyboards, from Italy, Germany, Belgium, and the Netherlands, include a unique Ruckers harpsichord at quint pitch. Clavichords are less numerous, but there are some seventy grand, square, upright, cabinet, and console pianos.

A 1627 Andreas Ruckers single, the only extant harpsichord from that family pitched a fifth above normal, is analogous to a quint virginal. It is disposed 1×8′, 1×4′, although in this case it is obvious that these designations cannot be taken in any absolute sense. The Ruckers shops produced various standard models, but we cannot say if this little instrument is truly unique or simply the only one of its kind left. It is in fine condition: it has most of its block-printed papers, and its soundboard painting is still in good repair. The edifying lid motto, "Sic transit gloria mundi" (Thus

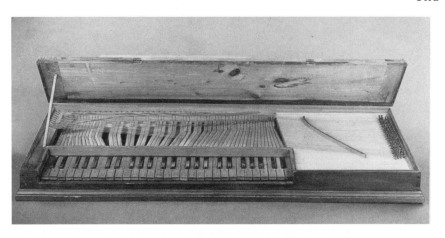

Anonymous early 18th-century fretted clavichord

passes the glory of the world), was used frequently by the Ruckerses. Its attractive balustrade stand is probably original.

At one time the keyboard of the 1627 quint was altered and another 8' register was added, but it is now back at the original pitch level and C/E–c³ compass. While much the same could be said of a 1639 Andreas Ruckers single, which had been changed from its original 1×8', 1×4' C/E–c³ design to a 2×8', 1×4' double with a compass of GG–d³, the comparison would be misleading. To paraphrase O'Brien (pp. 265–66), as it now stands the 1639 is in a historical limbo, reflecting no single period of its life. The original seventeenth-century compass has been restored and the eighteenth-century disposition has been changed back to 1×8', 1×4', but the scalings represent neither period. The keys and many other parts are eighteenth-century. When the upper manual was removed in the restoration, the large gap now existing between the keyboard and the bottom of the nameboard was filled with a wide namebatten. But despite the changes to which it has been subjected, it is a fine-sounding Ruckers, reverberating with a youthful vigor that belies its multifaceted history.

A 1639 octave virginal, originally part of a mother-and-child combination but now orphaned, was also altered, probably in the eighteenth century. Its compass was widened by three notes, and although it has been returned to its original range, some of its parts are replacements.

Two Ruckers "5-voet" muselars, built to sound a major second above normal pitch, are a 1640 by Ioannes and 1667 by Andreas. Both short-octave C/E–c³ compasses were later expanded chromatically, the additional notes fitted in by moving the case brace on the bass side of the keyboard and adding on to the keyframe. Both lids have mottos, but the one on the earlier instrument, "Musica laborum dulce levamen" (Music sweetly lightens labor), is original, while the 1667's "Omnis spiritus laudet Dominum" (Let all spirits praise the Lord), dates from the eighteenth century, when the lid was replaced. Both instruments have balustrade stands that are probably originals, even if not with these particular muselars.

The museum owns a 1740 clavicytherium identified only by the initials M. C. H. on the inside of the door. Unexceptional in both appearance and sound, it is assumed to be of Dutch origin. A double dated 1669 and signed Petrus Ioannes Couchet is probably not by that builder, although it bears a rose from a Couchet virginal. Originally a single-manual with a GG/BB–d^3 compass, it was given a second keyboard and the range was altered to C–f^3. O'Brien (p. 197) notes that while there is little about it to suggest a Ruckers-Couchet origin, it does show similarities to another Flemish builder, Joris Britsen (there were three Britsens, all named Joris).

A ca. 1769 clavicytherium by the Tournai builder Albert Delin is spectacular looking. The elegant painted and gilded case (the decoration, especially the carved filigree on the case door, probably dates from the late nineteenth century), the stand with graceful cabriole legs, and the tastefully flowered soundboard painting are unforgettable. As with the two other extant Delin clavicytheria, in the Musikinstrumenten-Museum in Berlin and the Musée Instrumental in Brussels, the end blocks are "sandwiches" of ebony between two pieces of ivory. And as with these other uprights, the stunning burst of sound from so close to the player's ears is thrilling, while its fluent action is a tactile pleasure. Its two 8′ ranks are reasonably well differentiated, and a buff stop for one of them provides further contrast.

A 1787 five-octave double by Abraham Leenhouwer of Leyden has upper guides projecting through the cheek, like those of its Flemish predecessors. By that time all schools had abandoned this direct method of changing registers in favor of levers on the wrestplank or through the nameboard, if not *genouillères* or pedals.

The museum's many Italian plucked keyboards include a 1575 inner-outer polygonal virginal by Dominicus Pisaurensis. The end panels on its lid depict conventional landscapes, but the design in the center appears to have been done in a twentieth-century nonrepresentational style. The case is probably original to the instrument, but the lid painting must have been done at a later time.

A 1589 false inner-outer virginal by the Venetian Giovanni Celestini,

Ca. 1769 clavicytherium by Albert Delin

with half-inset keyboard, is a visual and tonal delight. With delicately cut moldings, an intricate geometric rose, and the plan view of its polygonal case outlined in ivory buttons, it exemplifies the architecturally oriented beauties of Italian virginals. A recumbent Venus is painted on the central panel of the lid, flanked by a bespectacled man on one side and a monkey on the other, each reading a book. It remains an excellent musical instrument, with the usual sixteenth-century Italian range of C/E–f^3 and a velvety, resonant, center-plucked tone. This 1589 is another confirmation of the late-Renaissance Italian tendency to decorate smaller home instruments more finely, elaborately, and expensively than harpsichords, suggesting that nobility and wealthy bourgeoisie preferred them as domestic possessions. It may also help explain the popularity of virginals in Elizabethan England, whose court was fascinated by Italian trends.

A large imposing harpsichord with Giovanni Celestini 1605 on the nameboard had long been accepted as genuine, although its wide range—FF, GG–f^3 (no FF-sharp)—unusual for that early date, was thought to have been the result of some kind of extension of an earlier compass. But Denzil Wraight, in "The 1605 Celestini Harpsichord: Another Misleading Instrument," *The Organ Yearbook* 19 (1988), pp. 91–103, argued convincingly that the harpsichord is neither by Celestini nor as early as 1605. Wraight noted that the molding on the nameboard was not matched by those on the rest of the instrument, and that its moldings were different from those on other Celestinis. Thus, Wraight was able to reject the authenticity of the signature and date, and other factors led him to the conclusion that this harpsichord was probably not even made in Venice. Further examination, particularly of the builder's construction lines on the bottom boards, allowed him to infer that the range was indeed authentic and original to the instrument. It is now dated from about the middle of the seventeenth century.

An anonymous early eighteenth-century triangular octave virginal is unusual in that its sides are no higher than the soundboard. The jack-rail, attached to holders set on the soundboard, seems to bear little similarity to the rest of the case; either it was built in this odd way, or the sides were damaged at some point and simply cut off. We know of one other instrument with such sides, a 1532 virginal in St. Petersburg's Musical Instrument Museum, which is probably attributable to Brunetto dalli Organi.

Johann Heinrich Silbermann, the Strasbourg nephew and student of Gottfried, is survived by seven or eight bentside spinets. We have not seen them all, but those we have are handsome and lovely sounding instruments. They closely resemble the Gemeentemuseum's example, which, although undated and unsigned, is probably by Silbermann or someone in his orbit. It has a floating-panel lid, book-matched veneers, and cabriole legs with carved knees.

An otherwise charming little octave virginal showing an encircled angel on the interior of the lid looks suspiciously like some of the Franciolini representatives in other museums, although it cannot be attributed to his workshop with any certainty. "Aloysius Ventura, 1533, Venice" is inscribed on the back interior wall (an uncommon place for a builder's signature), but the instrument's provenance is unproven.

The museum's pianos number a dozen grands, 1794–1924; over thirty squares, 1749–1865; thirteen uprights, including giraffes and pyramids, 1804–40; and miscellaneous types such as upright consoles. A typical five-octave fortepiano, dated 1794, by Johan Lodewijk Dulcken of Munich (grandson of the Antwerp and Brussels builder Johann Daniel Dulcken), is double-strung from bottom to top. It has a paneled lid, damper-lifting on both knee levers, and four tapering square legs. At some point it had been converted to a harpsichord, but during a recent restoration it was turned back into a piano and given a copy of a Stein action.

A spectacular 1808 Érard decorated in Empire style was made for Hortense de Beauharnais, wife of Louis Bonaparte, king of the Netherlands from 1806 to 1810. This piano will reward close study: with divided bridge and nut; a range of FF–c^4; triple stringing; four pedals operating damper, moderator, lute, and *una corda*; plus a knee lever for a bassoon stop, it is a fine-sounding and versatile instrument. And with its carefully book-matched mahogany veneers, Empire-style bronze ornaments, lyre-medallions, and gilt and painted glass mounts, it is also a splendid example of a builder's attention to visual detail.

Southern Germany is represented by some outstanding pianos. A Ferdinand Hofmann grand of ca. 1785–1800 has bone naturals and an ornate brass grillework nameboard. A ca. 1805 Johann Schantz is a later version of the instrument Haydn recommended as a good, quiet home piano. A Christoph Friedrich Schmahl *Tangentenflügel* of 1791 appears to have its original strings. Of the lowest five bass notes, one string of each pair is overwound, but the other is of plain thinner wire—perhaps an octave string. A 1778 square by Johann Gottlob Wagner with an elaborately veneered case and four stops was called a "Clavecin Roïal" by its builder. A Schubert-era six-octave grand with triple stringing and pedals for damping and *una corda* is attributed to J. Sailer of Munich.

A splendid Pleyel dated 1847 has a full seven-octave AAA–a^4 compass, five tension bars, and the usual damper and *una corda* pedals. With their subtle colors and response, sustaining qualities, damping abilities,

1808 piano by Érard

and touch, there are no better instruments for Chopin's music than Pleyels. Preferred for their tonal response to that of the bolder, more powerful Érards, they were his favorites for salon performances.

There is a ca. 1880 seven-octave down-striker by Benedictus Schleip (probably related to J. C. Schleip, who was famous for lyre-pianos); although it is braced by a full metal frame, it is still straight-strung. A 1906 Bösendorfer still has a Viennese action, and a 1924 Hamburg Steinway still has only two pedals.

The earliest of the vertical pianos are upright grands by Stodart (1804) and Broadwood (ca. 1817), both with *una corda* as well as damper pedals. The Stodart's two case doors are covered in the usual cloth, and its keywell is inlaid with satinwood, while the Broadwood's mahogany case features a decorated nameboard. A second Broadwood upright grand has a fine mahogany veneer and fabric covering for its case front. The museum has other cabinet pianos, as well as many giraffes and pyramids.

An unusual ca. 1829 five-octave Conrad Graf pyramid with opulent decor has been much cited and pictured in books about the history of the piano. In Empire style, its silk-backed open-work upper case sports a Hapsburg double eagle below a gilt crown, a large lyre with five gilt bars for strings, and a pedestal and vase surmounting all. At each side of the case two female Moorish figurines, with gilt hair, necklaces, and skirts, each present a candelabra. The nameboard features a porcelain insert on the right side (the left one has been lost) depicting Grecian women playing musical instruments. The keyboard, with mother-of-pearl naturals and tortoise shell sharps, rests on caryatids; like the figurines above, they are bare-breasted and wear golden necklaces and skirts. The lower case—also silk-backed—has an exuberant sunburst at the front. It has been reported that it was ordered by a Hungarian businessman who wanted "something unusual." His wish was abundantly fulfilled.

Squares include a ca. 1770 anonymous instrument of probable London provenance, with hand stops both for damping and lute. Other London squares—a 1773 by Johann Christoph Zumpe & Gabriel Buntebart, a ca. 1780 Christoph Ganer, and a 1780 Adam Beyer—also have hand-stop damping (the Beyer's are divided for treble and bass). A 1782 Longman & Broderip has, in addition to the hand stops, three pedals for lute, swell, and Janissary. Square pianos were very practical instruments, and were designed for household use. They were made in great numbers in England and Germany. By the end of their heyday, around 1865, they had grown to a range of seven octaves with full metal plates; the museum has some of that type from Holland, and even one from the United States.

Ca. 1829 pyramid piano by Conrad Graf

Curiosities include a three-octave sewing-box piano with dancers playing tambourines flanking a mirror on its raised lid.

Informative, though dated, illustrated booklets are Rob van Acht and Wouter Scheurwater, *Old Harpsichords: Their Construction and Restoration* (1977, issued by the museum); and Clemens von Gleich, *Pianofortes from the Low Countries* (1980, also issued by the museum, in cooperation with the Frits Knuf). Both booklets have English as well as Dutch texts. Also available, entirely in English, is Clemens von Gleich, *A Checklist of Pianos: Musical Instrument Collection, Haags Gemeentemuseum* (The Hague, 1986). Unfortunately, all these books are out of print, but *Checklist of Harpsichords, Clavichords, Organs and Harmoniums* (1989), also by von Gleich, is still available. For information on recent acquisitions of keyboard instruments in the museum, the *Jaarboeks* (Yearbooks) of 1991 and 1993 have interesting articles.

CHAPTER XI

Norway

Oslo

 Norsk Folkemuseum

Address: Museumsveien 10, N-0287 Oslo 2; hours: May 1 to May 30, 10 A.M.–5 P.M.; June 1 to August 30, 9 A.M.–6 P.M.; September 1 to September 30, 10 A.M.–5 P.M.; October 1 to April 30, 11 A.M.–3 P.M. Monday to Friday, 11 A.M.–4 P.M. Saturday and Sunday; telephone: 22 12 37 00 or 22 12 36 66; fax: 22 12 37 77.

With acres of old wooden buildings moved to the site from throughout the country, the outdoor Norwegian Folk Museum aims to preserve the past not only with the artifacts normally found in museums but also with churches, schools, homes, barns, and other structures. It has a small collection of early keyboards, all of which are in storage.

The museum has a 1778 Shudi & Broadwood harpsichord it has owned since 1898. It was restored some years ago. Aside from the clavicytherium discussed below, the only other plucked instrument is a rebuilt anonymous seventeenth-century virginal. There are nine clavichords, mostly eighteenth-century, including a 1747 five-octave Johann Adolph Hass with the usual bass register of 4′ strings and an "Apollo and the Muses" lid painting. A 1749 four-octave instrument is by the Lübeck builder Ludwig Franck. The museum has some late eighteenth-century square pianos.

A small, single-strung, somewhat crude-looking clavicytherium is of fifteenth- or sixteenth-century origin. It has a partial soundboard; the area marked off by cutoff bar (had there been one), spine, and bellyrail is occupied by an ornately carved grillework of a contrasting wood.

The clavicytherium's past is shrouded in some mystery. It seems to have descended from a slightly different upright instrument, one with a partial soundboard. This gave it something of the appearance of a harp with a rather thick post; indeed, in this manifestation it was referred to as an *arpichordium*. There is some evidence that it was strung in gut and to have been supplied with metal pins or hooks called brays, which touched the strings near the nut to produce a buzzing sound. Both gut strings and brays are characteristics of the Renaissance harp, and the *arpichordium*, which was described and pictured in 1511 by the German theorist Sebastian Virdung in his book on musical instruments, *Musica getutscht und Ausgezogen* (literally, "Music Germanized and Summarized"), might well have been considered a keyed version of the harp. Only three partial-soundboard *arpichordia* are extant, all seeming to be in the German tradition. The first, from ca. 1480, in the Royal College of Music Collection in London, has the distinction of being the oldest known plucked keyboard. The second, in Stockholm's Musikmuseet, has the maker's name and date— Henning Hake, 1657—inscribed on the back of the belly rail, which is exposed because of the partial soundboard. The third is this one in Oslo's Norsk Folkemuseum.

TRONDHEIM

🎔 Ringve Museum

Address: Lade Allé 60, Trondheim; guided tours in English and other languages; write in advance to the museum at P. O. Box 3064 Lade, N-7002 Trondheim; telephone: 7392 2411; fax: 7392 0422.

With its picturesque buildings set in the rolling hills of Lade, a peninsula overlooking the city of Trondheim and its fjord, Ringve was for centuries a working farm. The estate and its contents were willed to the people of Norway as a Museum of Music History by its last owner, Christian Bachke, and his Russian-born wife, Victoria, both of whom were music lovers and instrument collectors. After Christian's death in 1946, Victoria Bachke undertook to turn Ringve into the museum she and her husband had visualized. When it opened in 1952 it was still a working farm, but in the space of ten years, with new acquisitions and the constant need for more space, the animals were removed. The collection was considerably augmented in 1967 with the purchase of a collection of 130 instruments, including some early keyboards, from Buenos Aires, Argentina. From its inception, the museum has included demonstration and performance on its instruments.

The strength of the Ringve Museum's keyboard collection lies in its more than sixty pianos; it also has two harpsichords, two spinets, a virginal, and four clavichords, which are not without interest.

An eighteenth-century harpsichord is attributed to the Paris builder Antoine Vater (an expatriate German), but it is unlike Vater's other work. It has a thin-walled bentside, molded bridges, an extraordinarily high 8′ hitchpin rail, a crude replacement rose, a natural wood keywell with a replacement nameboard, and other anomalies that would indicate an interesting history. It also has an attractive lid painting of a castle by a river.

With a typical disposition of 2×8′, 1×4′, lute, and buff, a 1767 Jacob Kirkman still plays well, even though, like so many other English instruments, its cheek is severely cocked. A fancy little anonymous 1684 triangular octave spinet, Italianate in style, was formerly attributed to Pietro Faby. A Venetian polygonal virginal, probably from the late sixteenth century, and a bentside spinet from the seventeenth, both anonymous inner-outers, complete the list of plucked keyboards. The virginal is a typical specimen, with a particularly dainty Gothic rose, although it has suffered from some inept repairs. The outer case, thought to date from the next century, has a lid painting of a Madonna and Child in a cartouche, surrounded by a starry background. The small spinet is nicely turned out, with round ivory buttons set into the backs of the ebony sharps and, at regular intervals, into the top molding and cheeks. The naturals and arcades are also ivory, with inlay banding and ebony and ivory designs on the nameboard. The lid has a painting on a mythological subject.

Two of the clavichords are from Hamburg, a 1728 Johann Christoph Fleischer and a 1756 Johann Christian Gerlach, the only extant instrument by this maker. A third is a Copenhagen instrument attributed to Hartwich Müller, 1775, who built the 1769 clavichord in Copenhagen's Musikhistorisk Museum. The nameboard of the 1775 is pierced by evenly spaced holes, a curious but attractive decorative touch. The rigidly centered lid painting of an outdoor concert is said to depict one of the islands in the Trondheim fjord. The Fleischer and the Müller have identical stands; one was probably copied from the other, or both from a third, proving once again that stands are one of the more ephemeral elements of harpsichords and clavichords—easily traded, lost, destroyed, and replaced. An 1807 instrument signed by Otto Joachim Tieffenbrun, Copenhagen, completes the clavichord holdings.

Containing only eleven Norwegian pianos—of which nine are upright consoles—the Ringve Museum is something of an exception to our statements that instruments tend to be found in the areas in which they were built; but it may be that not many pianos were built in Norway. Further-

1775 clavichord attributed to Hartwich Müller

more, Victoria Bachke, who collected most of the instruments, seemed more interested in developing a representative European aggregation than in preserving the work of local builders. In a recent book, *Piano i Norge-"et uundvaerligt Instrument"* (Oslo, 1985), Peter Andreas Kjeldsberg lists forty-two Norwegian piano makers, so the dearth of Norwegian pianos in this collection could be misleading.

The earliest signed piano is a 1783 Johann Andreas Stein, with the typical wide music rack, vertical grain veneer, and gracefully turned and fluted legs. Its lid is veneered with a checkerboard pattern, a Stein specialty. A ca. 1826–27 Conrad Graf has a dust cover sitting loosely above the strings on little blocks glued to the sides of the case. The Viennese builder Joseph Böhm, represented here by a ca. 1825 grand, was perhaps more famous for his invention of a foot-controlled page-turning device than for his pianos. English grands are exemplified by a Robert Stodart of 1786, an 1805 John Broadwood & Son, and an 1870 Érard.

Other grand pianos in this collection come from Poland (Wiszniewski, Danzig, ca. 1840); France (Pleyel, Paris, 1845–50; and Érard, Paris, ca. 1905); and the United States (Steinway and Sons, New York, ca. 1915, with an

Anonymous late 18th-century square piano

Aeolian reproducing mechanism). Only two are Scandinavian: a ca. 1815 Richter & Bechmann and a ca. 1855 Hornung & Möller, both from Copenhagen.

Five of the Ringve Museum's square pianos were made in Scandinavia: two from Norway, both early nineteenth-century and built by C. F. Waarum; two from Stockholm, an 1810 by Lindholm & Söderström and a ca. 1865 by Rosén; and from Copenhagen a late 1800s Hornung & Möller. The museum has four anonymous German squares; one, with rounded sides and a lid painting, is reputed to have belonged to Wanda Landowska, and another bears a false "Andreas Stein" label. Signed instruments are by Alexander Brettschneider (Leipzig, ca. 1830), Meyer (probably Andreas Meyer, ca. 1845), Johannes Witte (Lübeck, ca. 1865), and J. J. Wagner (Hamburg, ca. 1865).

Six more squares come from London: two unsigned from the late eighteenth century and ca. 1810, an Adam Beyer of 1788, a Clementi & Co. of ca. 1818–20, a Collard & Collard of ca. 1845, and a late nineteenth-century Isaac Carter. From Paris are two Pleyel square grands dated 1845 and ca. 1865.

Most of the museum's Norwegian pianos are upright consoles, with two by Mads Jansen from ca. 1865 and six by Brödrene Hals with dates ranging from ca. 1850 to the early twentieth century. London is represented by only one, a Ralph Allison & Son, ca. 1860. German examples include an anonymous from ca. 1850, a Roenisch (Dresden, ca. 1860), a Blüthner (Leipzig, ca. 1900), and a Feurich (Leipzig, ca. 1900). The remaining five upright consoles are all from Paris: Ignace Pleyel & Co. ca. 1850, ca. 1858, and ca. 1865; Henri Herz ca. 1850; and Érard ca. 1855.

Verticals include a cabinet piano by Wood, Small & Co., Edinburgh & London, ca. 1825; another by Baumgardten & Heins, Hamburg, ca. 1840; and a lyre piano by Johann Christian Schleip, Berlin, ca. 1840.

The Ringve Museum also has a particularly beautiful harp piano from ca. 1870–90, by the Brussels builder Christian Dietz. He was the grandson of Johann Christian Dietz, who developed the first commercially viable harplike instrument plucked from a keyboard. This particular instrument boasts a striking polychrome chinoiserie (or perhaps more precisely at this late date, Japonaiserie), on a black ground. The rail partway up the string band, found on many harp pianos, is often described as a damper; but its true function is to stop the strings lightly at their mid-points, as a guitarist touches a string to produce a harmonic, and in fact is called a "flageolet stop." With the connection of the harp to both the Bible and classical antiquity, with the familiarity of a keyboard-controlled action, and with the space-saving advantages of an upright instrument, harp-pianos graced many nineteenth-century drawing rooms.

When the Argentinian collection was purchased in 1967 several modern instruments came with it: an octave spinet and a harpsichord by Luis Gineste of Buenos Aires, and clavichords by Wittmayer and by the Dutch organ builder C. G. Klop.

The museum has published a checklist of all its holdings, including the keyboards: Peter Andreas Kjeldsberg, *Musikkinstrumenter ved Ringve Museum: The Collection of Musical Instruments* (Trondheim: Ringve Museum, 1981). It is in Norwegian, but it includes a short list of terms with

1870–90 harp piano by Christian Dietz

English equivalents. The museum has also published a small coffee-table book: *Ringve Museum, Trondheim: Utgitt av Ringve Museums Venner*, 1988. Written in Norwegian, English, German, and French, it contains color photos and short descriptions of representative instruments in the collection. The Dietz harp-piano is on the cover.

CHAPTER XII

ℙORTUGAL

LISBON

🏛 Museu da Música

Address: Estacaō Alto dos Moinhos, Metropolitano de Lisboa,
R. dos Soeires, 1500 Lisbon; hours: 1 P.M.–8 P.M. Tuesday to Saturday;
telephone: 778 8074; fax: 778 8069.

Early Portuguese keyboard instruments are rare, and little is known about them. A few are scattered in other museums and private collections, but with three harpsichords, four grand pianos, some squares, and eleven clavichords, Lisbon's Museu da Música has the largest single aggregate, in itself enough to assure distinction. In addition it houses about fifty non-Portuguese pianos and a fair number of other plucked instruments and clavichords.

The museum was created in 1915, with the gift of the collection of Alfredo Keil, a German who lived in Portugal, wrote Portuguese national opera, and collected musical instruments. Keil's holdings were soon joined by the those of Michel'angelo Lambertini, Antonio Lamas, and a few others. The collection has been moved several times; in 1936 it was installed as part of the Conservatório Nacional, but in 1975 it was moved to the Biblioteca Nacional. Some years later it went into temporary storage. At present, the Museu da Música occupies a large space in the atrium of the Alto dos Moinhos station of the Colégio Militar-Sete Rios subway line. When we visited, this new facility was in preparation, but it is now completed and open to the public. Our descriptions are limited to what we saw then, from information we were able to glean from checklists kindly supplied by the museum, and from the publications listed at the end of this section.

The name José Joachim Antunes looms large in eighteenth-century

Portuguese harpsichord and piano making; it is found on one of the museum's three locally made harpsichords. That instrument, dating from 1785 (rather than the recorded date of 1758), resembles a strongly built, one-manual, heavy-case 2×8′ Italian, with no moldings and just a suggestion of an inner-outer decor. A wide 8′ hitchpin rail, a feature also found on Antunes pianos, is immediately noticeable, and reminds one of the similarly wide rails on Cristofori pianos. On Cristofori's instruments the rail "floats" above the soundboard and is not attached to it; here, however, the rail is undercut, glued to the soundboard in the area over the liner, but cantilevered over the board. Like all the Portuguese harpsichords and pianos in this collection, its exterior is painted a dark green, while the areas above the soundboard and in the keywell are veneered with a light, naturally finished wood, probably tulip. Another Joachim Antunes harpsichord from 1785, with characteristics similar to this one, is found in the Finchcocks Collection near Goudhurst.

The collection also owns a 1789 harpsichord by a Manuel Antunes (the relationship, if any, between him and Joachim is unknown). Also a 2×8′, and also with an austere inner-outer allusion, it is superficially similar to Joachim's instrument of 1785. This is the only late Portuguese harpsichord or piano with a painted soundboard, but the bridge goes directly over some of the painting, indicating that the soundboard was probably painted first, before the bridge was glued in place. Since painted soundboards are thoroughly outside the southern tradition anyway, this feature presents something of a mystery.

The third Portuguese harpsichord, listed as "eighteenth century, school of Antunes," does not have the wide, undercut hitchpin rail of the 1785 Antunes.

Non-Portuguese harpsichords include a 1785 two-manual Longman & Broderip, complete with lute stop, Venetian swell, machine, and pedals. A 1690 two-manual Italian instrument bears the name of the Florentine builder Nicolaus de Quoco, the date of 1690, and the improbable range of B–a². Given the scarcity of genuine Italian two-manual harpsichords and the bizarre range, it seems more than likely that this is yet another Franciolini fabrication.

The collection has other plucked keyboards, including Italian and Flemish virginals. The first is a 1670 square inner-outer by Giovanni Landi of Siena. The shape of the inner instrument is oblong, with its upper-right corner "cut off." Inner-outer virginals normally were polygonal in shape, while the false inner-outers tended to be square, often with a tool box in the upper-right corner; so this one is unusual. It is attractively decorated, with human figures growing out of acanthus leaves (a motif going back to the early Renaissance) on the exterior of the outer case, and a lid painting depicting activities around a ship anchored in a bay.

The Flemish virginal is a mother-and-child muselar, with child missing, signed "Hans Ruckers, 1620." O'Brien (p. 279–80) affirms that it is not a Ruckers; still, it is a valuable instrument, since there are so few virginals extant by other Flemish builders. The style and subject matter of the lid painting—courtiers enjoying themselves in a variety of outdoor activities—is similar to the ca. 1600 Ruckers virginal in Milan's Museo degli Strumenti Musicali. The area around the keywell is painted in a black-and-white design of the type later imitated by Flemish papers. Painted designs, also found on the 1550 Karest virginal in Rome's Museo Nazionale degli Strumenti Musicali, and the 1581 mother-and-child muselar in New York's Metropolitan Museum, may have been typical of the earliest Flemish virginals. The evidence of the lid painting and keywell, therefore, suggests that the date of 1620 may not be accurate; the childless muselar probably dates from before the seventeenth century.

The Museu da Música has two plucked instruments at octave pitch. The first is an anonymous eighteenth-century inner-outer triangular spinet, probably Italian. The inner case is attractively decorated in gold filigree on a red ground, while the outer has a decoupage polychrome chinoiserie on a pale yellow ground. The second is a Flemish-looking 2×4′ harpsichord, short and squat because of its deeply curved 4′ bentside and heavy northern construction. Although it has the standard Flemish painted soundboard and the equally typical bone naturals with dimples separating two pairs of scored lines, there are many non-Flemish anomalies. There is no rose, for example, and the ubiquitous blue borders outlining the elements of the soundboard are also missing. This instrument was the subject of a short article by L. A. Esteves Pereira, "An Octave Harpsichord at the Instrumental Museum-Lisbon," *The English Harpsichord Magazine* 2/2 (April, 1978), pp. 30–32.

An undated piano by Joachim Antunes, built about the same time as his 1785 harpsichord, looks very much like its plucked cousin. It is painted a dark green, is double-strung, and has the same sort of undercut hitchpin rail. The obvious difference, however, is the row of piano hammers hinged to the belly rail, an action reminiscent of those found on many square pianos. Another Antunes piano, dated 1767, is in South Dakota's Shrine to Music Museum. A similar, but more problematic example, is this museum's anonymous late eighteenth-century Portuguese piano, with the same sort of primitive action. Its bridge is both mitered and curved in the bass, a feature worth mentioning not only because of its rarity but because the builder might have made that unnecessary gesture in the spirit of pure fun. An iron tension bar in the treble is undoubtedly a later addition.

That builders moved from the countries of their birth has been noted many times. Nevertheless, it is difficult to fathom the migrations of the harpsichord and piano builder Henrique van Casteel, who was born in Tournai, Belgium; moved to Lisbon to build instruments while in his thirties; and moved back to Belgium, before he was fifty, to build there. Lisbon owns one of his pianos, made in 1763. With its modified false inner-outer appearance and dark green exterior, it superficially resembles the other Portuguese harpsichords and pianos in this collection. Its beautifully made action is modeled after Cristofori, while its internal bracing is northern in concept. Accordingly, it combines elements of Portuguese, Italian, and northern building practices. The instrument is described in L. A. Esteves Pereira, "A Forte-piano at the Instrumental Museum-Lisbon," *The English Harpsichord Magazine* 3/4 (April, 1983), pp. 67–70; and in Stewart Pollens, "The Early Portuguese Piano," *Early Music* 13/1 (February, 1985), pp. 18–27.

A 1786 fortepiano by Mathias Boster, with a range of GG–g³, and a square by Antonio Pedrozo complete the list of Portuguese pianos. Also in the collection are almost thirty squares, by Astor (London), Baumgardten & Heins (London), Breitkopf & Härtel (Leipzig), Clementi (London), Collard & Collard (London), Dörner (Stuttgart), Érard (Paris), Gunther (London), Mayer (Hamburg), Pape (Paris), Pohlman (London), Rädecker & Lunau (Lübeck), Traumann (London and Hamburg), and Watlen (London). Grands are by Astor (London), Broadwood & Sons (London), Clementi (London), Boisselet (Marseille), Érard (Paris), Pape (Paris), and Sailer (Trieste). The handsome 1844 grand by Boisselot & Fils has an ornate three-desk music rack—one facing the keyboard player and two at either end and at right angles, facing out to the sides. We are told that this piano accompanied Franz Liszt on one of his concert tours and was left in Lisbon after his last recital there on January 15, 1845.

The Museu da Música also has a ca. 1865 Gustave Baudet *piano-violon*, supposedly similar to the one at Halle's Händel-Haus. Later versions, called the *piano-quatuor*, are found in Leipzig's Musikinstrumenten-Museum and Stuttgart's Württembergisches Landesmuseum.

The three anonymous and undated Portuguese clavichords we saw are all presumably from the late seventeenth or early eighteenth centuries. Despite their painted exteriors, these small fretted instruments strongly resemble the simple clavichords common in seventeenth-century Germany. One is simply painted black, another has yellow flowers on a black ground, and the third, also black, has a bucolic lid painting. The collection owns another dozen clavichords, almost all Portuguese and all anonymous except for a 1783 instrument by Jacintho Ferreira of Lisbon and a 1796 by Manuel Carmo of Porto.

The Museu da Música publishes a slim but attractive coffee-table volume with brief descriptions and pictures of some of its holdings. Although instruments of all kinds by Portuguese makers are featured, it also includes other Western and many non-Western examples: *Colecção de Instrumentos Musicais, Antevisão de um Museu* (Lisbon: Ap-Edições, 1989). A smaller booklet of a similar sort, *Com Eles se Fez Música: Instrumentos de uma Colecção Esquecida* (Lisbon: Instituto Portugués do Património Cultural, 1989), was published for an exhibition of musical instruments. It has pictures and generic descriptions of many instruments, but shows only two keyboards. The latest catalog was produced for the inauguration of the museum's new space: *Fábriea de Sons: Instrumentos de Música Europeus dos secs. XVI-XXI* (Lisbon, Sociedade Lisboa 94, 1994). All three publications are in Portuguese.

$\mathcal{S}$PAIN

BARCELONA

Museu de la Música

Address: 373 Avenida Diagonal, 08008 Barcelona; hours: from July to September, 10:00 A.M.–2:00 P.M. Tuesday to Sunday; from October to June, 5:00–8:00 P.M. Wednesday; telephone: 3 416 11 57; fax: 3 217 11 06.

Barcelona's Museu de la Música, established in 1921, first acquired housing in 1946, when it was lodged in the Conservatory of Music. In 1983 it moved to its present address, a lovely old building in a commercial area on a corner of a wide, bustling boulevard. Unlike some of the other museums discussed in this book, Barcelona's Music Museum is relatively new. Its collection is sizeable, even if not in keyboards, which number seven clavichords, six harpsichords, and fifty pianos. As might be expected, many of these last are Spanish, particularly from the nineteenth-century Barcelona builders Munné and Bordas. The museum catalog lists more than eighty individuals who have donated instruments, but most of the keyboards came from the collection of Folch i Torres-Baget, which were donated to the museum in 1947.

This collection has only one spinet, a twentieth-century Neupert acquired in 1980. The other five plucked instruments, all harpsichords, are quite interesting, although they tell us little about Spanish building practices. Only two are signed, and both are by Hamburg builders: a 1720 Carl Conrad Fleischer and a 1737 Christian Zell.

The single-manual 2×8′, 1×4′ by Carl Conrad Fleischer (brother of Johann Christoph Fleischer, the builder of the 1×8′, 1×4′ single in Berlin's Staatliches Institut) has a characteristic North German rounded tail, and its exterior is finished in a faded red—perhaps at one time a *faux* tortoise shell—with narrow black bands. It has an extremely wide wrestplank, wider than on any comparable instrument we have seen, and its gap slants upward from cheek to spine. As a result, the plucking points of all three of its registers are deeper into the strings by far than those on other Hamburg harpsichords—or most harpsichords of any ilk, for that matter. We have not heard the instrument, but its individual registers as well as its ensemble would probably be somewhat hollow and fluty, though bold. This feature is in marked contrast to the only other extant Carl Conrad Fleischer, a 1716 single in Hamburg's Museum für Hamburgische Geschichte, which has a more normal wrestplank, a gap paralleling the nameboard, and, probably, a more conventional sound. Both Fleischers have almost identical upside-down wedding-cake roses.

The 1737 two-manual Zell is one of the three surviving harpsichords by that maker (the others are the 1728 in Hamburg's Museum für Kunst und Gewerbe and the 1741 in Aurich's Museum Ostfriesische Landschaft). Its exterior is finished in a badly faded polychrome chinoiserie, but the lid painting, similarly finished, is in better condition. The interior of the case is natural wood with some ebony banding and veneers set in diamond patterns in the keywell. Strangely, this instrument has no soundboard painting, a decoration that is to be expected on an eighteenth-century North German harpsichord. Perhaps it was obliterated at one time; but if so, there is no sign that it ever existed. Another possibility is that the original soundboard was replaced in a restoration. It is disposed 2×8', 1×4', with large wooden stop levers operated on the wrestplank. In common with other German and Italian harpsichords, the gap slants upward to the left, away from the player in the bass, but only slightly. The effect is to pull the bass plucking points away from the nut, but not as strongly as in the Fleischer. The bits of leather for the buff stop are mounted on tiny individual molded pieces of wood—a nice, if somewhat fastidious touch. The Zell sits on an unusual stand: its moderately wide apron has seven turned legs with no stretchers or other members connecting them.

Museums often have "mystery instruments": the Museu de la Música has three. The first looks suspiciously like an eighteenth-century Central German harpsichord. It has a five-octave, FF–f³ range, keyboards with ebony naturals and bone or ivory-topped sharps, a bentside curve of medium proportions, a mitered tail, moderately thin case walls of natural wood, a bottom molding, a top molding that overlaps the inside of the case, a paneled lid, a Saxon-style symmetrical rose based on a triangle, and an 8' bridge that is straight in the bass. All these characteristics can be found in the 1776 Silbermann harpsichord in Berlin's Staatliches Institut; but this harpsichord has some North German, French, and Italian

1737 harpsichord by Christian Zell

characteristics as well. Central German harpsichords do not normally have decorated soundboards, but this one does, and its distinct North German style includes a large vignette featuring what seems to be a burial vault or crypt between the gap and the rose. Nevertheless, the floral motifs are arranged in groups, as on a French harpsichord. Moreover, the 8′ hitchpins are placed in front of, rather than into, the molded hitchpin rail, a distinct feature of Italian harpsichords.

There are other curious things about this instrument. Although its lid is paneled, it has but a single floating board, rather than the more usual two or three (the Silbermann mentioned above has three). Finally, the upper quarter of the 8′ bridge was at some time built out toward the gap with additional wood. Surely the intent was to shorten the scale in the treble, but one can only speculate about why that was considered necessary, why it was done by adding wood instead of moving the bridge, and on the effect the added mass would have on the sound of those upper-register notes. One can also speculate about this harpsichord's origin. Because of its anomalies it is easy to assume that it might have come from a Spanish shop, but it could also be a Central German instrument that fell into the hands of someone who thought it needed a soundboard painting. But that explanation does not account for the strange lid, the placement of the 8′ hitchpins, and the built-out portion of the 8′ bridge.

It could be a little easier to ascribe a Spanish origin to the two remaining harpsichords. A graceful 1×8′, 1×4′ single manual, with a slender rounded tail, is assigned to the eighteenth century. Its short-octave, C/E– c³ range is rather old-fashioned, but not unheard-of for that late date. On the other hand, since its place of origin is uncertain, there are few benchmarks by which its age may be gauged, and it could well be older. It does not have a soundboard painting or a rose; but it does have a rose *hole*, surrounded by an inlaid border of the type one might expect to see encircling a guitar sound hole. The sharps are of tortoise shell, and the note names are written on the bone or ivory naturals, as they were on early seventeenth-century Flemish and Italian instruments.

The fronts of the keys are undercut with two semicircles. The exterior wall on all sides of the case are framed with natural wood moldings, and inlaid cap moldings overlap both sides of the case. The exterior of the case and lid are painted with gold acanthus leaves on a blue ground, and there is a painting on the interior of the lid. The fronts of the cheeks are gently slanted, at an angle far less acute than that found on Viennese fortepianos. The interior of the case and the keywell are natural wood, and the nameboard is inlaid with diamond-patterned veneers not dissimilar in concept to those on the 1737 Zell. The registers extend through the cheek. There is a buff stop, but no molding around the soundboard. Finally, the wrestplank is several inches wider than seems necessary, adding to the length of the case for no apparent reason.

The last of the "mystery harpsichords" is a 2×8′ GG/BB–c³ single-manual with a rounded tail and a deeply but unusually curved bentside. Its soundboard grain is at a 45-degree angle to the spine, an idiosyncrasy sometimes seen in Italian harpsichords but rarely in others. Surprisingly, its rose is of the Saxon type described in connection with the first of the "mystery instruments." As in the harpsichord just discussed, all sides of the plain black case are framed with red moldings, and a cap molding overlaps both sides of the case walls. The interior surfaces of the case and keywell are covered with paper, upon which are printed colorful chinoiserie-like scenes. The nameboard is cut down to the level of the wrestplank, and two register levers extend over it, one on each side. The bottom of the nameboard has cutouts to receive the back ends of the black-stained sharps, a characteristic often found on German pianos but rarely on harpsichords. The naturals are of boxwood. This instrument also has a wider wrestplank than would seem necessary, adding an inch or two to the length of the case.

Finally, it is obvious that at some time both the bridge and the nut were moved toward each other. This may have been done so that the stringing could be changed from iron to brass (at present it is not strung at all), or so that a new or rebuilt keyboard could be placed in the instrument in order to shift the apparent range upward without changing the actual pitch. The hitchpins are positioned in Italian style, in front of the narrow soundboard molding. Like the previous two instruments, this one partakes of many traditions. Whether it and one or both of the others are simply anomalies, or represent a yet dimly understood Spanish tradition, cannot be answered in a book of this nature; but those harpsichords are worthy of further study.

Of the Museu de la Música's six clavichords, four are thought to be of Spanish origin, one is of undetermined provenance, and one is an undated eighteenth-century instrument signed by the Spanish builder José Grabalos. Although the soundboard area is smaller than on eighteenth-century German and Scandinavian clavichords, the Grabalos instrument has an unusual FF–f⁴ six-octave range. The dovetailed case is finished in natural wood.

Fully half of the museum's pianos are by Spanish makers, and these are all squares, verticals, or upright consoles. Represented by four instru-

1805 desk piano by Josef Martí

ments each are the names of Munné (Lorenzo and Juan) and Bordas (Manuel and Gerónimo); and with two each, Antonio Lladó and Oller y Kyburz. Josef Martí, Rafael Gabriel Pons, Miguel Slocker, Fernandez, José Colmenarejo, Giacomo Balbi, Chassaigne Frères, Agustín Altimira, and Juan Ayné are each represented by one piano.

Ca. 1830 square piano by "J. V."

An 1805 desk piano by Josef Martí of Barcelona is literally a square piano fitted into a desk, like a drawer. On a lovely 1828 six-octave square by Fernandez of Madrid, the ends of the nameboard curve out to meet the front of the case, thereby shortening the last few keys on either end to mere stubs. Although form overwhelms function here, the instrument is attractive. An anonymous cabinet piano from ca. 1820, which the catalog identifies as either French or Spanish in origin, is an unusual piece, with openings at the top and bottom of the case designed to reveal the fact that such instruments are constructed upside down, with the tail at the bottom and the wrestplank on top.

The few surviving pianos of the Viennese builder Martin Thim are gracious, refined instruments, with high-quality woodwork, beautifully painted scenes on sensuously curved nameboards, ebony and gold caryatid legs, and elegantly proportioned pedal lyres. The ca. 1820 example in the Museu de la Música has seven pedals: *una corda*, mute (buff), bassoon, dampers, moderator, second moderator, and Janissary stop. A heavy-looking ca. 1830 square of unknown origin has a "bentside" at the right, in the area of the wrestplank. The curve serves to break up the rigidity of the oblong shape, even though it serves no musical purpose. The same sort of charming conceit is regularly found on the square pianos by the earlier South German builder Johann Matthäus Schmahl.

A large, beautifully produced catalog is available, in Catalan: *Museu de la Música 1/Catàleg d'instruments* (Barcelona: Ajuntament de Barcelona, 1991). Each instrument is briefly described, and occasionally a small color photo is supplied.

$\mathcal{S}$WEDEN

STOCKHOLM

 Stiftelsen Musikkulturens främjande

Address: Riddargatan 35–37, S-114 57 Stockholm;
hours: by appointment only; telephone: 8 661 71 71.

Unlike most of the collections discussed in this book, the instruments of the Swedish naval officer and collector Rudolph Nydahl have not ended up in a public museum; instead, in 1920, Nydahl created a private foundation, The Stiftelsen Musikkulturens främjande (The Foundation for the Furthering of Musical Culture), in which his treasures were to be cared for and available to the public for study. The foundation is in a business-residential section of Stockholm, not far from the harbor. The Nydahl collection is not large, but it does have an interesting group of harpsichords as well as clavichords and pianos by Swedish builders.

Some of the earliest recorded harpsichords, virginals, and clavichords are ascribed to the Venetian builder Dominicus Pisaurensis, and there are more instruments bearing his name than those of any other Italian maker. Wraight surmises that only fifteen of the twenty-eight instruments ascribed to him are genuine. But by carefully comparing molding profiles, Wraight was able to assign the Stiftelsen Musikkulturens främjande's early (ca. 1563–70) but unsigned single-manual, inner-outer Italian harpsichord to Dominicus. The newer (perhaps by as much as two or three centuries) outer, is more eye-catching than the older inner. The case and stand are finished with black and gold chinoiserie on a red ground, with a lid painting of King David playing his harp, surrounded by a circle of dancing *putti*.

Wraight provides an attribution for yet another virginal in this collection. By comparing its molding profiles with those of a signed 1590 virginal

in Nuremberg's Germanisches Nationalmuseum, he was able to identify
the builder as either Donatus Undeus or his son Hieronymus, from Bergamo, with a tentative date of 1623 or later. Both instruments also bear
the initials IB on their jackrails, and Wraight postulated that they stood
for Ieronimo (the I substituting for the J in Jeronimo, a Latinization of
Hieronymus) Bergomensis (of Bergamo).

No attribution has been provided for an Italian inner-outer harpsichord, probably built around 1700, but with a nameboard claiming the
instrument was made by Ioannes Antonio Baffo in 1581. It is likely that
the signature and date were faked by a nineteenth- or twentieth-century
dealer—perhaps Franciolini, but he was by no means the only one involved in such shady dealings—simply to increase the instrument's value.
The same would be true of the harpsichord signed "Hans Ruckers, 1644,"
which is not a Ruckers and is probably of German or French origin. It
originally had two manuals, but is fitted with only one now, and the
soundboard is a replacement. Nevertheless, it is beautifully decorated and
sits on an ornate stand.

An otherwise handsome seventeenth-century false inner-outer single-
manual Italian harpsichord was turned into a tangent piano by substituting wooden tangents for jacks. It differs from other such conversions described in this book. An additional set of strings was added, making it
3×8′; and each of the two ranks of jacks was replaced by a tangent with
a flat leather button on top. This means that the each course of strings
is struck by two tangents, one behind the other. However, by withdrawing
the keyboard slightly, only the first set of tangents is activated. The reason
for such an arrangement is unclear. The instrument has been redecorated
with an olive-green paint with panels and legs that screw to the case. The
lid painting is yet another "Apollo and the Muses." The flap is also
painted, with a defiant Prometheus bound to his rock, a man and woman
by a wooden box (presumably his son Deucalion and niece Pyrrha), a
helmeted messenger on a winged horse (presumably Hermes), and a dis-
traught-looking sea serpent.

For years a beautifully decorated harpsichord in the Nydahl collection
was thought to have been built around 1680 by Ioseph Ioannes Couchet
and rebuilt by Pascal Taskin in 1768. Then, for a time, it was thought not
to be an original Couchet. Current opinion is that it is indeed a Couchet,
one of the last from his shop, and that it did undergo a *ravalement* by
Taskin. It is not difficult to understand the confusion: the instrument is
much longer than the usual Couchet, looking almost like a long-tailed
Italian. Originally a 1×8′, 1×4′ single, it was converted to a 2×8′, 1×4′ by
some unknown party, then made into a double by Taskin. The label, on

1680/1768 harpsichord by Couchet/Taskin

which Taskin proclaims himself a harpsichord maker, custodian of the king's instruments, and student and successor to Blanchet, can still be seen on the inside of the bentside. The case is decorated with a fine lid painting in the style of Teniers (perhaps biblical in nature), floral patterns on a red ground, and a carved and gilded Louis XV Rococo stand.

The Nydahl collection has two clavichords by Hieronymus Hass. The earlier, built in 1740, with a C–d³ range, has an exterior finish of chinoiserie on a ground painted to look like grey slate or stone. The stand has the same finish, with a cutout in the middle of the apron rather than under the keyboard. Both stand and finish may not be original. Even though the clavichord is fretted, the bass has a course of 4′ strings. The soundboard painting is somewhat unusual, with a little vignette of a woman playing a lute in a wooded area in the lower left-hand corner of the soundboard. As expected on Hass instruments, the keywell commands attention, with natural wood veneers and ebony and mother-of-pearl inlays. The naturals are covered with tortoise shell, the sharps are topped with mother-of-pearl, and the arcades are ivory. The tool box lid combines them all: natural wood, tortoise shell, ivory, and mother-of-pearl.

1740 clavichord by Hieronymus Hass

The other Hass clavichord, from 1744, has a wider range, FF–f³, is un-fretted, and also has a bass course of 4′ strings. The decor is a little more sedate: the dark exterior, which is not original, contrasts with the red interior, and both are set off by a fine lid painting of the Muses. The soundboard painting consists mostly of leaves, and the instrument is missing what was undoubtedly a colorful nameboard. The natural covers are ivory, the sharps are tortoise shell, and the tool box lid is veneered with tortoise shell, ebony, and mother-of-pearl.

The foundation has one more Hamburg clavichord, a 1722 by Johann Christoph Fleischer. There are five Swedish clavichords: two by Pehr Lindholm (1789 and 1794); one by Lindholm and his son-in-law Henric Johan Söderström (1808), which is still playing with original strings; one by Johannes Broman (1769); and one by Carl Jacob Nordqvist (1818). These late instruments are large and were often used as substitutes for the more expensive square piano.

The Nydahl collection abounds in Swedish pianos, particularly squares from Stockholm. All of Mathias Petter Kraft's five extant squares are in Stockholm, with the 1788, 1803, and 1805 here, and the other two in Stockholm's Musikmuseet. The 1811 and 1814 squares of Lorents Mollenberg are his only surviving instruments. Others are by Pehr Lindholm (1786), J. E.

Berglöf (ca. 1830), George Rackwitz (ca. 1796), and H. G. Becker (n.d.), who built in Ystad, on the southern coast. There are also two cabinet pianos, both undated, and an 1839 grand with machine screws for tuning pins, all three by P. Rosenwall of Stockholm. An anonymous square is thought to have been built by a Swedish amateur in the nineteenth century; the nameboard bears a poem dated 1829.

Three of the grand pianos are undated Viennese: Johann Fritz, Johann Michael Schweighofer, and Conrad Graf. Another bears the signature of C. C. Lose, a Copenhagen dealer who probably imported Viennese grands for resale. Other grands are by Kisting & Son (Berlin, n.d.) and John Broadwood (1797). A Paris grand by Ignace Playel from after 1844 is reputed to have been owned by Chopin. If so, he did not enjoy the instrument very long, since he died in 1849.

An upright console by Alphonse Blondel, Paris, was called a "ship model" because its keyboard folded up when not in use, presumably to provide more room in the cabin. Other Parisian uprights are by Klopfer and Pape, both undated. Two claviorgana are a 1797–98 Longman & Broderip (London) and a 1771 instrument by Johannes Klein of Freiburg. A lyre by Johann Christian Schleip (Berlin) and a giraffe by Gregor Deiss (Munich) are both undated.

🎵 Musikmuseet

Sibyllegatan 2, S-103 26 Stockholm; mailing address: Box 16326;
hours: 11 A.M.–4 P.M. Tuesday to Sunday; closed on some Swedish holidays;
telephone: 8 666 45 30; fax: 8 663 91 81.

Stockholm's museum was founded at the turn of the twentieth century, bringing together several private collections, mainly those of Carl Claudius and Johannes Svanberg. The museum is now housed next to the royal stables, in an old but attractive building that was formerly an army bakery. As far as we know, the Musikmuseet is unique in that it houses an interactive children's exhibit, where youngsters can bang on a variety of drums, gongs, and bars, blow through tubes, and pluck and bow string instruments.

The museum has some harpsichords of more than passing interest, but it is particularly rich in local clavichords; all of its twenty-eight examples are Swedish, almost all of them from Stockholm. Most of its clavichords are in storage, so a good deal of the information given below is taken from a checklist kindly supplied by the Musikmuseet and from an authoritative book on Swedish clavichord building by Eva Helenius-Öberg, *Svenskt Klavikordbygge, 1720–1820* (Stockholm, Almqvist & Wiksell International, 1986).

The clavichord was important in Scandinavia in the late eighteenth and early nineteenth centuries, but nowhere did it assume the significance it did in Sweden. Early Swedish clavichords were built in the manner of the North German school; but after the middle of the eighteenth century a distinctively local version appeared, characterized by a soundboard whose grain ran at an oblique angle to the case walls, a characteristic S-shaped bridge, the frequent use of a 4′ register in the bass, relatively plain painted or natural wood exteriors, undecorated soundboards, and compasses of up to six octaves. These clavichords were loud, capable of producing a volume close to that of many square pianos.

The Musikmuseet has the earliest extant Swedish clavichord, a 1688 four-octave instrument with a broken short octave by George Woytzig. Even with its fairly generous soundboard area, it is indistinguishable from most late seventeenth-century German fretted clavichords. But in contrast to those relatively plain instruments, the exterior of the Woytzig's case is carved in bas relief with acanthus leaves, and the interior of the lid is graced with a mythological painting. Another, slightly later instrument, by Elias Wittig, in a rather dilapidated condition, seems close to the Woytzig in concept.

Two early eighteenth-century examples are a 1736 Erich Månsson German and a 1738 Daniel Stråhle. With ranges exceeding four octaves, partial fretting, 4′ registers in the bass, and soundboard grain parallel to the front and back case walls, both instruments resemble contemporaneous Hamburg clavichords. The German has a painted case (although that might have been done in an 1896 restoration), while the Stråhle is finished in a painted "natural wood," with a graceful matching cabriole stand. Both have nice lid paintings, and the Stråhle even has a soundboard painting.

Philip Jacob Specken was another German-born maker who learned harpsichord and clavichord building at home (Dresden) but then practiced his craft on foreign shores. The museum has four of his clavichords, from 1741, 1743, and ca. 1745, and one undated. The 1741 serves to highlight some of the differences between mid-eighteenth-century North German and Swedish versions of the instrument. While the Specken has the large soundboard area and general proportions of a Hass clavichord (but without a 4′ register in the bass), it is painted a single color and has neither a soundboard painting nor an eye-catching keywell. The soundboard grain runs at an oblique angle, and the bridge has the curve configuration characteristic of the Swedish clavichord. It has an excellent lid painting

1806 clavichord by Mattias Peter Kraft

of the genre known as "country pleasures," in this case a young couple dancing to a flutist.

A 1752 four-octave clavichord by Lars Kinström is closer to North German ideals than are Specken's instruments. It is partially fretted, its exterior is painted with an attractive design, and it has a well-executed lid painting and a painted soundboard. But a 1756 instrument with much the same range by Johannes Broman has the Swedish attributes discussed above, and is characterized by Helenius-Öberg as "The prototype of the Swedish clavichord" (p. 176).

Pehr Lundborg built lutes and harps as well as keyboard instruments. The museum has three of his clavichords, from 1787, 1803, and 1790. The first, pictured in Helenius-Öberg's book (p. 171), is simply painted, although the natural wood nameboard bears some marquetry, and the interior case walls are also in natural wood. The soundboard area is very large. As is common with late Swedish clavichords, it appears to have two tool boxes, one on either side of the keyboard, but the right-hand one is painted onto a wood plate to provide visual symmetry. The museum also has 1792 and 1806 clavichords by Lundborg's student Mathias Peter Kraft, who became one of the best-known builders of his time. The large, plainly finished 1806 has a range of five and a half octaves, a tool box on the left, and a "dummy" on the right. It makes a surprisingly big sound; it is, in fact, the loudest clavichord we have heard, achieving volume at the expense of the clavichord's traditional sensitivity. Like most Swedish builders, Kraft also made pianos, but because clavichords could be turned out more cheaply and were not burdened with the adjustment and maintenance requirements of pianos, they were popular among his middle-class nineteenth-century countrymen.

With six clavichords (1785, 1787, 1803, 1807, 1808, and 1811), Pehr Lindholm's work is well represented in the Musikmuseet. The three instruments dating from the opening decade of the nineteenth century are co-signed with Henric Johan Söderström, Lindholm's son-in-law. An 1816 clavichord is signed by Söderström alone. The examples we saw had the "double" tool boxes mentioned above, which were probably standard on most Swedish clavichords by this time. These are large instruments, plain but imposing.

One of the latest clavichords in the museum's collection, dated 1821, by Eric Wessberg, is also large, plain, and imposing and in the tradition of the Lindholm school. An 1832 instrument by Adam Bergstedt probably represents the final stage of Swedish clavichord building.

One of the most fascinating instruments in the Musikmuseet is a small single-strung clavicytherium with partial soundboard, similar to the ones in Oslo's Norsk Folkemuseum and London's Royal College of Music. Unlike the last two, however, which provide no clues as to maker, date, or provenance, this one is signed, on the back of the exposed upper belly rail, "Henning Hake in Riga/Me fecie Anno 1657." In an article dealing with these three instruments, "A Contribution to the History of the Clavicytherium," *Early Music* 6/2 (April, 1978), pp. 247–59, John Henry van der Meer tentatively assigns a German origin to all three clavicytheria. The Henning has three roses between the keyboard (which is missing) and the upper belly rail, a structural member that marks the terminus of the soundboard area; and the soundboard is decorated with flowers. Van der Meer offers an excellent summary of what is known about these small upright harpsichords with partial soundboards and provides pictures of the instruments.

Two of the museum's more conventional harpsichords are Swedish, a 1748 Philip Jacob Specken and a 1756 Johan Broman. The two-manual, 2×8', 1×4' round-tailed Specken was mounted on a wall when we saw it, and without keyboards; but next to it were a series of photos showing a copy under construction. Clearly, this instrument and probably most Scandinavian harpsichords were built in the tradition of the Hamburg School, with sides overlapping the bottom, a heavy spine and thinner bentside, and a series of structural members combining bottom braces with knees.

Built along North German lines, with a rounded tail and relatively thin bentside, but with a length of nearly twelve feet, the Broman is an eye-catching instrument. Bjarne Dahl, in "Harpsichord of Note," *The Harpsichord* 2/1 (February, March, April 1969), pp. 10–15, reports that the instrument was painted dark blue; but when we saw it in 1992 it was in natural wood. The keywell is quite attractive, with marquetry floral designs on burl veneers and with ebony borders. The naturals are ivory-covered, and the sharps are of tortoise shell. Like the 1726 Hass in Copenhagen, the Broman is disposed 3×8′, 1×4′, with four sets of jacks. It has only one 8′ bridge, but that undoubtedly has a bilevel arrangement, or something similar, to accommodate the third 8′ string.

This instrument has experimental elements that are neither North German nor Scandinavian. The most obvious is its expanse, which results from a scale that is Pythagorean for almost the entire five-octave, FF–f^3 compass. Further, the bridge pins are so arranged that the three 8′ strings in each course are as close to the same length as possible. And rather than being hitched to their own rail glued to the underside of the soundboard, the 4′ strings pass through cutouts in the 8′ bridge and are hitched to the 8′ rail. Although in North German harpsichords, the stop levers were invariably mounted on the wrestplank, in the Broman, four levers run under the wrestplank and protrude from the nameboard, presumably using the system found about the same time in the harpsichords of Johan Daniel Dulcken. There are two horizontal coupler knobs projecting from the front of the upper-manual endblocks, and the upper and lower halves of the upper manual can be coupled independently to the lower. The buff rail is operated by a lever on the wrestplank. Reportedly, this instrument differs little in sound from a harpsichord of ordinary length.

Among the non-Swedish harpsichords is a little 1738 2×4′ instrument of three and a half octaves by Jean Goermans. The only 4′ harpsichord built by Goermans—or by any other Parisian builder as far as we know—it is exceptionally well proportioned and is decorated all over with chinoiserie on a light red ground. Rather than the normal gilding on the moldings, they are painted red. The soundboard painting is nicely executed, and despite the small area available, it incorporates a bird scene.

Also included in the Musikmuseet's collection is a 1642 Ioannes Ruckers muselar. Its keyboard was made chromatic in the eighteenth century but was changed back to the original short-octave bass during the twentieth.

1738 octave harpsichord by Jean Goermans

$\mathcal{S}$WITZERLAND

BASEL

🏛 Historisches Museum

Address: Historisches Museum Basel, Steinberg 4, CH-4051 Basel;
hours: Wednesday and Friday 2 P.M.–5 P.M.; Sunday
10 A.M.–Noon and 2 P.M.–5 P.M.; telephone: 271 05 05; fax: 271 05 42.

The address given above is the central office for the Historisches Museum; the Musikinstrumenten-Sammlung is located at Leonhardsstrasse 8, an attractive, residential-style building in which the early keyboards are beautifully displayed. Founded in 1878, this collection has had a complicated history. It is not large—ten plucked keyboards, eight clavichords, eight pianos from before 1800 and a few after that date, and a *Tangentenflügel.* Since its founding it has been considerably augmented, particularly by the holdings of Maurice Bedot-Diodati and Otto Lobeck. Among its more interesting instruments are some from the Swiss Brosi family, a rare non-Ruckers Flemish virginal, and a Silbermann bentside spinet with a beautiful other-worldly sound.

Peter Fridrich Brosi was a German builder who trained under Silbermann in Strasbourg and then came to Basel, where he became a Swiss citizen and opened a shop. The Historisches Museum has an unsigned and undated bentside spinet ascribed to him, with a geometric triangle-based Saxon-style rose. In an unusual conversion, the spinet has been turned into a piano by substituting a Viennese action for the jacks.

Peter's son, Johann Jacob, who spelled his last name Brosy, is represented by a 1775 bentside spinet and a 1790 square piano. Unlike Silbermann's spinets, Brosy's is not dressed up with book-matched veneers; nevertheless the wood on the case and lid seem to have been carefully selected for attractive grain patterns. Except for its mildly curved cabriole legs, the piano is quite plain. Father and son are the subject of a monograph by Veronika Gutmann, *Zum Schaffen der "Instrument und Orgelmacher" Peter Fridrich Brosi und Johann Jacob Brosy: Ein Beitrag zum Basler Instrumentenbau im 18.Jahrhundert*, Volume XI of *Basler Jahrbuch für Historische Musikpraxis* (Winterthur: Amadeus, 1987).

The Historisches Museum has a fascinating 1572 anonymous virginal; if it is Flemish, it would be the only one from that area at quint pitch by a non-Ruckers builder. The museum counts it as a Flemish instrument but John Koster, in his as yet unpublished *Early Netherlandish Harpsichord Making from Its Beginnings to 1600*, thinks it is more likely German. The pitch level is uncertain: the museum sees the virginal as a quint instrument, but the pitch could be higher than a fifth above normal pitch—whatever "normal" pitch may have been. Its $C/E-a^2$ range is the usual one for a Flemish instrument at that early date. It is pretty, with a lid and a front flap to cover the keyboard area. The exterior is apple green, with a pomegranate painted to the left of the flap and two apples to the right. The soundboard has a faded painting, but no rose. The interior of the case and the jackrail are red with gold scroll work. A Latin motto graces the jackrail. The sharps have the same sort of nicks or dimples found on the naturals—again a common feature of early Flemish instruments—but the fronts of the naturals have carved trefoils rather than applied arcades. A lid painting of Orpheus charming the beasts is complemented by a nameboard painting of the very same Orpheus at the entrance to the Underworld. The instrument is the subject of a pamphlet by Veronika Gutmann, *Das Virginal des Andreas Ryff* (Basel: Baumann & Cie, Banquiers, 1991).

An anonymous Italian inner-outer harpsichord at rare quint pitch, dated ca. 1600, at some point had its inner glued into its outer. The instrument has a so-called hollow wrestplank, with that member only wide enough for the wrestpins and the nut on a free soundboard. Archival information often tells of harpsichords covered with leather, but few such examples have survived. An exception is a 1696 inner-outer harpsichord by the Venetian Giovanni Andrea Menegoni, whose outer case not only still has its leather covering but also the brass stud fasteners. The note names have been inked on the naturals, a mannerism common in earlier instruments.

Johann Heinrich Silbermann, the famous nephew and student of Gottfried Silbermann, built all sorts of keyboard instruments, but most of those that survive are bentside spinets and clavichords. The five-octave spinet from ca. 1770 in the Basel collection is typical of his meticulous work, with book-matched veneers on the exterior, a floating-panel lid,

Ca. 1770 bentside spinet by Johann Heinrich Silbermann

graceful cabriole legs with nicely carved knees, and the triangle-based geometric Saxon-style rose on the soundboard. But visually attractive as this instrument is, its sound is almost overwhelming. The bass notes have a resonance unlike any we have ever heard on a bentside spinet, and one must wonder if it sounded as well when it was first built, or if quirks of fate and circumstance conspired to age it that way.

An anonymous C/E–c³ fretted 1723 clavichord is prized not so much for its musical values, which are minimal, but for its history. It is alleged to have belonged to a nun, Ignatia Aloisia von Sury de Bussy, who lived in an abbey not far from St. Gall. Its exterior and lid interior are decorated somewhat amateurishly with floral patterns, and in the center of the lid is a painting of a kneeling nun, supposedly Sister Ignatia herself.

A 1782 clavichord by Christian Gottlob Hubert is an entirely different sort of instrument. Despite its range of only four and a half octaves and its partial fretting, it is large, with an expansive soundboard area; and what we might see as limitations were probably perceived as worthwhile compromises. In common with other Hubert clavichords, it does not have a set of 4′ strings in the bass. Typical of Central German instruments, it has a paneled lid and makes good use of handsomely grained wood.

Johann Andreas Stein, his son Matthäus Andreas, and his daughter Anna Maria (better known as Nannette) are represented by three pianos: the father by a 1792 instrument made in his shop in Augsburg; his son and daughter by an 1800 piano built after they established their partnership in Vienna; and an 1816 by Nannette, with bassoon stop, four pedals, and dust cover.

Basel has a plain-looking 1782 Zumpe square, a good example of a piano without much pretension. It allowed a middle-class family to own a genuine musical instrument, something previously reserved for the rich and high-born. An 1824 Graf grand has the columnar legs popular at that time and a dust cover. Its four pedals are neatly housed in a lyre attached to stretchers running between the front legs. The museum has a ca. 1830 lyre-piano by Schleip, with the seven wooden rods in the lyre (varnished to look like brass) representing the seven tones of the diatonic scale. A

1782 square piano by Johann Christoph Zumpe

ca. 1850 grand by Érard has five metal tension bars, securely screwed to the wrestplank and the metal hitchpin plate, to counteract the pull of its triple stringing.

A small booklet by Walter Nef, *Alte Musikinstrumente in Basel* (Basel: Stiftung für das Historische Museum Basel, 1974), in German, French, and English, offers brief descriptions and color photos of some of the instruments, including a few keyboards. A nicely illustrated book by Otto Rindlisbacher about Swiss keyboard makers would be of interest to anyone visiting collections in Switzerland: *Das Klavier in der Schweiz: Klavichord, Spinett, Cembalo, Pianoforte: Geschichte des Schweizerischen Klavierbaus, 1700–1900* (Bern and Munich: Francke Verlag, 1972).

CHAPTER XVI

UNITED KINGDOM

EDINBURGH

🌼 Russell Collection of Early Keyboard Instruments,
University of Edinburgh

*Address: St. Cecilia's Hall, Niddry St., Cowgate, Edinburgh EH1 1LJ;
hours: Wednesday and Saturday 2 P.M.–5 P.M. except for public holidays
(including some specifically Scottish); Monday to Saturday 10:30 A.M.–
12:30 P.M. during the Edinburgh Festival (usually the last three weeks of
August); special openings for large groups and scholars, by appointment;
telephone: 131 650 2805; fax: 131 650 2812.*

Edinburgh's Russell Collection represents a unique collaboration between
a dedicated collector and a far-sighted educational institution. Raymond
Russell (1922–64) was highly selective in his acquisitions, and through
many years of buying and selling, he assembled a choice and representative
aggregation of antique keyboards. Russell hoped to see his collection become a living museum of restored instruments, serving as a center for
the study of historical keyboard organology and performance practice at
a British University. To this end, he engaged in lengthy negotiations with
the University of Edinburgh, which purchased St. Cecilia's Hall in 1959
and converted it into a museum. With its elliptical Concert Room and
generous display areas, it is an elegant space.

Shortly after Russell's early death, in 1964, his mother donated most of
his instruments to the University, which has greatly expanded the original
holdings by subsequent purchases and loans. The collection now includes
fifteen harpsichords: six one-manual, eight two-manual, and one (spurious) three-manual; seven English or Scottish bentside spinets; four virginals; an octave spinet; six clavichords; three grand pianos and six squares;
a cabinet piano; and an upright console.

John Barnes pointed out in "The Flemish Instruments of the Russell Collection, Edinburgh," in *Colloquium: Restauratieproblemen van Antwerpse Klavecimbels* (Antwerp: Ruckers Genootschap, 1971), pp. 35–39, that the French did everything necessary to bring older instruments up to date; but the English, while intending to make them more useful for modern music, nevertheless altered them as little as possible, even to the extent of leaving some of them as singles with compasses of less than five octaves. Barnes's comment fairly describes the eighteenth-century English alterations to the collection's 1637 1×8′, 1×4′ Ioannes Ruckers single with an original chromatic C–c³ keyboard. Over a period of time the case was widened, a second 8′ register was added, and with eight more keys, the compass was expanded to AA–f³. The case's red and gold decor and trestle stand probably date from these modifications. The lid lacks a painting, but its flap depicts St. Cecilia at the organ.

The Russell Collection owns a 1638 Ioannes Ruckers, one of only two surviving non-aligned doubles by this maker. Since except for its redecorated case exterior, it has been little altered and never restored, it is an exceptionally important document. Its papers, soundboard decoration, lid painting, and keyboards are largely intact, although the original Ruckers rose has been replaced by an Italianate one. O'Brien (pp. 116–17) has a schematic diagram and an interesting picture of the keyboards, showing how the upper manual short-octave keys were made to reach over the lower manual keys to play the appropriate pitches. (The other non-aligned Ioannes double, from 1637, is in Rome's Museo Nazionale di Strumenti Musicali, and though it does not play, it has been restored.)

Like the 1638, an Andreas I of 1608 was originally a non-aligned double; but about 1680 it met the fate of nearly all such surviving instruments and was turned into an aligned double with an added 8′ register. A century later the upper keyboard and all the jacks were removed, and it was converted into a piano. It became a harpsichord once again in a 1928 restoration, but an even later rebuild provided it with new keyboards, a shove coupler, and a GG/BB–d³ (no c-sharp³) compass. Its papers are not original, little remains of its soundboard painting, and its exterior is now green and gold. Its slightly naughty lid and flap paintings are thought to be by the artist Pieter Codde.

A 1645 Ioannes Couchet is the earliest-known instrument by this member of the Ruckers dynasty. Originally a typical C/E–c³ 1×8′, 1×4′ single, it was subsequently enlarged and given another 8′ register and a compass of AA, BB–f³ (no BB-flat); it was not, however, converted to a double. It was later "restored" to a C–c³ chromatic compass, but as O'Brien points out (p. 271), the instrument is now "in a state of organological purgatory, awaiting a purification and return either to its original or to its eighteenth-century condition." Sadly, many such instruments have shared a similar fate.

The earlier of the museum's two Italian harpsichords is an anonymous ca. 1620 2×8′ inner-outer with a chromatic C–d^3 compass. The original balance rail survives, indicating that the instrument was built with a broken short octave, and with split sharps for d-sharp/e-flat and g-sharp/a-flat in the middle two octaves. The accidentals in the present top octave were made by gluing the parts of these split sharps together. The bass portion of the bridge is independent of and parallel to the main section, a feature seen from time to time on other Italian harpsichords. Curiously, the bass strings are not hitched in the usual manner, but exit the case through holes in the tail, and are fastened to pins set into the case exterior. This instrument also has a hollow wrestplank—in this case, a normal wrestplank hollowed out on its upper surface so that most of the nut sits on free soundboard veneer. Evidence suggests that Cristofori, or at least his workshop, was involved in updating the instrument to eighteenth-century standards. The lid painting of the outer case, an "Apollo and the Muses," probably dates from the beginning of twentieth century.

Few major European museums are without a Franciolini deception, and the Russell Collection's three-manual Italian is one of his late-Victorian works. It was originally a single, probably 2×8′, built in 1627 by Stefano Bolcioni, to which Franciolini fitted three keyboards, perhaps from a French organ. He also gave it a crude, massive 4′ bridge and a lid painting and finished it in *vernis martin*. Regardless of its lineage, it is a spectacular-looking harpsichord. Not quite as elaborate and with a different decor is a three-manual Franciolini fraud attributed to Cristofori in Munich's Deutsches Museum, and yet another is in the University of Michigan's Stearns Collection in Ann Arbor.

The 1769 double-manual harpsichord by Pascal Taskin may be the most influential historical keyboard instrument of our time. Celebrated from the very beginning of the harpsichord revival, it was restored in 1882 by Louis Tomasini. Louis Dièmer borrowed it from time to time for public concerts in Paris in the late nineteenth century. It was exhibited at the 1889 Paris Exposition, then lent to the Érard firm for study, as a model for new production of harpsichords. During the German occupation of France in the 1940s, it was sent to Vienna's Kunsthistorisches Museum, but it was returned to Paris soon after 1945. Russell acquired it in 1952. Its decor is comparatively restrained, with a gold-banded green exterior and a pale salmon interior; however, recent analysis has shown that these colors are not original. Its soundboard painting is one of the most beau-

"1627" harpsichord by "Bolcioni"

1769 harpsichord by Pascal Taskin

tiful, and it has been copied often. With an FF–f³ compass, it is disposed 2×8′, 1×4′, with buff for the upper-manual 8′. Its rich, persuasive tone and responsive action have inspired many copies, and for years it has represented the epitome of the mature eighteenth-century French harpsichord.

A 1764 double by either Jean Goermans or his son Jacques also has a noteworthy history. It was acquired by Russell in 1962 and sold to the collection by his mother in 1974. In 1783–84, when the instrument was only two decades old, it was rebuilt by Taskin, who altered the initials *IG* in the rose to look like *IC*, the initials of Ioannes Couchet. Taskin knew full well that regardless of its quality, a rebuilt Couchet was worth many times a rebuilt Goermans. For years it was assumed to be a Couchet, but when Grant O'Brien restored the instrument in 1976, other clues told him that the rose could not possibly be Couchet's, and that attribution was rejected. The deception was confirmed a few years later by Sheridan Germann, who discovered the *G* to *C* alteration. She was further able to identify the instrument as a Goermans based on the style of the soundboard painter. Her research is described in " 'Mrs Crawley's Couchet' Reconsidered," *Early Music* 7/4 (October, 1979), pp. 473–81.

Surviving Hass harpsichords are rare, with only two singles among them. The Russell Collection's 1764 Johann Adolph has the classical disposition of 2×8′, 1×4′ plus buff, with hand stops and a five-octave compass. Like most German harpsichords, its wrestplank-mounted stop levers do not protrude through the nameboard. The exterior herringbone mahogany veneers and six fluted legs are modern, probably dating from a 1935 renovation. Most of the rest of the decor is original, as is the tastefully muted soundboard painting. There is no rose. Like the few other Hasses we have heard, it is an excellent instrument.

The collection has six English harpsichords, all of them of interest. A 1720 Thomas Hancock (London, 1720) with a range of GG–e³ belongs more to the English tradition of the previous century than to the Shudis and Kirkmans to follow. Its 2×8′ disposition, thin case walls, lack of crossbanding veneers, applied top molding overlapping into the case, and deeply curved bentside are all characteristics of the seventeenth-century International School, of which England was a part. Its keyboard, with ebony naturals, skunk-tail ivory sharps, and spinetlike end blocks, also refers to an earlier tradition.

The ca. 1725 Francis Coston double has many characteristics in common with the Hancock, and in addition has a painted soundboard, which is almost exclusively limited to counterfeit Ruckerses and is rare in English harpsichords. Its ivory naturals, exterior of walnut veneer marked off into panels with ash stringing, and upper and lower internal bracing are closer to the eighteenth-century tradition; but its overlapping sides hark back to the seventeenth-century International style. This instrument is described in a detailed and wide-ranging article by Grant O'Brien, "The Double-Manual Harpsichord by Francis Coston, London, C. 1725," *The Galpin Society Journal* 47 (March, 1994), pp. 1–42.

A 1755 Jacob Kirkman is one of the most elaborately embellished English harpsichords. Its crotch walnut veneers are beautiful (even the spine was lovingly veneered and cross-banded), but the really spectacular part of the decoration is the walnut-on-sycamore marquetry in the keywell, on the case walls over the soundboard, and on the jackrails. Although it does not imitate the motifs of Flemish papers, the effect is similar. A Kirkman harpsichord in the Finchcocks Collection, dated a year later, has the same marquetry but in reverse. Clearly, the marquetarian cut through both layers of veneer at once and used all parts to good advantage.

A 1773 harpsichord that also bears Kirkman's name was made by the London builder Robert Falkener, whose signature appears on the underside of the soundboard. Two years earlier Kirkman had brought legal proceedings against Falkener, seeking to halt the unauthorized use of his name, but it seems not to have deterred the counterfeiter. Nevertheless, it is a beautiful instrument and a fine-sounding one as well. It originally had hand stops only, but the two left-most knobs were replaced by two pedals and a machine stop in ca. 1790. Pedals in twos usually operate a machine stop and a swell; but this instrument has no swell, and the two pedals are used to achieve an extra variety of registrational changes.

Burkat Shudi, a Swiss-born joiner, emigrated to England while still in his teens. He was trained as a harpsichord maker by Herman Tabel, the expatriate Fleming generally regarded to be the father of the eighteenth-century English school (Kirkman also worked for him). Later, the Scotsman John Broadwood found employment with Shudi, married his daughter, and became his partner. On Shudi's death, his son, also Burkat, continued the partnership. Hence, the 1766 Shudi double and the 1793 Broadwood single are from the same shop, similarly disposed with 2×8', 1×4', lute, machine, and swell (the swell on the 1766 was added later; Shudi's patent on the device dates from 1769). Although it is not the last English harpsichord made, the 1793 instrument is the last surviving harpsichord of Shudi & Broadwood; by that time the firm had begun mass production of fortepianos.

The collection's earliest virginal is a 1585 C/E–f^3 inner-outer polygonal instrument by the Venetian Alexander Bertolotti. It reposes in an elaborate outer case that includes four lidded boxes for tools and spare parts and a painting of a hunting scene on the lid. Ivory buttons decorate the

1585 virginal by Alexander Bertolotti

moldings and jackrail, and also outline the keyboard. The soundboard's geometric rose is especially finely wrought.

A false inner-outer triangular Italian octave spinet is signed "Petrus Michael Orlandus Anno 1710" on the back of the nameboard; its front bears the motto "Du(m) vixi tacui mortua dulce cano" (In life I was silent; in death I sing sweetly). The riddle would have been clear to almost any literate person who lived with musical instruments: the wood speaks of its muteness while a living tree, but of its ability to make music, as a harpsichord, after its death.

There is also an anonymous enharmonic virginal from Italy, ca. 1600–20. Its C/E–f³ compass with broken short octave in the bass has divided accidentals for three d-sharp/e-flat and g-sharp/a-flat pairs. Since each of these notes had its own key, jack, and string, a properly tuned meantone triad could be heard in all tonalities normally recognized as usable.

A 1668 virginal by Stephen Keene with a vaulted lid, embossed and gilded papers, applied moldings, and colorful decor both in painting and casework, though fairly typical, is one of the more opulent examples of

1668 virginal by Stephen Keene

the genre. Its ebony naturals have embossed and gilt arcades, and the sharps are solid bone or ivory. The case and jackrail are outlined in ivory buttons, a decorative touch otherwise seen only on Italian instruments. The bass strings are hitched at the left and tuned from behind the jackrail, while the rest of the strings have the normal arrangement. The beautifully decorated soundboard contains four geometric roses, and the lid painting of a country scene is of high quality.

A second virginal, rather somber in appearance and believed to be of Scottish origin, is in marked contrast to the Keene. It has few of the latter's amenities, and is probably the only "English" virginal without a representational painting on the lid. Still, the lid interior is nicely decorated, painted a dark reddish brown, with six painted diamonds framing birds and flowers and surrounding a motto in praise of music, "Per aures ad animum" (Through the ears to the soul).

The six bentside spinets cover a period of some seventy-five years, the height of that design's popularity in England. The earliest, an anonymous

London instrument in plain walnut from ca. 1705, has a GG/BB broken short octave. The original compass went to c³ in the treble, but both a c-sharp³ and d³ were added later, probably about 1720. The keyboard has the traditional seventeenth-century ebony naturals and ivory sharps. A Thomas Hitchcock spinet of ca. 1728 has a double-curved bentside. Others, with the more usual squared-off tails, are by John Harrison (1757), Baker Harris (1776), Christian Shean (1782), and Neil Stewart (1784). The Hitchcock, Harrison, and Harris are from London; the Shean and Stewart, Edinburgh. They are all five-octave designs, some FF, GG–f³ (after the English fashion, without FF-sharp); the others, GG–g³.

Fretted and unfretted clavichords are represented by a small ca. 1700 anonymous German and a large unfretted Johann Adolph Hass (Hamburg, 1763). The first has the normal C/E–c³ four-octave compass; its plain walnut case contains but twenty-two pairs of strings to serve forty-five keys. The Hass, with an FF–f³ compass and 4′ strings for the lowest nineteen notes, has a luxuriously adorned silver-on-red chinoiserie exterior, a lovely lid painting, a decorated soundboard, an olive wood interior, naturals of tortoise shell, and sharps topped with mother-of-pearl. The stand is modern.

Other clavichords include a fretted instrument by the important Polish-German maker Christian Gottlob Hubert (Ansbach, 1784), once the property of Sir Donald Francis Tovey. A large, unfretted Georg Christoffer Rackwitz (Stockholm, 1796), in typically late-Scandinavian fashion, has a wide compass (FF–c⁴) and 4′ strings in the bass. There is also an anonymous ca. 1770 German clavichord and one of the earliest Dolmetsch instruments, built in 1896 and based on a Hass.

Square pianos include a 1767 and a 1768 by Johann Christoph Zumpe, a seminal figure in early piano design. The second has his typical divided hand stops for treble and bass dampers, single action without escapement, a compass of FF, GG–f³ (there is an apparent GG-sharp, but it is a dummy), and a small soundboard. Its trestle stand is original. A larger square by Longman & Broderip (London, ca. 1785) with FF–f³ compass, still uses hand stops for split treble and bass damping. Another knob operates a harpsichord-like buff stop. A later square, by Andrew Rochead (Edinburgh, ca. 1805), with a compass of FF–c⁴, has an elegant mahogany and satinwood veneered case. The collection also owns a Broadwood (London, ca. 1790) and another finely decorated Rochead square (ca. 1815).

A commanding cabinet piano by Broadwood & Sons, London, 1834, has a six-octave, CC–c⁴ compass and damper and *una corda* pedals. Its rosewood case front is inlaid with brass, and the keyboard rests on spiral-turned legs. Its wooden stickers, from keys to hammers, are very long,

1772 piano by Americus Backers

and the resulting feel is a bit cumbersome—perhaps one of the reasons the more familiar upright console types eventually superseded upright grand and cabinet piano designs.

The collection has only three grand pianos, but one of them, an Americus Backers of 1772, is the earliest extant English grand. Backers, who emigrated to London from Holland before 1763, is widely credited with inventing the action initially adopted by Broadwood and Stodart for their early grands. The piano still has a fluent response and a fine tone. The two pedals, attached to the front legs, operate dampers and an *una corda*. The mahogany case is veneered in typical English style, and the trestle stand, through which pass the rods connecting the pedals to the action, is evidently original. It has a soundboard rose, so it is only the three iron gap stretchers that identify this as a piano to the casual observer. A detailed description of this instrument is found in Warwick Cole, "Americus Backers: Original Forte Piano Maker," *The Harpsichord and Fortepiano Magazine* 4/4 (October, 1987), pp. 79–85.

A Thomas Loud grand (London, 1808–10), compass FF–c⁴, is triple-strung throughout. It has pedal-operated split dampers and a true *una corda*: by raising a hand-operated latch at the right of the keyboard, the left-pedal action-shift is allowed enough added movement for contact with one string rather than two. Shortly after building this instrument, Loud emigrated to Philadelphia, where he resumed the production of pianos (an example from 1815 is owned by New York's Metropolitan Museum).

The collection's only Continental piano is a Viennese-action grand by Ignatz Heinrich of Olomouc (now in the Czech Republic, Olomouc is about one hundred miles northeast of Vienna). The walnut veneered case houses a string band of six and a half octaves, with *una corda*, damper, and two moderator pedals.

Only those items of the original Russell Collection are included in a guidebook by Sidney Newman and Peter Williams, *The Russell Collection of Early Keyboard Instruments* (Edinburgh: Edinburgh University Press, 1968). It includes photos—eight in color—of the instruments, as well as biographical sketches of the makers, string scales, and plucking points. A more complete work, though without pictures, is *A Brief Guide to the Russell Collection of Harpsichords and Clavichords in St. Cecilia's Hall* (Edinburgh: The Friends of St. Cecilia's Hall, 1994).

GOUDHURST

Finchcocks Collection

Address: Goudhurst, Kent, TN17 1HH; hours: 2 P.M.–6 P.M. Sundays from Easter to end of September, bank-holiday Mondays, and Wednesdays to Sundays in August (individuals can often join a group); or by appointment; telephone: 01580 211 702; fax: 01580 211 007.

Finchcocks is a manor house forty-five miles southeast of London in the county of Kent. A restored red brick building in Georgian Baroque style, it was completed in 1725 and sits in splendid isolation amidst the English countryside. Since 1971 its high ceilings and oak-panelled walls have housed the fine private collection of antique keyboard instruments of Richard and Katrina Burnett, who own and maintain the entire enterpise as a labor of love. A visit to Finchcocks differs from the average museum experience. First, a tasty lunch in the basement restaurant (arranged by prior reservation) is highly recommended, as is afternoon tea. Second, while visitors are free to roam about and examine the instruments, many of them playable, Burnett usually provides an entertaining discussion and demonstration of some of the pianos, harpsichords, and chamber organs on display. Third, one discovers that the manor house, despite its broad, impressive façade, is only one room wide; hence, it is not large enough to display all the instruments in the collection, and those on public view are changed from time to time. Finally, Finchcocks's beautiful garden is well worth a stroll before departing this idyllic site.

The strength of the collection is in its fifty-five pianos, two-thirds of them from England; but its two late clavichords and seven plucked instruments are interesting and should not be overlooked. The clavichords, for example, though built only a year apart, represent two opposing trends in the late instrument. The earlier, built in Stockholm in 1806 by Lindholm & Söderström, is typical of nineteenth-century Swedish examples: more than six and a half feet long, unfretted, with a wide FF–c⁴ compass, a 4′ set of strings for the lowest seventeen notes on a separate bridge, and two tool boxes (the right one a dummy) flanking the keyboard. It represents the culmination of European clavichord building, when, particularly in Scandinavia, the instrument competed with the square piano for popularity. The 1807 German exemplar by Georg Friedrich Schmahl of Ulm, on the other hand, is much smaller, has a compass of only C–f⁴, and is double-fretted. It continues an older tradition in clavichord building, one in which stability, ease of tuning, and sensitivity of touch were valued more than range and volume.

Plucked keyboard types include two bentside spinets: a ca. 1700 with a broken short octave GG/BB–d³ compass, signed "C. A." on the lowest key and attributed to the London maker Cawton Aston; and a five-octave 1742 Joseph Mahoon. Also from England are two large double-manual harpsichords, by Thomas Blasser (1744) and Jacob Kirkman (1756). Both are handsome instruments. The Blasser is veneered in a striking mahogany burl, with a burl-walnut interior, and the end blocks and the batten separating the upper and lower manuals are decorated with vine and leaf marquetry. The Kirkman also has an attractive exterior, of burl walnut; but the eye is drawn to the case's interior surfaces, which are covered with striking sycamore-on-walnut marquetry, the reverse of the pattern on the 1755 Kirkman in Edinburgh's Russell Collection. Using a technique not uncommon among marquetarians, sycamore and walnut veneers were laid one atop the other, and the patterns were cut through both simultaneously. The 1755 got the dark on light, while the 1756 was given the opposite.

Honofrio Guarracino is survived by seven or so virginals, all of the type known as Neapolitan and characterized by a half-inset keyboard and a wrestplank and wrestpins behind the jacks (rather than at the right side of the case). Finchcocks's 1668 example is particularly fine and well preserved, with a splendid geometric rose. A 2×8' single-manual harpsichord by Aelpidio Gregori has a date of 1797, but in the catalog to the collection it is noted that the first 7 appears to have been scratched out and replaced by a 6. This may have been an attempt by Franciolini or one of his ilk to make the instrument appear older and thus fetch a higher price.

In our discussion of Lisbon's Museu da Música we note the scarcity of Portuguese harpsichords as well as the prominence of the name Joachim José Antunes. Finchcocks has one of the few Antunes harpsichords in existence, looking very much like Lisbon's and, like that example, also dated 1785, (see the description in chap. XII, "Portugal"). The Finchcocks instrument seems better preserved, and it has a fine lid painting as well. Disposed 2×8' with buff, the one register and the buff are operated by two pedals, reconstructions of the missing originals.

Both Broadwood and Clementi grand pianos are well represented in this collection, with six by the former and four by the latter. Ranging from 1792 to ca. 1850, they illustrate the growth of the London piano during that crucial six-decade period. The compasses, for example, expand from an early five-octave FF–f^3 to a mid-century seven-octave AAA–a^4. Some, like the 1848, with its exotic veneers and gilt carvings, are quite ornate.

A ca. 1800 Clementi already extends the treble up to c^4. Ca. 1821 and 1822 Clementis both descend to CC, and both have "harmonic swells," a pedal-operated device intended to provide sympathetic resonance from the area of the string band behind the bridge, which is normally silenced by listing cloth. Other London grands include two from ca. 1835 by Collard & Collard (the successors to Clementi). One is done in rosewood; and the other, which sits on a six-legged stand, is attractively carved and veneered with various woods on a birds-eye maple background. Both are bichord, which is unusual for this late date. The Stodart family is represented by two grands, an early 1787 by Robert and an 1802 by William

1668 Neapolitan virginal by Honofrio Guarracino

& Matthew. A straight-strung, powerful ca. 1866 Érard rounds out the English grands. A graceful 1801 Paris Érard Frères has the same FF–c⁴ range as the ca. 1800 Clementi, but it adds bassoon and moderator to the damper and *una corda* pedals.

Austro-German pianos are also well represented. A five-octave Tirolean grand, dated 1793, by Sebastian Lengerer from Kufstein, in western Austria, is something of a geographical rarity. Like Stein fortepianos, its Viennese action lacks the back checks that prevent the hammers from rebounding, suggesting that these instruments were not intended to be played too vigorously. A ca. 1800 Michael Rosenberger (Vienna), with its knee levers, slanted cheeks, and vertical-grain veneer, has the look of the classic fortepiano, but its compass is an extended FF–c⁴. An elegant Johann Fritz, Vienna, ca. 1815, tastefully adorned with ebony and gold, has the six-octave "Schubert" range (FF–f⁴). It has a Janissary stop as well as pedals for moderator, *una corda*, and dampers. Its bassoon stop is activated by a knee lever. Two Conrad Grafs, ca. 1820 and 1826, have in common a range of CC–f⁴ and pedals for moderator, damper, and *una corda*. They differ in that the earlier has a bassoon and the later a "cembalo"

1785 harpsichord by Joachim Antunes

Ca. 1835 piano by Collard & Collard

Ca. 1800 piano by Michael Rosenberger

effect (perhaps intended to imitate the by now obsolete harpsichord, this stop placed stiffened leathers, rather than silk or parchment, against the strings). A walnut-veneered ca. 1840 instrument by Carl Henschker is the collection's youngest grand with a Viennese action.

One of the Grafs, four of the Broadwoods, and three of the Clementis allow playing on all three strings, or two, or one (*tre corde, due corde,* or *una corda*), effects called for by Beethoven in his late sonatas and undoubtedly regularly used by experienced pianinsts to effect color changes implied by the music, whether or not indicated. The *una corda* available to today's pianists (actually a *due corde,* whose effect is perhaps due as much to the application of smoother hammer surface to the strings than the reduction from three to two) offers only a pale imitation of the color changes available on those older instruments. It is part of the price paid for the modern pianos's potential for enormous volume. The moderator so commonly found on Austro-German pianos is another color mutation one misses when playing Classic and early Romantic works on modern instruments.

Of the many verticals in the collection a ca. 1810 upright grand by Jones, Round & Co. (London) stands out for its quiet beauty and classical lines. Done in mahogany veneers, with a satinwood nameboard and pale silk coverings on the door frames, it is another piano offering a keyboard shift to *due corde* and *una corda.* Finchcocks also has a ca. 1825 lyre-piano, anonymous but almost certainly by Johann Christian Schleip. A ca. 1805 pyramid by the Prague builder Leopold Sauer features a clock in the center of the open grillework of its case front.

There are many early English squares, by Beyer, Broadwood, Ganer, Longman & Broderip, and others, most with compasses extending to f^3 in the treble. Later ones go to c^4, or the full six–octave f^4; however, none add "extra" tones in the bass: FF is the lower limit. The earliest have hand stops for dampers, the later ones usually only a single pedal for damping (color mutations were usually controlled by hand stops). An exception is a 1792 Revolutionary-era Paris Érard, with knee levers for damping and buff. A favorite of Finchcocks visitors is a tiny, single-strung ca. 1800 portable square by Anton Walter & Sohn, with a compass of C–f^3. It is diminutive in size and tone, with a bell-like quality that never fails to charm.

A catalog, *The Finchcocks Collection*, compiled in 1990 by William Dow, is a slim but handy checklist of the holdings. Also available is a color-illustrated guidebook, *Finchcocks, Past and Present,* by the Burnetts. Many of Finchcocks's instruments have been recorded.

Ca. 1810 upright grand piano by Jones, Round & Co.

LIVERPOOL

🏛 Liverpool Museum

Address: National Museums & Galleries on Merseyside, William Brown Street, Liverpool L3 8EN; hours: 10 A.M.–5 P.M. Monday to Saturday; Noon–5 P.M. Sunday; telephone: 0151 207 00 01; fax: 0151 478 43 90.

Perhaps better known as the home of the Beatles, Liverpool also has a nice if small collection of early keyboards. It owes much to William Rushworth, head of the Liverpool piano firm of Rushworth & Dreaper, who established an educational collection of early keyboards in the 1920s. The museum purchased the collection in 1967 and has added to it regularly.

The museum has only four plucked keyboards, three of which, a bentside spinet and two harpsichords, are English. The five-octave spinet, by John Kirshaw of Manchester, dates from ca. 1750–60. Graced with walnut crossbanding and burl wood, it is a typically handsome example of English spinet making. Its real importance, however, probably comes from its place of origin. London builders so dominated the keyboard industry that any English instrument from outside that area takes on a certain significance.

A 2×8', 1×4' Jacob Kirkman double from 1767 has a lute stop and a machine. The latter was originally operated by the usual pedal, but at some time, probably in the twentieth century, the pedal was removed and a knee batten was installed in its place. Mahogany veneers divide the bentside into three panels. A single-manual 1774 Shudi & Broadwood is also veneered in mahogany, but with two bentside panels. It is interesting to note that even at this late date, and even with lute stops, machines, and Venetian swells vying to present a variety of tone colors, the English were still building basic one-manual, 2×8' instruments. Cost may have been a factor, but no shortcuts were taken with the beautiful mahogany case veneers and the sycamore keywell.

The last of the plucked instruments is an oblong inner-outer virginal from ca. 1610–20 inscribed with the name of the Venetian Giovanni Antonio Baffo, but attributed to the Florentine Francesco Poggio. The attribution was made by Wraight, who identifies the work of Italian builders by close examination of cheek and molding profiles and key arcades. This instrument originally had a broken short-octave compass of C/E–f^3, with split keys for the E-flat/D-sharp and G-sharp/A-flat accidentals in the two middle octaves, requiring a keyboard of fifty-six notes. About a century later it underwent a renovation, and the keyboard was changed to a chromatic C–f^3 range without split sharps. This required a fifty-four-note keyboard, and since the original had fifty-six, two register slots were plugged. Late in the nineteenth century the virginal passed through Franciolini's shop, where it may have acquired the floral patterns painted on the nameboard and the interior of the case.

Liverpool has only one clavichord, a 1783 Hubert. Once again, we see a late eighteenth-century instrument with what might be considered a limited, partially fretted, C–g³ four-and-a-half-octave range. And again, we need to realize that builders like Hubert—and those who purchased instruments from him—recognized that the larger the clavichord became the more it lost its intimacy. Like all his clavichords, this one is finished in natural wood, with herringbone veneers on the case exterior and a floating-panel lid.

A small square piano—a *Tafelklavier*—by Schrader & Hartz, London, ca. 1795, makes an interesting contrast to Hubert's 1783 clavichord. The range of the piano is about the same, but it is smaller than the clavichord and finished much more plainly. It would not have been considered as elegant or expressive an instrument as the clavichord, but it would bring music to a middle-class family at an affordable price. A ca. 1840–45 square by Robertson & Co., London, is considerably larger and heavier, with a compass of six and a half octaves. Also intended for a middle-class clientele, it is a more serious instrument, suitable for the music of Schumann and Chopin. An anonymous early nineteenth-century sewing-box piano, almost a third the size of the Schrader & Hartz square and with a two-and-a-half-octave range, could not possibly have been considered a serious instrument; nevertheless it expresses our culture's fascination for combining utilitarian objects with music-making contrivances.

Liverpool has two grands—a ca. 1810 Austrian (or perhaps South German) and a ca. 1840 Broadwood. The first looks very much like Walter's instruments, except that the sides are of solid wood rather than being veneered; thus, the grain pattern runs horizontally rather than vertically, something rarely seen on pianos of that vintage. The Broadwood, built only about thirty years later, looks much more like a modern piano, with cutout cheeks, three massive legs, and a pedal lyre. The five iron tension bars seem to have done their job, since the cheek shows little sign of having cocked.

Of Liverpool's six upright consoles, two are rather elegant models by Dreaper & Son, ca. 1860, and W. H. & G. H. Dreaper, ca. 1878. The first is a somewhat uneasy marriage of a boxy upright with Rococo ornaments, but it has some beautiful veneers and a pair of caryatid legs. The second, with an ebonized finish, derives all effect from ornaments such as carved sphinxes for endblocks and fluted pilasters with gold capitals for legs.

Ca. 1860 upright console piano by Dreaper & Son

Both have interesting origins, since the first was commissioned to match a particular room, and the second was designed by the Liverpool architects William and George Audsley.

Three of the other consoles are by London companies: Broadwood (1853), H. Justin Browne (ca. 1870), and George Rogers & Sons, ca. 1909. The fourth is a pianola—an American ca. 1930 player piano—by George Steck. The collection also owns two twentieth-century plucked instruments—a 1910 triangular octave spinet by Dolmetsch-Chickering and a 1926 Gaveau bentside spinet.

We have not seen this collection, but have derived our information from a fine catalog: Pauline Rushton, ed., *European Musical Instruments in Liverpool Museum* (Merseyside: National Museums & Galleries, 1994).

LONDON

🖼 The Benton Fletcher Collection, Fenton House

Address: Hampstead Grove, NW3 6RT, London; hours: March, Saturday and Sunday only, 2 P.M.–5 P.M.; April through October, Saturday, Sunday, and bank-holiday Mondays, 11 A.M.–5 P.M.; Monday, Tuesday, and Wednesday, 2 P.M.–5 P.M.; telephone: 0171–435–3471.

Fenton House, accessible from downtown London by an easy ride on the "tube" (subway), was built in 1693 and acquired by the National Trust in 1952. It contains the remarkable collection of keyboard instruments assembled by Major George Henry Benton Fletcher, a career soldier who also wrote and illustrated travel books. Fletcher first placed his collection in a building called Old Devonshire House, in Bloomsbury, and in 1937 presented both house and contents to the National Trust. During the 1941 London blitz, Fletcher moved most of his collection to the country; nevertheless, many original stands, outer cases, portraits, manuscripts, and other valuables, along with two chamber organs and a clavichord, were lost when Old Devonshire House was hit. After the war the collection was placed in another house owned by the National Trust, in Chelsea; but in 1952 the contents were moved to Fenton House in Hampstead Grove, a fashionable suburban spa during the Georgian era. The dwelling now contains not only Fletcher's instruments but also its former owner's furniture and china; and like Finchcocks, it also has a garden. Many of the instruments have been restored to playing condition and are accessible for intimate recitals, scholarly research, and to some extent even for practice by serious

1770 harpsichord by Shudi & Broadwood

students of early keyboards (it was Fletcher's wish that they be used for that purpose).

The collection is dispersed throughout the house. On the ground floor a large Concert Room has been made of two adjoining parlors, in which instruments can be centered at the front for performances. Its regular occupant is a huge 1770 Shudi & Broadwood double-manual harpsichord, with extended bass range to CC, similar to the 1775 in Vienna's Kunsthistorisches Museum. It is nearly nine feet long, with buff stop, lute register, machine stop, Venetian swell, and pedals to complement the standard 2×8', 1×4' ranks. The stunning walnut burl and mahogany veneers cover even the spine, which is normally left in plain wood on the assumption that it would be placed next to a wall and thus unseen. This example, one of fewer than a dozen of its model known to have survived, is ravishing both in looks and sound.

A remarkable 1612 Ioannes Ruckers double, on loan to Fenton House by permission of the Queen, is also usually found on the ground floor. Once a non-aligned double, according to O'Brien it was pitched a fifth lower than normal, with the second keyboard transposing a whole step, rather than the usual fourth. Furthermore, it seems likely that it originally had only three registers rather than the normal four, with a single doglegged 8′ between two 4′s serving both manuals. It was given an English *ravalement* in the eighteenth century, exhibited at the International Inventions Exhibition of 1885, and extensively restored in 1977–81. The aligned keyboards now have a GG, AA–f³ compass. In English fashion, the 4′ register is farthest from the player, and the 4′ strings find their way to their tuning pins through holes in the 8′ nut. O'Brien (pp. 178 ff. and 243) goes into some detail about this unique instrument.

The rooms (and even large closets) on the upper floors, including those in the "attic," host various instruments, with most of the larger ones being more English harpsichords. The Rockingham Room contains another Shudi, from 1761—a single-manual FF, GG–f³ 2×8′, 1×4′ with hand-stop buff as well as pedal-operated machine, but with no lute. Its handsome burl-elm veneer is cross-banded with walnut.

The Northwest Attic contains a 1762 Jacob Kirkman, and the Blue Porcelain Room (so named because of the Delftware in its case) has a 1777 Jacob & Abraham Kirkman. Both are doubles, disposed 2×8′, 1×4′, FF, GG–f³, with lute, pedal-operated machine, and a buff. The right-hand pedal of the 1777 operates a nag's-head swell. A 1752 2×8′ Jacob Kirckman single in the East Attic has the same compass as its sisters, but it lacks their color-mutation possibilities; nevertheless, its tonal response is impressive. Another single, of the same disposition and compass, was made for Longman & Broderip by Thomas Culliford in 1783. In this instrument pressing a pedal (not original) produces a color change by activating the buff stop and, at the same time, canceling one of the 8′s.

Post-baroque English harpsichords are versatile instruments that convincingly render English music of their time; but they serve mid-century Italian, Spanish, German, and French works as well. Advocates of the French school prior to 1760 may argue that Franco-Flemish instruments are the only appropriate media for that repertoire; but as viable alternatives to late French and other Continental doubles, these English harpsichords hold their own.

Smaller English instruments include a beautiful-sounding and elaborately decorated Robert Hatley virginal of 1664, with an FF, GG–c³ compass. Its soundboard has two roses, its interior and exterior are graced by embossed gilt papering, and the lid and fallboard are painted with bucolic scenes. There are also two GG–g³ five-octave spinets: an undated anonymous and a John Hancock, also undated but of late eighteenth-century London origin.

Anonymous, and thought to be either of South German or North Italian provenance, a well-preserved and quite early harpsichord is in nearly original condition. It is an enharmonic instrument, with a broken short octave and split keys for the F-sharps and G-sharps, enabling one to play in more than just the most common meantone tonalities. It was single-strung, and still retains that disposition, even though most enharmonic harpsichords were later rebuilt with a second 8' register and wider compass. After at least four hundred years of life, its tone is still robust and singing.

Italian inner-outer polygonal virginals include a cypress instrument with C/E–f³ compass signed "Marcus Siculus . . . MDXXXX" (Marco Siculo . . . 1540) on the jackrail, although the date and the authorship are in question. This very early instrument has an intricate upside-down wedding-cake rose. Another anonyme was, for no apparent reason, once ascribed to Baffo of Venice. A third virginal, probably from seventeenth-century Italy, was originally removable from its outer case but has now been fixed in place. It is unusual in that it is double-strung, with two 8's.

Fenton House's three pianos include an Americus Backers grand, trichord throughout, with a compass of FF–f³. It is undated, but since Backers was known to have been in London from 1763 to 1778, the instrument is probably from the same period as the superb 1772 Backers grand in Edinburgh (Clinkscale dates it at 1776). Unfortunately, its stand and damper-lifting mechanism were lost in the war. The collection's catalog (p. 15) claims that "this instrument may well be the earliest existing instrument of its type," but that statement was obviously made before the 1772 Backers was loaned to the Edinburgh collection by the Duke of Wellington. Warwick Cole, in "Americus Backers: Original Forte Piano Maker," *The Harpsichord and Fortepiano Magazine* 4/4 (October, 1987), pp. 79–85, compares the two extant Backers and calls the authenticity of the Fenton House piano into question.

There is also a big 1805 Broadwood grand, also trichord throughout, with two pedals and a five-and-a-half-octave FF–c⁴ range. At this date Broadwood's pianos were externally indistinguishable from his harpsichords, and this instrument, veneered and cross-banded in mahogany, with a satinwood keywell, is no exception. Like his harpsichords, the pianos are vulnerable to cheek-cocking. An attempt has been made to brace the instrument's frame with metal inserts, but the instability may be impossible to rectify.

The last piano is a late eighteenth-century Christopher Ganer square, double-strung throughout, FF–f³ compass, with hand stops for dampers and mute.

Finally, there are two clavichords: an anonymous fretted example, probably seventeenth-century, with a C/E–c³ compass; and a 1925 Arnold Dolmetsch with an unfretted C–d³ range, a case of English walnut, and a soundboard painting by Mabel Dolmetsch.

A catalog of some twenty pages is available: Raymond Russell, *A Catalogue of Early Keyboard Instruments: The Benton Fletcher Collection at Fenton House* (London, Curwen Press, 1981). An earlier version (1957) has black-and-white photographs.

🏛 Museum of Instruments, Royal College of Music

Address: Prince Consort Road, London SW7 2BS; hours: Wednesday, 2 P.M.–4:30 P.M. when in session, except January; or by appointment; telephone: 0171 589 3643; direct, 0171 591 4346; fax: 0171 589 7740.

The two dozen keyboard antiques at the Royal College may not be as diverse or as numerous as the holdings of some other European collections, but they include both unique and representative items. They are housed since 1970 in customized, climate-controlled bi-level quarters, with most of the early keyboards standing on the main floor. But a small, anonymous clavicytherium with a partial soundboard, presumably of German origin and provisionally dated ca. 1480, is displayed behind glass. Long famed as the earliest extant harpsichord, it is one of only three surviving examples of a rare upright instrument, the *arpichordium*; the others are in Oslo's Norsk Folkemuseum and Stockholm's Musikmuseet.

The London instrument, an inner with an outer case, resembles many small portative organs portrayed in contemporary paintings. It has one set of strings plucked by a simple action: a vertical sticker rising to a horizontal jack is affixed to the rear of each key. Each tripartite unit pivots, and the return is effected by gravity. The jacks have no provision for dampers, so the instrument must have sounded rather like a psaltery. The partial soundboard has two Gothic windows, one of which retains its decorative grillework, as well as a third hole for a rosette. The forty-note compass (originally something like E, F, G–g², now C/E–g²), parallels the range of the human voice. The museum has a replica of this antique, whose sound and short sustain are quite suitable for literature such as that found in the Buxheim Organ Book and other sources of the mid-to-late fifteenth century. The outer case also exists, although its paintings are of a more recent date.

The arpichordium may have been more common than might be assumed from the evidence of this rare survivor. The fragility of thin wood

Ca. 1480 anonymous clavicytherium

and a diffident attitude toward "old" things in past centuries may account for the instrument's present scarcity.

Among the earliest dated Italian harpsichords is a 1531 inner-outer by Alessandro Trasuntino of Venice, now disposed 2×8', with a GG/BB–c³ compass. In "The Specious Uniformity of Italian Harpsichords," in *Keyboard Instruments: Studies in Keyboard Organology, 1500–1800*, edited by Edwin M. Ripin (Edinburgh, Edinburgh University Press, 1971 [reprint,

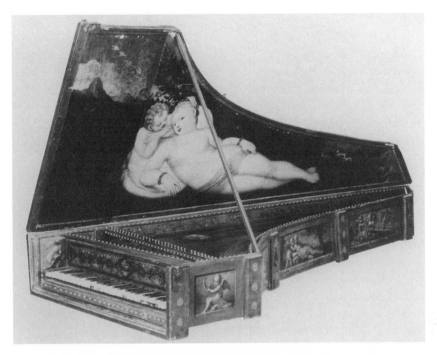

1531 harpsichord by Alessandro Trasuntino

Dover, 1977]), John Barnes cites such conversions as typical of those made during the seventeenth century to suit "modern" taste; in this instance, to make the harpsichord a more effective continuo instrument. The outer case is decorated in *grisaille*, with a Venus and Cupid lid painting. The inner walls and keywell are done in an intricate painted and inlaid moresque flatwork, and the soundboard is graced by three geometric roses. But despite its lavish decor, its original disposition was the usual sixteenth-century $1\times8'$, $1\times4'$ with the C/E–f^3 compass. X-rays reveal the outer case of the instrument to have had no fewer than three repaintings.

A similar change was wrought in the collection's other early Italian harpsichord, a ca. 1600 anonymous "inner" with a C/E–f^3 (no e-flat^3) range. At first a $1\times8'$, a second $8'$ was installed at some later time, and the compass was changed to C, D–d^3. In fact, the instrument bears signs of having been rebuilt three times in the seventeenth century. But rebuilt or not, it sings with a marvelously warm and singing tone, its 400-year-old wood retaining little of the high-frequency tonal response common in newer harpsichords. Its interior case walls and nameboard are richly decorated with bird and leaf patterns in gold on a green ground, and its keyboard is flanked by cheeks disguised as buxom maidens.

An outstanding example of the elaborate decor expected by aristocratic owners of early Italian virginals is found in a 1593 polygonal false inner-outer by Giovanni Celestini of Venice. The interior is covered with particularly sumptuous moresque strapwork decoration, and the three oval miniatures set into the nameboard depict Apollo's contest with Pan, Apollo pursuing Daphne, and Orpheus taming the beasts. The partially inset keyboard, C/E–f³, has artfully arcaded key fronts.

Two big, late harpsichords are a 1773 double-manual by Jacob & Abraham Kirkman and a ca. 1775 single by Ferdinand Weber of Dublin. The Kirkman has the usual 2×8′, 1×4′ hand-stop registers, as well as hand stops for lute and buff. Pedals activate a nags-head swell and a machine-stop, offering many registrational possibilities. An 1869 restoration is indicated on one of its keys. The 2×8′ Weber has hand stops for each 8′ plus lute and buff; a Venetian swell operated by a knee lever was added near the end of the century.

There are four bentside spinets, including a Restoration-era GG/BB–d³ Stephen Keene (London, ca. 1680; ideal for Purcell), with skunk-tail sharps and a substantial string length in the bass. An anonymous 1708 has marquetry decor and a broken short octave. A ca. 1750 John Hitchcock spinet is larger yet, with a full five-octave compass. Tradition places it briefly in Handel's possession.

The clavichords are also associated with famous names: a 1794 by the Viennese Johann Bohak is reputed to have belonged to Haydn. Unfortunately, in restoration attempts in the 1830s and again in 1912, its original bridge, tangents, and tuning pins were removed. A copy of a Hass clavichord was made in 1894 for Sir George Grove (of *Grove's Dictionary* fame) by Arnold Dolmetsch. It is a tribute to the work of that pioneer and a fascinating insight into his first revival replicas. Now over a century old, it is a historic document in its own right.

Viennese pianos are represented by a small anonymous ca. 1760 square and a large, six-octave Jacob Bertsche grand of 1821. The latter, a recent accession to the collection, has five pedals: damper, keyboard shift, two moderators, and bassoon. In excellent condition, it aptly serves for the Viennese literature and composers of the late Classic and early Romantic periods.

Both horizontal and vertical English grands are displayed, as are early squares. An imposing and sumptuously veneered 1799 FF–c⁴ Broadwood grand is triple-strung throughout, with leathered hammers and two pedals on the front legs of its trestle stand. A big 1825 Broadwood cabinet piano

1821 piano by Jacob Bertsche

is a type which, along with squares, was eventually superseded by more conventional upright console designs later in the century. The long-sticker vertical action, albeit cleverly designed, feels neither like a grand nor the later uprights.

English squares are represented by an 1824 Clementi and a ca. 1840 Collard & Collard, the successor to Clementi & Co. Such modest pianos were staples in Victorian parlors in Europe, as well as in European-emigré areas such as the United States, Canada, and Australia. Though they lacked the power and solidity of grands, they played a major role in the post-aristocratic cultivation of keyboard music, and their place in collections is amply justified by their historical significance.

In 1984 the museum published a fifteen-page *Guide to the Collection* by Elizabeth Wells, citing holdings not only in keyboard, but also in wind, stringed, and non-European instruments.

National Collection of Musical Instruments, Victoria and Albert Museum

Address: Cromwell Road, South Kensington, London SW7 2RL; hours: 10 A.M.–5:45 P.M. daily; telephone: 0171 938 8279; fax: 0171 938 8341.

Formerly known as the South Kensington Museum, the Victoria and Albert, or the V & A, as it is popularly known, has some extraordinary holdings. Under its earlier name, the museum acquired its first instruments from the Great Exhibition of 1851, where plucked keyboards were demonstrated as a foil to the presumed technological superiority of the mid-century piano. It also received keyboards from the private assemblage of the Victorian-era musicologist Carl Engel, a German-born scholar living in England. The institution's holdings have doubled since Engel's death in 1882.

The V & A is primarily concerned with the decorative arts, and from its beginnings it has tended to emphasize instruments with important visual elements. Hence, many of its keyboard holdings have especially elaborate decor, as well as intrinsic organological interest and historical significance. The museum owns more than fifty stringed keyboards: ten virginals, six spinets, and ten harpsichords in the plucked family; two clavichords; seven square pianos; nine verticals; seven grands; and a claviorganum. Some instruments have been restored, and a few have been recorded; but much of the collection is behind glass or otherwise protected, and thus rarely heard.

One of two sixteenth-century Italian harpsichords, a 1521 Hieronymus Bononiensis ("Jerome of Bologna," despite having been made in Rome) was long considered the oldest dated extant Italian. (A slightly older one has recently been identified and described by Denzil Wraight, in "Vincentius and the Earliest Harpsichords," *Early Music* 14/4 [1986], pp. 534–538.) In a leathered case of tooled and gilt strapwork designs, this instrument seems more impressive than its modest resources would imply. Its present 2×8′ disposition and C/E–d^3 compass have misled many into assuming a 250-year Italian tradition of 2×8′, four-octave brass-strung designs; but more recent scholarship has revealed that the original disposition was 1×8′, with a probable compass of C/E–f^3. During the Baroque era there was a modernization which included additional internal bracing, a second 8′, new jacks, a new keyboard, a new scaling, a new pitch level, and probably a change from iron to brass strings. The lives of many such old instruments were similarly extended; indeed, their survival into our museums was made more likely by the rebuilding process.

The other Italian is a somewhat larger 1574 inner-outer single by Giovanni Antonio Baffo of Venice. Its most arresting feature is a lid painting resembling the ceilings of Venetian palaces, with colorful grotesques on a white background centered on an "Apollo and the Muses." The exterior of the outer case is lavishly decorated in gilt moresques, with ivory buttons outlining the inner. Fine veneers and inlays of various woods on the interior of the inner case also contribute to its appearance. Once 1×8′, 1×4′ with a C/E–f^3 compass, the 4′ was later replaced by a second 8′ and the present typically Baroque GG/BB–c^3 compass was installed. Presumably, pitch levels and string materials were changed, too. The tail was probably mitered, as in most early Italians, but it has been shortened and squared off. Howard Schott, author of the latest catalog of the collection, notes that despite repeated rebuilding, Baffo's original jacks and guides still fit flawlessly.

Another sixteenth-century instrument, the harpsichord part of a 1579 claviorganum, was built not in Italy but in England, by Lodewyk Theewes (alternately rendered as Theeuwes, Thewes, Tyves, or Teeus, and apparently pronounced either "Taves," as in *caves*, or "Tayus" as in *Deus*), a Flemish builder working in London. The earliest-known harpsichord made in England, it may have influenced the subsequent course of building there. It is the oldest-known three-rank 2×8, 1×4′, and certain of its characteristics indicate practices discontinued by later eras. Sitting atop a large ornate organ chest, it embodies many curious traits: First, the case is made of oak, a wood not normally used in the Flemish or Italian traditions, but common in later English instruments and possibly pointing to an earlier, unknown English practice. Second, unlike the short-octave convention of Flemish and Italian building, it has a chromatic C–c³ range. Third, it has three sets of strings, 2×8′, 1×4′, a disposition that was common in the later seventeenth century and in the eighteenth but was unusual in the sixteenth. Fourth, one of its 8′ choirs seems to have had an "arpichordum" device to alter tone color in the manner of Antwerp muselars. Fifth, like a small number of Italian harpsichords (and at least two Germans: the 1537 Hans Müller in Rome, and a ca. 1600 anonyme in private ownership), its upper jack guides are fixed mortises cut directly into the soundboard, which is extended to cover a narrow wrestplank, allowing the nut to sit on a freely vibrating portion of the soundboard. Some of these conclusions were drawn from scant surviving evidence, since the keyboard is missing, and only one sticker, one 4′ jack and parts of others, and a single pipe from the organ's (presumably) five ranks remain.

The museum's two Ruckerses have differing histories. The first, by Andreas the elder, is possibly from 1631, despite a "1651" prominently inked on the soundboard. Although it was built as a normal 1×8′, 1×4′ C/E–c³ single, it is now a two-manual 2×8′, 1×4′ with a compass of GG, AA–f³ (no GG-sharp). Certain obvious features, such as keyfront arcades of boxwood molding and the doglegged front 8′ jacks, point to an English *ravalement*; the keyboards, pinning, registers, and jacks all support that conclusion. The entire case has been repainted, and mottoes, possibly copied from the original ones on the block-printed papers, were placed on the lid and flap (the fallboard was lost in the nineteenth century). Much of the original soundboard painting is still intact; it is, in fact, a board of some renown, since gathered in a circle at the tail of the instrument are five monkeys making music (although they may date from the *ravalement*).

Like the 1631, the second Ruckers (Hans, 1639) was originally a 1×8′, 1×4′ single; but it was built with a fully chromatic C–d³ compass. It was probably intended for export to England, where chromatic keyboards were more in vogue. It was later converted to a 2×8′, 1×4′, with a GG, AA–d³ range without widening the case. The keyboard and stand were lost in an 1853 fire at the Kirkman piano factory, where it was probably used as a rental instrument. It was once Crown property during the reign of King George III, and its fire-damaged Rococo decor dates from his era.

The museum has a third "Ruckers." The year 1634 is prominently featured on the lid and soundboard, and the nameboard reads "Ioannes Ruckers Me Fecit Antverpiae"; but it is an English harpsichord, a good instrument whose unknown maker tried to simulate a rebuilt Ruckers double. Now redated ca. 1730, it is at Ham House, Petersham, by courtesy of the V & A.

A two-manual walnut harpsichord of ca. 1725 by Thomas Hitchcock the younger is readily identified by its badly cocked cheek. Its GG–g^3 five-octave compass is more common in English spinets than the FF–f^3 found on harpsichords, and its skunktail sharps, soundboard grain running at an angle rather than parallel to the spine, double-curved bentside, and interior veneering also remind one of spinets. Although it would be fallacious to assume that Hitchcock did not know the "proper" way to build a harpsichord, he was indeed a spinet maker, and this is his only extant harpsichord. It is an important document, representing English harpsichord building just prior to its transformation by Kirkman and Shudi. At one point the jacks and registers were replaced, it was given a lute register, and the shove coupler was replaced by a dog-leg action.

Two large late eighteenth-century London harpsichords by J. & A. Kirkman (1776) and Shudi & Broadwood (1782) please the eye with tasteful veneers and stringing in expensive woods. Both have lute stops, pedals, machines, and nags-head (Kirkman) or Venetian (Shudi & Broadwood) swells. The Kirkman has the normal FF, GG–f^3 (no FF-sharp), five-octave compass; but the Shudi & Broadwood is chromatic down to the "great C" (CC), a Shudi specialty. Since no music of the time calls for the extra low notes, they may have been intended to facilitate doubling left-hand lines in octaves, a practice specifically referred to in C. P. E. Bach's famous 1753 treatise, *Versuch über die wahre Art das Klavier zu spielen* (Essay on the True Art of Playing Keyboard Instruments).

The V & A's 1681 double by Vaudry, the only known instrument by a member of that family (and thought to be by Jean-Antoine), is a particularly stunning example of a seventeenth-century French harpsichord. The case is extravagantly decorated in red, black, and gold-silver-bronze chinoiserie; unfortunately, the interior of the lid was later poorly redone, ostensibly to harmonize with the decor in the chateau that housed it. Disposed 2×8', 1×4', it was at one time part of a claviorganum. Still visible on its two front spiral-turned stand legs are inside cutoffs to accommodate a pipe case; and a series of holes was made below the bottom manual to allow for the insertion of organ-action stickers. It had a lower-manual shove coupler, an important innovation in its day, but during a 1976 examination by restorer Derek Adlam, that manual was found nailed in place. In "Restoring the Vaudry," *Early Music* IV/3 (1976), pp. 255–265, Adlam describes, among other details, why the harpsichord was returned to its original compass of GG/BB–c^3. The Vaudry is another important

1681 harpsichord by Vaudry

document, again from a period and regional school not as well known as the earlier Flemish and eighteenth-century French traditions.

An exquisite 1786 2×8′ single by Pascal Taskin, notable for the narrow octave span of its keys, was perhaps intended for a child or a woman with a very small hand. Resting on a beautifully carved, gilt Louis XVI stand, the black exterior and salmon-pink interior of the case are banded in gold and adorned with breathtaking chinoiserie. The EE–f³ compass is typical of Taskin after 1780. The lowest string is enigmatic, since no repertoire requires it. Perhaps it was intended to improve the tone quality of the FF, and may also have been tuned down to CC or some another bass note.

The V & A has a number of ornate virginals, some unique in decor. An anonymous early sixteenth-century Italian polygonal inner-outer virginal was long ascribed to Giovanni Francesco Antegnati of Brescia; but since the nameboard bearing the signature does not appear to be original, that attribution is now in doubt. Considerably altered during its long lifetime, its compass was originally F, G, A–f³, with the low F-sharp and G-sharp lacking. In one rebuild, a C/E–f³ range increased the number of notes from forty-seven to fifty; a restoration in the 1960s reinstated the F–f³ keyboard and was able to include the two lowest accidentals as well, but now, with forty-nine notes, one jack mortise remains empty. Under the lowest octave of keys, there are slots for pull-downs to a former pedalboard. The geometric rose has been carved directly into the soundboard and is marked off by tiny ivory studs. The inside walls of the virginal are beautifully decorated with raised gold scrolls and birds on a blue background. The outer case and inside of the lid, though probably not original with this instrument, are spectacularly decorated with a white moresque pattern.

Another Italian inner-outer built at about the same time, a 1555 Annibale dei Rossi of Milan with a C/E–f³ compass, is even more ornate. The inner case walls, the nameboard, and the side panels created by the half-inset keyboard are skillfully carved in shallow relief. Elongated lozenges are inlaid into the top portion of the case front. Exquisitely carved miniature musicians take the place of scroll-sawn cheeks, and the lower end of the jackrail is held in the jaws of a fanciful beast. Leather pads on its key bottoms, to receive stickers, suggest that at one time the virginal was part of a claviorganum. Its outer case is lacking.

A virginal similar to those described above is inscribed "Marco Jadra, 1568" on the front of the jackrail; but in a 1965 restoration the name of Francesco of Brescia and the date 1569 were discovered inscribed on the bottom of the soundboard. It has been speculated that this could be the same Francesco Antegnati whose name spuriously appears on the anonymous virginal mentioned above and that he was a supplier to Jadra. This is one of the mysteries surrounding many of these lovely instruments for which we may never know the answer. But, Jadra or Antegnati, the virginal is beautifully executed. Its anterior face is elaborately decorated in painted arabesques on ebonized cypress, suggesting that when the instrument was opened, the outer case (now lacking) revealed the entire front portion of

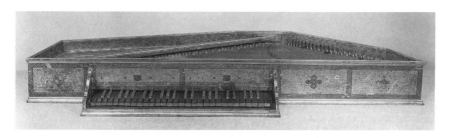

Anonymous 16th-century virginal (Queen Elizabeth's virginal)

the inner, rather than just the keywell area. Ebony moldings line the top and bottom of the case, with ivory stringing in the top. Ivory is also sandwiched between ebony panels in the scroll-sawn cheek brackets.

"Queen Elizabeth's Virginals," an anonymous, six-sided instrument from ca. 1570, is not a mother-and-child, as the plural name might suggest (the English fashion has long been to pluralize the word), but a normal Italian virginal. The ascription to ownership by Queen Elizabeth is unproven, but certainly credible, since the case bears both the Tudor arms and the emblem used by Anne Boleyn and Elizabeth I. The front and the interior walls of this sumptuous instrument are decorated in black, gold, red, and blue moresques, and the sharps are delicately inlaid with silver, ivory, and ebony. The compass is now GG/BB–c^3, but originally it was probably C–c^3, d^3, without the top c-sharp^3. Its outer case, believed to date from about a century later, is no less lavish: the interior is lined with silk and the exterior is covered with red velvet, except for the floral and vine patterns on the surfaces seen when the case is opened. Queen Elizabeth was reputed to have been a fine virginalist; this instrument would doubtless have been worthy of her.

A unique 1568 Flemish virginal is built into a walnut case resembling a heavy chest with in-curving sides. It is unsigned but bears the coat of arms of the Duke of Cleves, otherwise known as William the Rich—an appropriate sobriquet for one who owned so opulent an instrument. Its exterior is richly carved in various motifs, mainly musical ones. Mottoes grace the instrument's base, fallboard, jackrail, and lid, and the soundboard still has its painting. Its compass, now A–f^3, was almost certainly the usual Flemish C/E–c^3 at the time of its construction. Unlike most Flemish virginals, its recessed keyboard is in the middle of the case, rather than to the left or right, a feature found on no extant Ruckers virginals and only one other Flemish example (by Johannes Grouwels, in the Musée Instru-

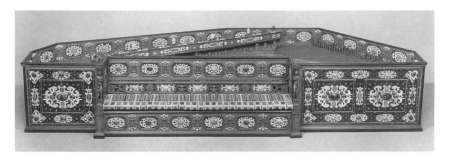

1577 virginal by Annibale dei Rossi

mental in Brussels). In addition to mottoes, its lid shows gold strapwork on a blue ground, with a medallion of the familiar "Orpheus charming the beasts" in the center. Guarding the keyboard at either end are fierce lion heads. Probably intended for table-top use, the virginal rests on four stubby legs.

Two other virginals are visual *tours de force*, among the most spectacular to be seen anywhere. The first, a polygonal inner by Annibale dei Rossi, Milan, 1577, is inlaid with more than 1,900 precious stones—emeralds, sapphires, rubies, lapis lazuli, pearls, turquoises, etc.—on every surface, including the half-inset keyboard itself. As with Rossi's 1551 virginal described above, the left end of the jackrail rests in a beastly maw. Although the instrument functions as a musical object, its use in that regard was probably always overwhelmed by the opulence of the decor. Words mean little in describing this instrument—it must be seen to be appreciated.

The same might be said of "The Glass Virginal," an anonymous ca. 1600 northern European (Flemish?) spinett-virginal. Although similarly extravagant, it is quite different: colorful metal and glass fantasies decorate the front, keyboard, interior, and lid, whose eighteen panels depict scenes from Ovid's *Metamorphoses*. There are many other virginals whose adornments have placed them in the category of *objets d'art*, indicating how highly smaller oblong instruments were valued during the late Renaissance, but these two triumphs of decorators' art are in a class of their own.

However curious the concept of playing only at 4′ pitch may seem now, *ottavini*, or octave instruments, were extremely popular, particularly in Italy. The V & A has two nice ones. The earlier is a tiny ca. 1600 anonymous Italian inner-outer triangular spinet, with a geometric rose and two gilded figures for cheeks. The nameboard is delicately decorated with knights and ladies in gold on black, in what appears to be an imitation

Anonymous 16th-century octave spinet

of late Medieval style. The cloth-lined outer case has a vivid lid painting of Arion and the dolphins, and a lid flap of *putti* musicians and dancing maenads. The spinet is a little gem, and that was the intention of its builder and decorator.

The second *ottavino* is a ca. 1625 anonymous German virginal, a true miniature, with a three-octave compass and a keyboard span too small for an adult hand. It was a desk as well as an instrument: a compartment in the lid and a secret drawer below the keyboard could house writing materials. Its silverwork and ornaments suggest that it was designed more for display than playing, a concept akin to the Bidermann wind-up spinet in Nuremberg's Germanisches Nationalmuseum, which it resembles. It is a charming reminder of a time that prized such well-executed dual-purpose curios.

Two later virginals of English origin have typical oak cases, inset keyboards, coffered lids with pastoral scenes on their undersides, soundboard paintings, and handsome embossed and gilt paper decoration. The 1642 Thomas White from London and the 1655 John Loosemore from Exeter demonstrate that, even during the English Civil War and the Cromwellian interregnum between Charles I and II, such instruments continued to be made and enjoyed.

Also of oak, but conspicuously plain in its decoration, a late seventeenth-century bentside spinet by John Player of London heralds the end of the virginals' heyday. A new design—with a single bridge, the longest strings at the rear, and the tuning pins and wrestplank at the front— brought to England about mid-century, lasted for nearly 150 years. The V & A's Player has a GG/BB–c^3 compass with broken short octave.

Four later, larger bentside spinets, although splendidly veneered and with wider compasses (typically GG–g^3) and elegant keyboards, are essentially similar. They are by Londoners Thomas Hitchcock (1740), John Crang (1758), Baker Harris (1770), and Joseph Mahoon (1771). A spinet on a trestle stand with a GG/BB–d^3 compass by Henry Hill, London, 1750, is scaled for 4′ pitch. Its ivory naturals, ebony sharps, and walnut veneer with sycamore stringing lend an air of quiet dignity to its miniature form; but it is in quite another world from the miniatures discussed earlier.

The V & A has only two clavichords. A large Barthold Fritz, Brunswick, 1751, typically North German, has an extended compass of FF–a^3, which is wide for that date. Its twenty lowest notes are reinforced by 4′ strings. The case exterior and the fluted, tapered legs are painted light green, but this decoration is not original. The lid is graced with a striking blue monochromatic hunting scene. A much smaller fretted clavichord is signed by "Peter Hicks," of whom nothing is known beyond this artifact. Another "mystery instrument," it stems from the latter part of the eighteenth century, when bentside spinets and early square pianos, not clavichords, were competing for the English public's attention and patronage. Since the tradition of English clavichord building is shadowy, and with this as the only known example, the Hicks is a rather doubtful anomaly. The well-made case and keyboard are in marked contrast to what appear to be amateurish soundboard and bridge repairs.

The museum's square pianos show a wide diversity of dates and types, and all but one are from London. A 1767 Zumpe, one of the very earliest by a leading member of the Apostles, signaled a new entrant for public favor among competing keyboard designs and innovations. Such simple instruments—double-strung, with a GG, AA–f^3 compass, hand stops for raising divided bass and treble dampers, and a primitive "English single-action"—became well established in Britain. Refinements such as widened compasses and pedals rather than hand stops came later.

Truly handsome decor, mainly in externally visible woods, may be seen in a 1773 Pohlmann, a ca. 1780 Ganer, a ca. 1795 Longman & Broderip, a 1801 Broadwood, a ca. 1815 Florez, and a ca. 1820 Clementi. Such concern for visual detail may be compared to that lavished on rectangular virginals and spinets from an earlier era. The 1801 Broadwood, with the piano itself as a "drawer" of a drop-leaf table, is at Ham House. The highly decorated square by the Madrid builder Florez, with gilt and brass accents for its exotic, sumptuous woods, no longer has its damper pedal but is otherwise intact. Florez's decoration was probably influenced by the famous Broadwood grand in Boston's Museum of Fine Arts, whose case was designed by Thomas Sheridan. It was commissioned in 1796 by the prime minister of Spain who is said to have presented it to his queen.

Of the museum's early grand pianos, far and away the most spectacular is a Georg Haschka (Vienna, c. 1815–20). Four atlantes bearing globes support the gilt Empire-style case; the lid is decorated with a dramatic "Samson and the Lion"; a back-curving nameboard depicts a bucolic Apollo; and eight pedals, cast as lion's paws, project from an ebony and gold lion's-mask lyre, supported by an ebony bow attached to the front legs. Its flamboyant decor and numerous color-altering stops may seem overdone to us, but in its time it was surely considered a masterpiece.

Two look-alike early Romantic London grands are a Thomas Tomkison (ca. 1815–20) and a William Stodart (ca. 1820). Both have compasses of CC–c^4, are nicely veneered, and were fitted with *una corda* and damper pedals. Their conservative English decor contrasts sharply with the Viennese Haschka.

An 1820 Van der Does giraffe (Amsterdam) and an anonymous 1840 English Euphonicon each emphasize the vertical harp configuration of the string band, but in different ways. In the giraffe the strings are enclosed by the case, which terminates at the upper left in the usual scroll; and a floor-to-scroll column, with a carved gilded lyre on its base, stands free of the case and reinforces the classical allusion. Following Viennese precedents, it has six pedals: bassoon, drum, damper, bells, *due corde*, and *una corda*. The Euphonicon, on the other hand, has three distinct components: in front is the console with the keyboard; behind that and to the left is the vertical harp, its strings exposed on an open cast-iron frame; and behind that, three soundboxes. It has two pedals—damper and keyboard shift.

There are three Collard & Collard verticals: a ca. 1840 upright grand,

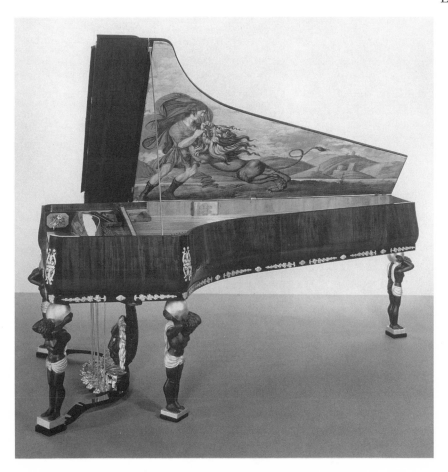

Ca. 1815–20 piano by Georg Haschka

a large upright console from between 1855 and 1875, and another console from ca. 1865. The grand's compass is CC–f^4, the two uprights are seven octaves, AAA–a^4. These three, along with a ca. 1860 Priestley, are especially noteworthy for their decor. The upper part of the ca. 1840 is flanked by columns topped with Corinthian capitals; the 1855–75 is a symphony of Victorian "gingerbread"; the design of the ca. 1865 has been attributed to Charles Bevan, who favored a neo-Gothic architectural style; and the Priestley was decorated in late-medieval style by the owner, artist Edward Burne-Jones.

A small 1867 Broadwood upright console was formerly aboard the royal yacht, the *Victoria and Albert*. There are also large late-Romantic grands:

Ca. 1820 giraffe piano by Corneille Charles Emanuel van der Does

a Wornum down-striker from ca. 1870, and two by Broadwood from ca. 1882 and 1883, again seemingly chosen as much for their decorative as their musical significance. A 1907 oak piano by Broadwood was made to harmonize in an oak drawing room in Jacobean style.

Two impressive exteriors grace otherwise normal later uprights: On a 1903 Broadwood, the keyboard is enclosed by the case doors and there is a modernist checkered pattern on the underside of the lid. In contrast, a quiet 1906 Römhildt has a case designed by Art Nouveau leader Henry van de Velde.

Recent catalogues of this collection include Raymond Russell's 1968 *Victoria and Albert Museum, Catalogue of Musical Instruments, Volume I: Keyboard Instruments*, and an updated survey with the same title by Howard Schott, 1985. James Yorke authored a somewhat less formal picture book, with eight color plates, entitled *Keyboard Instruments at the Victoria and Albert Museum*, first published in 1986. There is also an inexpensive 1959 "Small Picture Book No. 48" by Raymond Russell, once sold at the museum with the title *Victoria and Albert Museum, Early Keyboard Instruments*. More general in content, but containing a fair number of pictures of the keyboards, is Peter Thornton's *Victoria and Albert Museum, Musical Instruments as Works of Art* (1968; second edition, 1982). These books have been published either by the museum or by Her Majesty's Stationery Office, London.

OXFORD

Bate Collection of Historical Instruments

Address: Faculty of Music, University of Oxford, St. Aldate's, Oxford OX1 1DB; Hours: Monday to Friday, 2 P.M.–5 P.M.; telephone: 01865 276 139; fax: 01865 276 128.

Founded in the twelfth century by a group of scholars and monks, Oxford University today comprises thirty-seven colleges and includes such famed institutions as the Bodleian Library and the Ashmolean Museum. The city itself, near Shakespeare's Stratford upon Avon, is no less historic. Located in the Faculty of Music, The Bate Collection of Musical Instruments was named for Philip Bate, a twentieth-century collector of wind instruments and the author of some popular organological books. Having enjoyed the pleasures of collecting most of his adult life, in his senior years Bate gave all his instruments to Oxford University. Once established, the collection began to expand; and while it was traditionally renowned for its woodwinds, brass, and percussion holdings, recent accessions, particularly those from the Michael Thomas collection, have included some interesting and important antique stringed keyboards.

Many museums have historical replicas, and for the most part we have either referred to them in passing or omitted mention of them altogether—this is, after all, a book about *early* keyboard instruments; but the Bate Collection has reconstructions of two clavichords of such early design that no survivors exist. The first is found in a manuscript on musical instruments dating from ca. 1440 by the Burgundian astronomer and physician Henri Arnault de Zwolle. Arnault described and provided drawings for several stringed and keyboard instruments, including the lute, harpsichord, organ, and clavichord. While not problem-free, his drawings are sufficiently detailed so that the instruments can be replicated by a knowledgeable builder. Arnault's clavichord drawing has been reproduced in a number of sources, but perhaps the one most accessible to readers of this book may be in Edmund A. Bowles, "A Checklist of Fifteenth-Century Representations of Stringed Keyboard Instruments," in *Keyboard Instruments: Studies in Keyboard Organology, 1500–1800*, edited by Edwin M. Ripin (Edinburgh: Edinburgh University Press, 1971; Dover paperback reprint, 1977), pp. 11–18 (plate 4). This clavichord is somewhat different from almost all those described in these pages, with the exception of the earliest extant examples, such as those in Leipzig's Musikinstrumenten-Museum from a century later. Arnault's three-octave clavichord, calling for only nine courses of strings (although in the Bate reconstruction a tenth is presumed), is heavily fretted, and the soundboard extends the full length of the case. Unlike the Leipzig examples, it has a single high bridge. Judging from the iconographical evidence, this clavichord must have been a successful and common design. The replica makes a convincing sound, quite appropriate for literature from sources such as the fifteenth-century Faenza Codex.

The second reconstruction is a somewhat larger clavichord based on a ca. 1480 *intarsia* in the study of the Duke Federigo da Montefeltro, in his palace at Urbino. As famed as the Arnault instrument, this one has seventeen pairs of strings and a compass of F–f^3 (no F-sharp or G-sharp, and the lowest five notes are fret-free); otherwise, its design resembles Arnault's. Again, the *intarsia* has been widely pictured, and one is in the Bowles article, plate 14. A comparison of this and the Arnault clavichord can be found in Angelo Mondino, "The Intarsia of Urbino," in *De Clavicordio: Proceedings of the International Clavichord Symposium, Magnano, 1993*, edited by Bernard Brauchli et al. (Torino: Istituto per i Beni Musicali in Piemonte, 1994), pp. 49–55 and Plates 1–6 on pp. v–viii.

Two later unfretted clavichords are antiques: a large FF–f³ Hieronymus Hass, Hamburg, 1743, and a five-and-a-half-octave anonyme (FF–c⁴) from ca. 1810. The Hass has its usual lavish decor: ebony and ivory skunk-tail sharps; ebony, ivory, tortoise shell, and wood veneer on the tool-box cover; natural wood interior and painted exterior; and a lid painting. The twenty-two notes have a set of 4′ strings. The other instrument, probably from central Germany or Bohemia, is less elegant in decor but robust in tone.

Arnold Dolmetsch is represented by his Opus 1, dated 1894—a significant reminder of a second vigorous clavichord tradition, our own revival of historical keyboards. Unfortunately, its twisted case is unrestorable.

Of the harpsichords, the least elaborate is perhaps the most important. Made by William Smith of London, of whom little else is known, this ca. 1720 five-octave GG–g³, 2×8′ single is remarkably similar to one partially depicted in a 1731 portrait of Handel by Philippe Mercier. Long unknown, the instrument's recent bequest to the Bate Collection was the basis for a detailed article by Michael Cole, "A Handel Harpsichord," *Early Music* 21/1 (February, 1993), pp. 99–109. Each of the 8′s has a separate stop lever protruding through the nameboard; but without 4′, buff, or lute, the instrument relies on inherent color variety and the player's artistry, rather than "devices," for its musical effect. The quiet dignity of its walnut and sycamore veneers is relieved only by the keyboard's distinctive skunk-tail sharps. The first five of the 1720 Suites by Handel have been recorded on it.

Another early London harpsichord, perhaps as important as the Smith, is a 1700 Joseph Tisseran 2×8′, 1×4′ double, GG/BB–d³; one of its solid ivory sharps is split, the lowest E-flat. Originally fitted with a shove coupler, the second 8′ rank was later doglegged. The 4′ register is at the rear, behind the 8′s, in English fashion. The instrument has a soundboard painting, which is unusual for English harpsichords (but not for virginals), and the catalog notes that it may have been painted by the decorator who did the Coston in Edinburgh's Russell Collection. The keywell is also colorfully decorated. The imitation paneling on the case is not original, and the trestle stand, which dates from a later time, is painted to match it.

Little is known of Tisseran save this sole exemplar; but it is the earliest surviving two-manual harpsichord of English make, showing more similarity to instruments of the International School than to the harpsichords soon to be built by Hermann Tabel and his followers. Tabel was an expatriate thought to have been born in Flanders and trained in the Couchet shop in Antwerp. He established a new style of harpsichord building in London, superseding the models represented by Smith and Tisseran.

Burkat Shudi, a Swiss-born joiner, came to London, found work with Tabel, and began building harpsichords. He and Kirkman (who later also worked for Tabel) carried on the Flanders-based Tabel style, quickly replacing the older English school.

The Bate has a 1781 Shudi & Broadwood with all the accoutrements—lute, buff, machine, and Venetian swell. As usual, the case is handsomely veneered, in mahogany with the keywell in walnut burl. Unfortunately, the lute register is fixed in its gap; over the years the string tension has pulled the wrestplank forward, narrowing the aperture in which it once easily moved. There are several smaller English instruments: spinets by Benjamin Slade (ca. 1710–15), Thomas Hitchcock (ca. 1725–30), John Harrison (1749), and Baker Harris (1776). All but the Slade have five-octave compasses. The leather plectra on the Harris are thought by the museum to be original.

A somewhat mysterious ca. 1670 2×8′, 1×4′ double, probably of Franco-Flemish origin, has a chromatic compass of GG–c^3; its GG-sharp was originally lacking, but an early eighteenth-century *ravalement* added it by shifting the keyboard one step to the left and providing extra c^3 strings and keys. Since the soundboard painter has been identified as the same artist who decorated for the Parisian builder Richard at about that time, its builder may have been a Flemish emigré working in Paris. An extensive restoration was recently performed, and the harpsichord is now fitted with a new 4′ bridge, jacks with crow quills, registers, guides, and strings.

Larger, later, and unquestionably Parisian, is a 1750 Jean Goermans double with typical 2×8′, 1×4′ disposition and full five-octave compass (originally FF–e^3, but the top key and strings were added by narrowing the right cheek block). A buff stop mutes the front 8′ (on the upper manual). A lovely instrument, it has a blue and red decor, a gilt cast-metal rose with the builder's initials, a Louis XV stand, and an elegant soundboard painting. It has been restored to fine condition, and plays and sounds beautifully.

The Bate's four pianos are all squares with five-octave, FF–f^3 compasses: an Adam Beyer of 1779, a John Bland from ca. 1790–95, and a ca. 1790 Longman & Broderip. The Beyer is remarkably well preserved, needing little modern restoration. Three hand stops control split dampers and buff, and a pedal lifts and lowers the right portion of the lid for dynamic effects. There is an original dust cover of thin spruce, and its presence makes a discernable tonal difference. The Longman & Broderip features a double action, more sophisticated than the previous single types (John Geib, the inventor of that action, also made pianos for Longman & Broderip). This instrument also has a dust cover. The two six-octave (FF–f^4) nineteenth-century squares have noteworthy features. An 1818 Astor & Horwood, with a mahogany case, ormolu mounts, satinwood nameboard, painted dust cover, and fretwork panels, is fairly ornate. A large, heavy 1840 Broadwood has a projecting, rather than inset, keyboard. The catalog (p. 21) notes that "the damping is light enough to allow for good legato without pedalling in music such as Field's or Chopin's."

A pamphlet by Jeremy Montagu, *Bate Collection, Demi-Catalogue No. 1: Keyboard Instruments* (Oxford: Bate Collection of Musical Instruments, 1993), 23 pp., is detailed and informative.

Glossary

ACTION. Almost all grand piano actions derive from two basic types. The earlier, which was quite sophisticated, was devised by Cristofori and was also used by Silbermann and builders in Iberia. It separated the key and the hammer, with the latter mounted on a rail. It included an intermediate lever to increase the mechanical advantage of the finger, and an escapement—a means of allowing the hammer to fall away after striking the strings. Subsequent English and French actions were variations on Cristofori's invention, often simplified, as in square pianos, but usually with a great deal more complexity and adjustability, although sometimes without the intermediate lever. The modern grand action derives from this type.

The other action, and the only one in general use not based on the Cristofori model, was the Viennese (also called German), in which the hammer and its shank, facing toward the player, were hinged to the key itself. Escapement was provided for by a little lever that caught a beak on the hammer shank and set the hammer into motion when the key was depressed. Viennese actions were still available on some Austro-German pianos into the early years of the twentieth century.

ACTION GAP. In a harpsichord or grand piano, the space between the wrestplank and the bellyrail. The jacks occupy that space in a harpsichord, and the hammers and dampers in a piano.

AGRAFFE. *See* Down-striking action

ARCADE. A thin, ornamental piece of wood, ivory, or other material glued to the front of a key. Technically, it is only an arcade if it has a series of semicircles incised into its face; however, we have used the term more loosely, to refer to any sort of ornamental treatment to a key front, whether semicircular or not.

ARPICHORDIUM STOP. Found almost exclusively on Flemish Muselars, this stop consists of a narrow batten next to the straight (i.e., bass) portion of the right bridge, on which are mounted some soft metal staples. When the rail is moved forward the staples bear lightly against the bass strings, producing a metallic buzz when those strings are sounded. The term is thought to derive from the sound of the Renaissance harp, which used protrusions called brays that contacted the strings and produced the buzz.

ATLANTES. *See* Caryatid

BACKCHECK. *See* Check

BASSOON STOP. A device, usually pedal-operated, found on Viennese pianos from about 1790 to 1820. A bar covered with parchment or paper with cloth over it is suspended over the bass strings. When the bar is lowered, the strings buzz lightly against the parchment. While the resulting sound could be considered attractive, and useful in at least some musical circumstances, only by a stretch of the imagination could it be thought to resemble a bassoon.

BENTSIDE. The section of a harpsichord or piano between the tail and the cheek. Normally, at least part of its length is a portion of an arc.

BENTSIDE SPINET. *See* Spinet

BOMBÉ. Having an outward-swelling curve.

BOOK-MATCHED. Veneer panels are stacked as they come off the saw, and if they are glued to a substrate in this fashion the grain pattern repeats itself every panel. But if every other panel is flipped over, like pages in a book, then each pair reflects the pattern from the line of their joint.

BOX GUIDE. A fairly thick guide, slotted for the jacks which it carries, used mainly in Italian plucked keyboards, seventeenth- and some eighteenth-century German harpsichords, and English bentside spinets. The usual northern system of supporting jacks consisted of thin upper and lower guides.

BRIDGE. In a harpsichord or piano, the long, slender, shaped piece of wood attached to the soundboard whose purpose is to transfer the vibration of the strings to the soundboard. The sounding lengths of the strings are determined by the positions of the bridges and nuts. An instrument with one or two sets of 8′ strings normally has one bridge and one nut; but if a 4′ set of strings is present, another bridge and nut is required. The same holds true for a set of 2′ or 16′ strings. *See* Nut

BROKEN SHORT OCTAVE. *See* Short octave; Split sharps

BUFF STOP. A thin wooden batten set just behind the nut of a harpsichord or piano. Small pieces of leather or felt, one for each string, are glued to its surface. When the batten is moved the "buffs" contact the strings, muting them and producing a pizzicato effect. In England the stop is usually referred to as the "harp stop." Confusingly, the improper term "lute stop" is often used for this tone-altering device, perhaps because of the French (jeu de luth) and German (Lautenzug) equivalents. Ironically, the buff stop resembles the sound of neither a harp nor a lute. *See* Lute stop

CABINET PIANO. An upside-down vertical piano. The external form is a symmetrical, rectangular cabinet starting at floor level. The front usually has silk-covered doors concealing the soundboard and strings.

CABRIOLE. A gracefully curved leg shape, swelling out and then back, and culminating in an ornamental foot.

CAPO TASTO. *See* Down-striking action

CARTOUCHE. An ornamental enframement of some sort, into which may be placed inscriptions, armorial symbols, etc.

CARYATID. A vertical draped female figure, used in place of, or as part of, a column or support. A similarly clad male figure is an atlantes.

CHECK. A device to catch a piano hammer after it has struck the string, preventing it from rebounding. Also known as backcheck.

CHINOISERIE. A decorative effect imitating Chinese painting in an imaginative way, usually depicting Asians in a pseudo-Chinese setting, often playing Western instruments. Although chinoiserie was mostly restricted to France in the seventeenth century, by the next century it had become a universal decorative effect on wooden furniture. The lacquering technique often used in applying chinoiserie was called japanning.

CHROMATIC BARS. *See* Short octave

CLAVECIN BRISÉ. A traveling harpsichord that folds up into a box the size of a large suitcase, supposedly invented by the Frenchman Jean Marius at the beginning of the eighteenth century.

CLAVICYTHERIUM. An upright harpsichord in which all but the keyboard of a normal wing-shaped grand is transposed to an upright position.

CLAVIORGANUM. A combined harpsichord and organ, either in the same case or with the harpsichord placed on top of the organ. It is usually possible to play either of the instruments alone or both together. Handel is said to have favored the combination, and one could see its usefulness in accompanying oratorios and other theater works. *See* Organized Piano

COCKED CHEEK. A condition caused by the failure of the cheek-to-bentside joint of a harpsichord or early piano. The wrestplank is rotated up and into the gap, twisting up the cheek. English harpsichords and early pianos were particularly prone to it.

DÉCOUPAGE. Paper cutouts applied to a surface for decorative purposes. In Italy this practice was known as *arte povera* (poor-man's art).

DISPOSITION. The resources of a keyboard instrument. One element of disposition concerns the number of string choirs; thus, a harpsichord disposed 2×8′, 1×4′ has two sets of strings at normal pitch and one set an octave higher. Another element of disposition includes tone-altering devices, such as a harpsichord's buff stop or lute stop, and a piano's moderator or *una corda*.

DOWN-STRIKING ACTION. An action in which the hammer blow is delivered from above, rather than from below the string. It was patented in 1823 by Johann Baptist Streicher, the son and partner of Nannette Stein, but French and English were developed as well. In the early piano, the hammer blow tended to drive the string up, off the nut. On two pianos by Cristofori that survive, he counteracted this force by putting the nut (and hence the strings) underneath the wrestplank, rather than in its usual position on top. Accordingly, the hammer blow drove the strings *into*, rather than *off*, the nut. All the extant Silbermann pianos were built with this "inverted wrestplank." Similarly, the Streichers' down-striking action was meant to assure that the blow of the hammer would drive the string *onto* the nut, since it came from above. (As a bonus, it also removed the structural weakness resulting from the need for an action gap in the case.) The *capo tasto* (a metal bar pressing on the strings from above) and the *agraffe* (a metal stud with one or more holes in it through which the strings pass), which were invented about the same time, ultimately proved to be more appropriate ways of solving the string-nut problem.

A down-striking piano is a strange-looking instrument, with the section containing the string band at a conspicuously lower level than the action.

DUST COVER. Many early nineteenth-century pianos came with a thin soundboard-shaped, removable wood plate that sat on a few small blocks attached to the insides of the case, effectively hiding the soundboard and string band from view. Sometimes called a "second soundboard," its primary function was to homogenize the instrument's tone in the confines of a drawing room, where listeners were exposed to the direct sound of the piano. Its secondary function was to keep dust off the soundboard. The dust cover is one of the most ephemeral pieces of equipment on early pianos, easily lost and almost as easily replaced.

ESCAPEMENT. *See* Action

EUPHONICON. Invented by John Steward of Wolverhampton, England, the Euphonicon is a cross between an upright console piano and a harp-piano, with hollow resonators in place of a soundboard. Its upright console is foremost, but the vertical cast-iron open harp and strings behind it are its most prominent features. Behind the harp are its three resonators; their graduated sizes are reminiscent of members of the cello family.

EXPANDING JACK RAIL. This feature is found mainly on seventeenth-century South German harpsichords. The width of the jack rail increases from treble to bass, like a thick wedge. Actually, the essential element is not the jackrail but the registers and the sets of jacks themselves. They are close to each other in the treble, but spread as they move to lower registers, and at the bass side of the instrument they are separated by several inches. Obviously, the gap also needs to be wedge-shaped in order to accommodate the expansion.

FALSE INNER-OUTER. *See* Inner-outer

FLOATING-PANEL LID. Floating-panel construction is often used in furniture to ensure the structural integrity of large surfaces. A panel is fitted into slots in the interior edges of the frame and "floats"; since it is not glued in, it is free to contract and expand with changes in temperature and humidity. Floating-panel lids are found on some harpsichords, clavichords, and fortepianos built in eighteenth- and nineteenth-century Germany.

FRETTED AND UNFRETTED CLAVICHORDS. Until the eighteenth century, clavichord tangents were arranged so that two, three, or sometimes even four notes could be played on a single unison set of strings (because of the larger distances involved in fretting lower strings, the lowest octave or so on such instruments was usually unfretted). It was not until the beginning of the eighteenth century that unfretted clavichords, in which every course of strings was excited by its own tangent, began to appear.

GAP SPACER. *See* Gap stretcher.

GAP STRETCHER. An iron brace, spanning the action gap in a piano, usually in the form of an inverted *U* or half-circle. It helped resist the tendency of the gap to close from the tension of the strings, thereby rotating the wrestplank and cocking the instrument's cheek. Historically, gap stretchers preceded tension bars. Harpsichords were not subject to the same tensions, but for the same reason often had gap spacers, small bars, usually of wood, placed between the wrestplank and bellyrail.

GEIGENWERK. *See* Streichklavier

GENOUILLÈRE. 1. French for knee lever. 2. *See* Machine stop

GIRAFFE PIANO. An upright piano in which the normal grand shape is transposed to a vertical position, in a manner similar to the clavicytherium. However, a large rounded scroll-like embellishment, extending beyond the line of the spine, is almost always superimposed on what would normally be the tail of the instrument. With some imagination the cabinet could be seen as the neck of a giraffe and the embellishment as its head.

GLASSICHORD. A small keyed percussion instrument in which glass rods, rather than strings, are struck by piano-like hammers. Glassichords were novelties usually combined with an item of furniture such as a table or sewing box.

GRISAILLE. A grayish, monochromatic painting of sculptural motifs.

HAND STOP. A lever which, when moved, adds or subtracts a register (such as an 8′ set of strings) or tone-altering device (such as a buff stop) to the sound. Hand stops are usually found on the wrestplank and often protrude through the nameboard. In square pianos they are often found in a box on one or both sides of the keyboard.

HOLLOW HAMMER HEAD. A piano hammer usually made by rolling up parchment or cardboard with glue, letting it dry, and cutting it into individual hollow hammer heads. Sometimes hollow rings of wood were used. The heads were usually covered with leather.

INNER-OUTER. The combination of a thin-case harpsichord, virginal, spinet, or clavichord placed in a protective, lidded outer case. An instrument of integral-case construction which nevertheless projects the illusion of an inner instrument in an outer case is called a false inner-outer. These modern terms, coined by Frank Hubbard, are so descriptive they have been universally adopted.

INTERMEDIATE LEVER. *See* Action

INTERNATIONAL SCHOOL. In the sixteenth and seventeenth centuries harpsichord building tended to follow either a northern, southern, or International School. Flemish harpsichords practically defined the northern school, and Italian harpsichords did the same for the southern. French, English, German, and Scandinavian instruments tended to follow the building practices of the International School, although each region defined it in its own way. In general, instruments influenced by the International style tended to have deeper-curved bentsides than northern harpsichords; case walls overlapping the bottom boards as in the Italian style; bentsides, tails, and cheeks thinner than the spine; painted soundboards; and geometric non-metallic roses. Their exteriors were usually of natural wood, sometimes decorated with marquetry or applied moldings.

JACK. On a plucked keyboard instrument, the slip of wood that sits on the end of a key. The upper parts of the jack consist of a tongue, which carries the plectrum, and one or two dampers.

JANISSARY STOP. In an attempt to imitate the sound of cymbals, triangle, and bass drum made popular by Turkish military bands (Janissary bands), eighteenth- and early nineteenth-century makers of Viennese and German pianos often fitted their instruments with Janissary stops. The mechanism typically consisted of three elements: a metal bar that dropped down on the bottom two or so octaves of bass strings ("cymbals"); a set of nested bells struck with metal rods ("triangle"); and an internal drum stick that struck the soundboard or part of the case ("bass drum"), all usually operated simultaneously by a pedal.

JANKO KEYBOARD. Invented by the Hungarian Paul von Janko in 1882, this strange typewriter-like keyboard has doubled key levers, each with three tiers of touch plates, arranged in a whole-tone scale. All scales can be fingered alike, and intervals of more than a twelfth can be played by an average hand. Janko's invention was adopted by several European and American builders, but in the end it suffered the same fate as the Streichers' down-striking action.

JUST CURVE. The curve of a bridge that is bent in such a way that the lengths of the strings are doubled for each descending octave. Practically all stringed keyboard instruments are justly curved, or nearly so, in the treble; but southern European harpsichords tend to extend that curve down to c. Accordingly, a long, narrow, deeply curved bentside, closely following the bend of the bridge, is a southern characteristic. A just curve is also known as an exponential or Pythagorean curve.

KNEES. Triangular in shape, knees are interior structural members of Italian and International-style plucked keyboard instruments and early pianos. Their purpose is to transfer the thrust of the instrument's walls to the bottom.

LUTE STOP. The nasal sound produced by a row of harpsichord jacks plucking as close to the nut as possible. This may be achieved by cutting a gap through the wrestplank ("cutting" is a figure of speech; the wrestplank is made of two pieces, with the gap for the lute stop jacks between them) in order to bring the jacks right up to the 8′ nut, or by placing a set of 8′ strings on a second 8′ nut placed close to the near set of jacks in a normal gap. The term is sometimes improperly applied to the buff stop. The German word for lute stop is *Nasal*. In English the terms lute, buff, and *peau de buffle* are often confused (*see* Buff stop; Lute stop; Machine stop).

LYING HARP. A variety of late eighteenth-century square piano with a bentside at the right (wrestplank) side of the case and a spine narrowing inward toward the left. Also known as a *recumbent harp* (in German, *liegende Harfe*), it was the particular speciality of Johann Matthäus Schmahl.

LYRE-PIANO. An upright piano in which the cabinet is given a lyre shape and decoration. It could be thought of as a modified pyramid piano.

MACHINE STOP. An expressive device found on late eighteenth-century English and French harpsichords. On English instruments it enabled the player to preset registers (on both manuals) other than the ones being used. When the pedal was depressed it took off the settings in use and substituted the preset ones. It was possible, for example, to go instantly from the sound of the full harpsichord to that of the lute stop by depressing the pedal quickly. Operating the pedal slowly, on the other hand, could withdraw the ranks one at a time, producing a credible *diminuendo*. Reversing the process resulted in a *crescendo*.

The French machine stop was somewhat different. It consisted of five, or more usually six, knee-operated pommels (*genouillères*) arrayed under the front of the harpsichord stand. Four of these controlled the lower 8′ and 4′ sets of jacks, the *peau de buffle* (an additional row of jacks quilled in soft buffalo leather), and the coupler. The fifth raised the *peau de buffle* jacks (presumably in order to get their weight off the keys and lighten the action). The sixth pommel operated like an English machine stop and was capable of both sudden changes in registration and convincing dynamic nuance.

MARQUETRY. A technique applied to the flat surfaces of furniture and musical instruments in which thin pieces of wood, shell, bone, and sometimes metals are glued to a surface, forming pictures, floral patterns, and other designs.

MODERATOR. A muting device found on Viennese fortepianos, consisting of a leather or felt strip mounted on a thin rail set just under the strings, cut so that individual tongues of material coincided with each unison. It was normally set back, out of the way of the hammers; but when pulled forward (by means of a knee lever, pedal, or hand stop), the moderator interposed the tongues between hammers and strings at the strike points. In effect, the strings were struck by "softer" hammers and produced a darker, veiled, somewhat muted sound. Indeed, the device was sometimes referred to as a mute.

MOTHER AND CHILD. *See* Virginal

MUSELAR. *See* Virginal

NAGS-HEAD SWELL. *See* Venetian swell

NON-ALIGNED DOUBLE. The two-manual harpsichords of the Ruckerses and Couchets had an upper keyboard at normal pitch with a C/E–c³ compass. The lower keyboard, with a C/E–f³ compass, was pitched a fourth lower. Striking a c on the upper manual produced that pitch, but a c on the lower was located three naturals to the left and produced a g; hence, the keyboards were not aligned, and the arrangement is often called a transposing keyboard. During *ravalement* non-aligned keyboards were discarded or rebuilt into aligned doubles.

NUT. Similar in cross section to the bridge, the nut is usually placed on the wrestplank. Its purpose is similar to that of the bridge, but rather than transfer vibrations to another part of the instrument, it reflects them back to the bridge. *See* Bridge

OGEE. A molding profile shaped in a reverse curve, like the letter *S*.

ORGANIZED PIANO. A piano and organ combined in the same case. In the nineteenth century they were built as home instruments, usually uniting a square piano with one or more sets of pipes or reeds.

OVERSTRINGING. *See* Straight stringing

PANELLED LID. *See* Floating-panel lid

PEAU DE BUFFLE. *See* Machine stop

PEDAL PIANO. Late eighteenth-century and early nineteenth-century Austro-German pianos were sometimes supplied with organ-like pedalboards that operated a separate set of hammers. Sometimes the pedal hammers struck the same strings as the keyboard hammers, providing a means of playing bass notes independently of the hands but not a downward extension of range. In another type the pedal hammers acted on a separate soundboard and set of strings, thereby allowing a downward extension of range. In yet a third type, a separate pedal division was placed on the floor, beneath a regular grand piano. This last variant drew favor from Mozart, Schumann (who wrote a series of studies for the pedal piano), and Mendelssohn and Liszt (both of whom owned pedal pianos).

PIANINO. *See* Upright console

PUTTI. The plural of *putto*, a young boy. Groups of dancing, lounging, and instrument-playing *putti* was a common decorative device, particularly on Italian instruments.

PYRAMID PIANO. An upright piano in which the cabinet is shaped like an elongated isosceles triangle—like a pyramid, but with its top cut off. The angled sides are usually straight, but sometimes they curved inward gently.

QUERFLÜGEL. A piano in the shape of a bentside spinet.

RAVALEMENT. The practice of rebuilding and enlarging Flemish harpsichords. Although the technique was practiced throughout Europe, it is particularly associated with the eighteenth-century French school.

REGISTER. 1.The treble, tenor, and bass regions of harpsichords and early pianos have inherently distinctive tonal qualities, often identified as registers. 2. The term is also applied to the tonal qualities derived from the point at which a harpsichord string is plucked (a phenomenon not unrelated to the treble, tenor, and bass registers). The closer-plucking set of jacks on a French double, for example, is known as the front 8′ register; the set of jacks plucking right next to the 8′ nut on an English harpsichord is called the lute stop, or the lute register. 3. The slotted wood batten in which the jacks ride is also known as a register, as well as a guide or slide.

ROSE (ROSETTE). A decorative device of no acoustical significance set into the soundboards of many harpsichords, clavichords, and some early pianos. The geometric roses on Italian and seventeenth-century French and South German harpsichords were inspired by Gothic church windows and made of parchment, cardboard, leather, or wood. The roses in Flemish and eighteenth-century French and English harpsichords often portrayed an angel playing a harp or an organetto, with the builder's initials worked into the design. These were made of metal— usually lead or a lead alloy—and gilded. *See* Upside-down wedding-cake rose

SCALE. In stringed keyboard instruments the scale is the sounding length of a particular string, from which the length of most of the other strings can be determined. Although there may not always be historical justification for doing so, today that string is generally agreed to be an octave above middle C (c^2). In harpsichords, southern scales tended to be short—around 10–11 inches and intended for brass stringing. Northern scales were longer, around 14 inches, intended for iron strings in all but the bass. With the development of high-tension steel music wire, modern piano scales are about 17 inches.

SHORT OCTAVE. A C/E short octave allows the apparent low E to be tuned to C. The F-sharp is tuned to D and the G-sharp is tuned to E. Thus, the bass has the diatonic notes C, D, E, F, G, and A. From B-flat on, the keyboard is chromatic. A later GG/BB short-octave tuning sets the apparent BB to GG, the C-sharp to AA, and the E-flat to either BB-flat or BB, depending on the musical requirements. From C up the notes are chromatic. *See* Split sharps. The term *chromatic bass* applies to what we understand as a "normal" keyboard; that is, bass notes without a short octave and with all the chromatics.

SOUNDING LENGTH. The portion of the string between bridge and nut that determines its pitch.

SPINET. 1. A square, triangular, or bent-sided harpsichord (the last known as the *bentside spinet*). In plan view, the strings slant upward from left to right, at a shallow angle to the keys. The bass strings are in the rear of the instrument, farthest from the player. The jacks operate in a register in the gap in front of the wrestplank, as in a grand harpsichord. 2. The term *spinett* was used by the Flemish for the form of the virginal plucking close to the left bridge (*see* Virginal). 3. The term *spineta* was used by the Italians to describe the polygonal virginal.

SPLIT SHARPS. 1. In short-octave tuning, one or both of the accidentals set to diatonic notes are sometimes split, front and back, into two keys, each with its own key lever, strings, and jacks. This allows both the short-octave note and the nominal note to be sounded. Thus, in a C/E short-octave split-sharp tuning, the F-sharp would be split into D and F-sharp, and the G-sharp into E and G-sharp. Such a keyboard is described as broken short octave. 2. Some seventeenth-century Italian keyboards were given one or more split sharps in the middle octaves, in order to play both mean-tone versions of an accidental. Accordingly, the front section of a split g-sharp would produce that note, while the back would sound an a-flat. The highest octave usually was not so treated, and the lowest octave was almost always occupied with the split sharps of the short-octave tuning. Instruments with such keyboards are often called enharmonic.

SQUARE PIANO. A piano in oblong—but not square!—shape. While the grand piano traces its ancestry to the harpsichord, the square developed from the clavichord. *See* Tafelklavier

STRAIGHT STRINGING. A type of piano stringing in which all the strings run parallel to the spine. Harpsichords and early pianos were strung in this way, but the system was superseded in the nineteenth century by overstringing, in which the bass bridge was placed in a more central position on the soundboard and its strings were angled over the others.

STREICHKLAVIER. A piano- or harpsichord-like family of keyboard instruments in which the tone is initiated and sustained by some bowlike mechanism. A *Streichklavier* is able to sustain sounds and modulate dynamics in the manner of string instruments, and so represents a sort of marriage of the violin family with the keyboard. Its invention is credited to Hans Heiden of Nuremberg around 1575, although Leonardo da Vinci and others toyed with the concept. Heiden called his version a *Geigenwerk*. An early twentieth-century upright-console adaptation by the Baudet firm was called the *Piano-quatuor*.

STRINGING. In inlay patterns, the thin bands of contrasting wood, metal, ivory, or other material used to separate borders from field veneers. An entirely different meaning, of course, refers to the metal strings of an instrument.

TAFELKLAVIER. Literally, "table piano"; eighteenth- and nineteenth-century square pianos that were small enough to be placed on a table. In Germanic usage the term can also apply to larger square pianos, even square grands. The expression also refers to a piano of any size intended to function secondarily as a table.

TANGENT. 1. The thin metal blade mounted on the end of a clavichord key. When the key is depressed the tangent strikes the string and at the same time acts as a nut, establishing the sounding length of the left end of the string. 2. The jack-like slip of wood that strikes the string in a tangent piano. *See* Tangentenflügel

TANGENTENFLÜGEL. A "tangent piano," in which the action consists of leather-topped harpsichord-like wooden jacks, or tangents, which sit on the ends of the keys and are thrown up against the strings. As alternatives to the Viennese action, they had the virtue of practically maintenance-free operation. The principal maker of *Tangentenflügeln* was the Regensburg firm of Späth & Schmahl. In almost every other respect their instruments resembled Viennese fortepianos.

TENSION BARS. From about 1820 to the acceptance of the cast-iron frame, piano makers used metal bars running from wrestplank to hitch plate to help the frame resist the pull of the strings. Tension bars were first used by English and French builders.

TREFOIL. A stylized ornament consisting of a triangle of shapes, usually semi-circles.

UPRIGHT CONSOLE PIANO. The familiar upright home piano whose strings run at a gentle angle inside the case. This instrument was invented fairly early in the nineteenth century in an attempt to make the instrument even more space-efficient than the tall pyramids, giraffes, cabinets pianos, and upright grands. It is the most common piano found in today's households, varying in height from about three to five feet. Other names for this piano are *pianino* and "cottage piano."

UPSIDE-DOWN WEDDING-CAKE ROSE. A symmetrical, layered rose of some depth, usually made of parchment or leather, that descends into the instrument. With a little imagination it could be thought to resemble a tiered wedding cake turned upside down and hollowed out. Such roses are found primarily on Italian and seventeenth-century French and South German harpsichords.

VENETIAN SWELL. An inner "lid" with louvered slats, fitted to late eighteenth-century English harpsichords. When it was raised with the main lid, it had no effect on the instrument's sound; but when it was lowered to a horizontal position just above the strings, the louvers could be opened and closed by a pedal. By itself, the swell elicited sounds we might describe as muffled and unmuffled; but convincing and fairly wide-ranging dynamic nuance was possible when it was used in conjunction with the machine stop.

The Venetian swell was used almost exclusively on harpsichords (it did appear on a few English grand pianos), but the nags-head swell—in which all or part of a hinged lid could be raised or lowered—was found on both harpsichords and square pianos.

VERNIS MARTIN. A decorative style in which the object is covered with gold leaf, then painted with colorful garlands and grotesques.

VIRGINAL. A rectangular or polygonal form of the harpsichord, with two bridges on the soundboard. In plan view, the strings run upward from right to left at a shallow angle to the key levers, with the jacks thrusting upward through the soundboard. The jackrail, running from left to right at a more acute angle, follows the jacks underneath it. The bass strings are closest to the player. Italian virginals were often inner-outers in polygonal form. In Europe, it is fairly common to discriminate between virginals and spinets on the basis of shape, identifying the polygonal version as spinets and the square (actually oblong) shapes as virginals. It was old English practice to refer to a virginal in the plural, and one often still sees that usage.

The Flemish built three kinds of virginals; those with keyboards to the left of the case front (plucking close to the left bridge and producing a nasal sound) called *spinetten*, (or in English, *spinett-virginals*), those with keyboards in the center of the case front (sounding more like a conventional harpsichord); and those with the keyboard placed on the right, plucking close to the center of the strings (producing a hollow, fluty tone) called *muselars*. Both spinetts and muselars (but rare in the former) could have a compartment in the unused portion of the case front to house an octave virginal, a combination known as a "mother-and-child." The child could be played by partially withdrawing it from its mother, by removing it from its mother's case, or by placing it on top of the mother and playing both from the mother's keyboard.

Index of Names

Edward L. Kottick, Emeritus Professor of Musicology at The University of Iowa, is interested in the history, construction, and decoration of early keyboard instruments. A builder himself, he is the author of *The Harpsichord Owner's Guide*. With George Lucktenberg he has conducted tours of many of the museums visited in this book.

George Lucktenberg is Adjunct Professor of Music and Artist-in-Residence at Reinhardt College and a member of the keyboard faculty at the Interlochen Arts Camp. He has been director of the Aliénor Harpsichord Composition Awards since 1980, the same year that he founded the Southeastern Historical Keyboard Society.